JACKSON'S MMA
THE GROUND GAME

GREG JACKSON

with KELLY CRIGGER

LAS VEGAS

contents

SPORTS NUTRITION GUIDELINES

CHAPTER ONE: THE FULL GUARD

CHAPTER ONE, PART TWO: INSIDE THE FULL GUARD

INSIDE THE FULL GUARD: STANDING

CHAPTER TWO: GUARD VARIATIONS

BUTTERFLY GUARD

CHAPTER THREE: SIDE MOUNT

CHAPTER FOUR: HEAD CONTROL

CHAPTER FIVE: REAR MOUNT

CHAPTER SIX: FULL MOUNT

ACKNOWLEDGMENTS

First to my family, for being so kind and supportive: My dad, Jim Jackson, for teaching me so many things, especially how to be a leader. My mom, Kris Jackson, for never giving up on me, when a lot of moms would have. My brother, Matt Jackson, for always encouraging my imagination. My wife, Stephanie, for her constant love and inspiration. You are my rock I put my back to. And my children, Samantha and Jimmy, for understanding that their Dad has to work so much.

To my friends: Jim Dudley, for teaching me how to be a teacher, encouraging my intellect, and all the great walks. All my Quaker friends, it takes a village to raise a child. All my friends growing up in the South Valley of Albuquerque, thanks for keeping me alive and teaching me the meaning of friendship. David Rutchman, for countless hours of philosophical conversation aimed at self-improvement, not competition. Brad Valdez, and the whole Valdez family, for having my back since kindergarten, and introducing me to my love of combat. Itzolin Garcia, the first person to bring out the martial arts teacher in me, wish you were here. My best friend, Mike Helvie, for contributing to my mental sanity. Our adventures over the years have helped to keep my life in balance. Mike Winkeljohn, for being my mentor and giving his insights and always watching out for me. Thanks big bro! Chris Luttrell, for talking me into MMA competitions and being an unparalleled strategist and a great friend. Brad Ahrensfield and Tom Vaughn, whose belief and enthusiasm helped shape our school into what it is today. Rob DeBuck, for getting me involved with the Albuquerque Police and always keeping me smiling. Ricky Kottenstette, the great emancipator, for improving my quality of life. Julie Kedzie, the samurai, for your friendship and support. Nick Gonzalez, for selflessness and investing in the youth of our school. Steve and Terri Irwin and the whole Australia Zoo clan, your contributions to my life are deep and extraordinary.

To my vanguard pro fighters: Keith Jardine, who has been my friend through thick and thin, thanks brother. Diego Sanchez, for opening so many doors. Joey Villasenor, whose kindness and brotherhood mean so much to me. Floyd Sword, for being a ray of sunshine. Nate Marquardt, whose positivity and help have enriched my life. Dan Higgins, whose amazing gifts over the years have left me in awe. Rashad Evans, for your courage and generosity. Georges St. Pierre, whose passion for our art constantly inspires me. Damacio Page, Donald "Cowboy" Cerrone, Leonard Garcia, John Dodson, and Brant Gibbs for keeping me entertained. And all my pro fighters: thank you for allowing me to train you.

To my fellow coaches around the country: Phil "The Art" Nurse, Feras "the mastermind" Zahabi, Trevor "One Hit" Wittman, and John "the apocalypse" Chaimberg, your collaboration and genius are truly appreciated.

My sincere thanks to the Tapout crew for giving me so many opportunities and always believing in me. Charles "Mask" Lewis, you will always be in my heart.

To Kelly Crigger, for talking me into writing this book, doing all the hard work, and sharing a love of military history and strategy.

To all of my students old and new, you have made our school what it is today. You have all made so many contributions over the years, which I appreciate more than I can say.

To my longest continuous student "Crazy" Steve Schrenkel, who would have thought we would ever be here!

A special thanks goes out to Lance Freimuth for his tremendous editorial work on this book.

Sports Nutrition Guidelines

PR Cole MS, RD Candidate
Columbia University, New York City

A successful MMA athlete draws upon a unique arsenal in order to thrive as a practitioner or competitor. Technical skills, mental discipline, endurance, and perseverance are all vital aspects of training. A solid nutrition regimen is a crucial component that supports the skills necessary to thrive in MMA. Optimal sports nutrition offers a wide range of benefits to give the athlete a competitive edge during training sessions and competitions. The right types, amounts, and combinations of foods consumed at the optimal times will help prevent fatigue, joint/muscle injuries, and illness. Taking this type of systematic approach to nutrition also enhances recovery, muscle development, and overall performance. Whether you're new to MMA or an experienced fighter, you are surely familiar with the physical and mental demands of this sport. Since your training asks so much of you, give your body the quality fuel that it needs to push your potential to the brink.

I. General Nutrition

The three major nutrients that you should get to know are carbohydrates, protein, and fat. If by chance you decide to skip this section (which I don't recommend) here's what you need to know in a nutshell.

Carbohydrates—Carbs are the major source of fuel for BOTH endurance and resistance training.

Protein—While not a major source of fuel, protein (when combined with carbs) helps with the growth and repair of lean muscle tissue.

Fat—Healthy unsaturated fats support the cardiovascular and immune systems. They also help with the digestion of important vitamins.

Let's get to know these key nutrition players in more detail. While it's far more accurate to determine macronutrient requirements based on body weight, the following is a rough distribution of an ideal daily nutrient mix for a highly active fighter.

55%–65% Calories from high-quality carbohydrates
15%–20% Calories from lean proteins
20%–30% Calories from mostly unsaturated fats

It may surprise you to see that carb needs are higher than protein needs. This is one of the most common nutrition myths floating around gyms nowadays. The reasoning for this nutrient distribution will become clearer to you as we go along. It has to do with the role of carbs as a major fuel source, and the role of protein in tissue repair.

Carbohydrates

Much confusion exists regarding the role of carbohydrates in the diet. Athletes often shy away from carbs in favor of high-protein diets in the hopes of either losing or maintaining weight and building muscle. In actuality, carbohydrates are the preferred fuel for muscles during high-intensity exercise. This is true for both cardio and resistance training. Protein will help to repair and maintain lean muscle, but it all comes down to carbohydrates to energize the body through any type of intense exercise.

Popular diet mythology dictates, "Carbs lead to weight gain." You should note that weight gain boils down to overall calorie intake and energy expenditure. Taking in more calories than you burn over a weekly basis will cause weight gain. Athletes should rely on carbohydrate-rich foods before and after endurance workouts to provide fuel and to promote glycogen recovery. Glycogen is the storage form of carbohydrates found directly within muscles.

Carbohydrates come from grains, fruits, and vegetables. They differ in structure depending on their source and how they are processed. The two major types of carbs are referred to as "simple" and "complex" carbohydrates.

The highest quality carbohydrates that offer the most nutritional benefits come from vegetables, fruits, and whole grains. Oatmeal, 100% whole-grain breads/pastas, barley, and brown rice are just a few examples. Take the time to look at a food label to ensure the product says "100% whole grain," since a term like "multigrain" could mean that the product is mixed with refined (processed) carbohydrates.

Simple carbs include both monosaccharides and disaccharides. Examples of monosaccharides are glucose, fructose, and galactose. Disaccharides include sucrose (table sugar), lactose (milk sugar), corn syrup, and honey. Complex carbohydrates are larger in structure than simple carbohydrates. The starch and fiber from plants are examples of complex carbs.

At least half of the grains you eat each day should be whole grains since they offer more nutrients than refined grains that have lost most of their nutritional value from processing.

Estimation of daily Carbohydrate needs to maintain weight:

30 min–1 hr moderate exercise
~ 2 grams per pound of body weight

1 hr intense training/day
~3 grams per pound of body weight

1–2 hrs intense training/day
~ 4 grams per pound of body weight

Ultra-endurance athletes
~ 5 grams per pound of body weight

Fiber is a type of plant carbohydrate that cannot be digested but still offers numerous health benefits. Two types exist, soluble and insoluble. A minimum of 25 grams of fiber per day from both kinds is recommended for all adults (athletes and couch potatoes alike). Fiber helps to lower cholesterol, promotes regular bowel movements, and aids in weight control by curbing appetite, since it is digested slowly and thus promotes a favorable slow and steady release of sugars into your bloodstream for energy. High-fiber diets may also lower your risk of developing heart disease

Soluble Fiber: This is the type that helps to lower cholesterol. Sources include oatmeal, barley, beans, and brown rice.

Insoluble Fiber: This form of fiber helps to keep bowel movements regular. Sources include wheat bran, whole grains, and vegetables.

Protein

Both plant and animal sources of protein are made up of strings of amino acids. Animal-based protein is often called "complete" protein since it offers all of the essential amino acids required to build the proteins and tissues the body needs. On the other hand, the majority of plant-based protein contains an incomplete set of essential amino acids. Mixing both types of protein is important to maintain a healthy diet.

Protein in and of itself does not build muscle. Diligent strength and conditioning regimens are the most important aspect of increasing (and maintaining) lean body mass. Adequate, though not excessive protein will support that growth and maintenance. Extra protein intake beyond what the body needs is just extra calories. The element nitrogen, common to all proteins, cannot be used by the body and is processed by the kidneys and excreted in urine. Overconsumption of protein therefore puts added stress on the kidneys.

Estimation of protein needs:

Type of Adult	Grams of protein per pound of body weight
Sedentary (couch potato)	0.4
Casual exerciser (has a treadmill that mostly gathers dust)	0.5-0.7
Endurance athlete (triathlete)	0.6-0.7
Building muscle mass (body-builder)	0.7-0.8
Athlete restricting calories (fighter cutting weight)	0.8-0.9
Upper limit requirement for everyone	0.9

Top sources of lean animal protein:
+ Skinless chicken/turkey breast
+ Seafood: Chunk light tuna (avoid albacore), wild salmon, sardines, anchovies, tilapia, halibut, Pollock, shrimp
+ Lean beef (sirloin, tenderloin, bison, ostrich, venison)
+ Eggs/egg whites (up to 1 yolk per day)
+ Nonfat/low-fat dairy (milk, cheese, and yogurt)

Top plant-based protein sources:
+ Beans (kidney, pinto, lentils)
+ Nuts (almonds, walnuts, peanuts)
+ Tofu
+ Edamame
+ Quinoa
+ Soy milk
+ Whole-grain breads/pasta
+ Oats

Fats

Fat is vital for a healthy diet for numerous reasons. Dietary fat aids digestion of important fat-soluble vitamins like A, D, E, and K. Fat is also used as a fuel source during low-intensity exercise. Some fats like omega-3 and omega-6 fatty acids are essential in the diet because the body cannot synthesize them. Believe it or not, body fat stores are important to maintain since a layer of fat surrounds and protects delicate organs like the kidneys, heart, and liver.

Not all fats are created equal! Around 20–35% of total calorie intake should come from healthy fat sources. In fact, there is no benefit from consuming a diet that is less than 15% fat. Saturated fats are sometimes called "hard fats," and they are mainly found in high-fat beef and dairy products. Since saturated fat is harmful to heart health and can increase cholesterol levels, intake should be limited to no more than 10% of total calories in order to keep arteries healthy. Unsaturated fats on the other hand or "soft fats" are heart-healthy and are found in plants and fish. Unsaturated fats are either monounsaturated or polyunsaturated. (The degree of saturation refers to the chemical structure of the fat molecule.)

Essential fats like omega-6 and omega-3 fatty acids are polyunsaturated and are vital to maintaining immune function and overall health. Since omega-6 fats found in many plant oils are often used in food preparation, the average American diet contains enough of this nutrient. However, omega-3 fats, particularly the health-boosting EPA and DHA varieties, are generally found in much lower quantities in the average diet.

Currently, most people have a greater omega-6 intake compared to their intake of omega-3 fat, which is the opposite of what the body prefers. This backward ratio can promote systemic inflammation, so a focus on omega-3 fats is highly beneficial. A higher intake of omega-3s compared to omega-6s is preferable. While certain plants like flaxseed and walnuts offer omega-3 fats, these are not as potent as the fats derived from certain types of fatty fish. A mix of both is recommended.

Potential benefits of omega-3 fats
+ Reduced inflammation throughout the body
+ Maintenance of fluidity of cell membranes
+ Prevention of excessive blood clotting
+ Reduced risk of thickened arteries
+ Improved insulin response
+ Prevention of cancer cell growth
+ Improved immune response
+ Improved joint health
+ Improved brain health

Saturated fats to avoid (Bad Fats)
+ Animal sources——Red meat, lard, poultry skin, butter, whole milk, cream, cheese, ice cream, and other full-fat dairy products.
+ Plant sources —coconut oil, palm oils, cocoa butter.

Sources of monounsaturated fats (Good Fats)
+ Olive, canola, and peanut oils
+ Olives, peanut butter, nuts
+ Avocados

Sources of omega-6 fats (Good Fats)
+ Vegetable oils (corn, sunflower, safflower, soybean, cottonseed)

Examples of plant sources of omega-3 fats (Excellent Fats)
+ Oils (flaxseed, canola, walnut, wheat germ, soybean)
+ Nuts and seeds (butternuts, walnuts, soybean kernels)
+ Vegetables (soybeans)

Examples of animal sources of omega-3 fats (Amazing Fats)
+ Wild salmon, sardines, anchovies, and herring

Trans Fats (Really Bad Fats)
Trans fats are artificially created compounds that lower "good" cholesterol and raise "bad" cholesterol. These should be avoided at all costs. Sources of trans fats can include:
+ Fried foods
+ Commercial baked goods containing hydrogenated or partially hydrogenated oils, such as:
  • Shortening
  • Partially hydrogenated soy bean oil
+ Any foods containing the words "hydrogenated" or "partially hydrogenated"

So to sum it up, when it comes to fat we have . . .

The Good
Unsaturated fats: From vegetables, nuts, and certain types of seafood.

The Bad
Saturated fats: Fatty meats and full-fat dairy products and tropical oils (i.e., palm oil).

The Ugly
Trans Fats: Fried foods and commercially baked goods.

I once had a client who was "fat-phobic" during the end of his training camp, as he was trying to slim down for weigh-ins. He asked me if a short-term fat-free diet would rev up his weight-loss efforts. I explained to him that diets with less than 15% fat offer no advantages to athletes. Since healthy fats can boost immune function, taking them out of the diet increases the risk of getting sick from intense training that puts such stress on all body systems. I also reminded him that his weight loss was all about creating a calorie deficit and curbing his appetite and that since fat is such a filling nutrient, it can be used moderately to keep feeling fuller longer.

II. Estimation of Calorie Needs

Another client of mine called me up one day very concerned that he wasn't losing any weight. He was training more than three hours a day and ate extremely healthy foods. He couldn't figure out why those extra pounds weren't submitting. Once I took a closer look at his diet, I realized that it all came down to the calories. His food choices were exemplary, but he was just eating too much. Weight loss, maintenance, or gain is all a calorie game that needs to be played with precision.

Calorie Basics

Calories are a measurement of energy that determines weight management. Calories from food fuel basic metabolic needs and support physical activity. Body weight is maintained when an athlete consumes roughly the same number of calories that he/she burns throughout the course of a week. Weight is lost when fewer calories are taken in than what is burned over the week, since the body burns through fat stores to provide energy. Weight is gained when more calories are consumed than burned on a weekly basis.

Calorie needs can be estimated by current weight and level of physical activity. However, since so much variation exists between individual metabolic rates, it may take some trial and error to tweak the estimation of calorie needs to support personal weight-management goals.

The chart to the right shows a range of calorie needs to maintain body weight for given weights and levels of training. Those who have a difficult time keeping weight on probably fall at the higher end of the calorie range for the given weight and exercise regimen. Those who have more difficulty shedding pounds likely fall on the lower end of the calorie range.

Weight Loss

It's ideal to target body fat loss instead of lean muscle loss. This is best achieved by a diligent resistance training routine and by avoiding rapid weight loss. A more gradual loss helps promote a decrease in body fat percentage. One pound of fat is equivalent to 3,500 calories. In order to lose one pound over the course of a week, a daily deficit of 500 calories is required. For a loss of two pounds weekly, that deficit would need to be 1,000 calories. Unless someone is significantly overweight, a loss of two pounds per week is the maximum amount that should be lost in order to minimize muscle breakdown.

Here is an example of calorie estimation from the chart below of a 160-pound athlete with a moderate level of exercise (sixty to ninety minutes per day)

Weight management: 3,040 calories/day

1 pound weekly weight loss: 3,040 calories/day – 500 calories/day = 2,540 calories/day

2 pounds weekly weight loss: 3,040 calories/day – 1,000 calories/day = 2,040 calories/day

If this athlete experiences more or less weight loss than estimated, a few hundred calories will need to be either added or subtracted respectively. This is where the trial and error comes into play in order to find the ideal rate of weekly body fat reduction.

Estimated Daily Caloric Needs For Energy Balance			
	120 lbs	**160 lbs**	**280 lbs**
Low: (sedentary) (13–15 calories per lb/BW)	1,560–1,800	2,080–2,400	3,640–4,200
Moderate: 30–60 min/day **3-4 times/week** (16–18 calories per lb/BW)	1,920–2,160	2,560–2,880	4,480–5,040
High: 60–90 min/day **5+ more times/week** (19–21 calories per lb/BW)	2,280–2,520	3,040–3,360	5,320–5,880
Very High: 90+ min **6 or 7 days a week** (22-25 calories per lb/BW)	2, 640–2,880	3,520–3,840	6,160–6,720

Weight Cutting Concerns

Combat athletes have traditionally viewed the weight cut as a necessary part of training that helps improve performance by allowing a fighter to compete at the very top of his/her weight class. Typically, athletes make weight by significantly reducing food and fluid intake the week prior to competition. Severe dehydration from sauna use and intense exercise in heavy clothing is also common practice.

Please be aware that taking weight cutting to extremes offers no advantage and significantly detracts from athletic potential. Scientists have conducted numerous studies on boxers, wrestlers, and other combat athletes to determine the influence of rapid weight loss on serious athletes. Cuts greater than 5% of body weight have been associated with fatigue, tension, and higher scores of anger on psychological tests. In fact, depressed mood and irritability are well-documented side effects in weight-class athletes who undergo rapid weight loss in the week prior to competition. The studies also report that the majority of athletes performed far below expectations. A combination of dehydration, depleted muscle glycogen, and reduced lean muscle mass are all proposed as contributors that detract from performance. Other research has demonstrated a loss of anaerobic power from rapid weight reductions. Another potential side effect is impairment of muscle function and an increased risk for muscle tissue injury.

I highly advise a gradual weight loss regimen as opposed to a rapid cut that results in a loss of greater than 5% of total body weight. With all the grueling work and dedication that it takes in the months leading up to a fight, it would be a shame to throw all that away with a drastic cut. Any MMA veteran will agree that mental well-being leading up to a fight is of the utmost importance for focus. Taking the time to plan for weight loss before or even during the beginning of a training camp will help to promote a stable state of mind that will allow for maximum concentration.

While many fighters plan for weight loss during their camp, I don't recommend this approach. A professional training camp requires a level of elite workouts that can be taken closest to the brink when an athlete is eating to maintain weight rather than trying to lose weight. If possible, try to begin your camp at a weight at which you would fight tomorrow if you had to. Also try to keep your pre-weigh-in water cut to a minimum in a range of 2–5% of body weight.

III. Nutrition before, during, and after Workouts

Pre-Workout Nutrition
Pre-exercise nutrition aims to fuel the body with glucose (a major type of fuel), delay fatigue during long exercise, prevent dehydration, and satisfy hunger. Just as with calorie estimation, it may take a few tries to optimize the timing and composition of ideal pre-workout food and fluid. Some athletes can tolerate food thirty minutes prior to training, while others require a full hour for digestive comfort. In order to achieve peak performance though, food and fluids must be consumed in the time frame of thirty minutes to four hours before exercise.

Since exercise increases blood flow to working muscles and decreases blood flow to the digestive tract, it is important to avoid large servings of food and fluid close to the beginning of a training session.

Pre-Workout Food Guidelines
✦ The pre-workout meal should be low in fat, moderate in protein, but high in carbohydrates.
• Carbohydrates are the major fuel source during intense exercise, so it's important to prepare blood sugar levels for activity. Once blood sugar drops, muscle glycogen (the storage form of carbohydrates) is used, and then fatigue sets in. Going into exercise with low blood sugar will result in earlier fatigue.
• A low to moderate amount of pre-workout protein can help ensure that enough amino acids are present after the workout to minimize muscle tissue breakdown.
• Fat is digested slowly and can leave an athlete feeling sluggish, so high-fat meals before exercise should be avoided.

✦ Unless it's a morning workout, a meal should be eaten three to four hours before exercise, and a smaller snack consumed one to two hours beforehand.
• It generally takes three to four hours for a larger meal to digest, two to three hours for a small meal, one to two hours for a blended liquid meal, and one hour or less for a small snack.

✦ Two-thirds of the meal should ideally be made up of carbohydrate sources (whole-grain breads, pasta, rice, cereals, fruits, vegetables, reduced-fat yogurt and milk). The remaining third of the meal should consist of a lean protein source (poultry, fish, shellfish, egg whites, beans, nuts, or tofu.)

✦ Sample pre-workout snacks:
• A banana with 1 tablespoon of peanut butter
• Low-fat yogurt and a piece of fruit
• Oatmeal made with skim milk and fruit
• Trail mix with nuts and fruit
• Granola with low-fat milk and fruit
• A smoothie made with low-fat yogurt, fruit, and wheat germ or flax meal

Pre-Workout Fluid Guidelines
Adequate hydration is a significant contributor to a powerful workout but is often overlooked. During a training session, a drop in weight greater than 2% of total body weight due to sweat loss leads to a compromised performance. Dehydration may result in decreased muscle strength, speed, stamina, energy, and mental focus. Additionally, athletes who are dehydrated are at increased

risk for injury, physical/mental fatigue, cramps, cardiovascular strain, and heat intolerance. Paying attention to hydration needs helps to maintain a lower core temperature and lower heart rates to ward off exercise-induced fatigue.

✦ As a general rule of thumb, try to drink at least 2 cups of water (~ ½ liter) two hours before exercise and then another cup (~ ¼ liter) ten to twenty minutes prior.

✦ To be more precise, go for a range of 2–3 milliliters per pound of body weight two hours before your workout.

✦ Experiment with timing to determine what feels most comfortable.

✦ Get in the habit of stepping on a scale pre- and post-workout to assess body water loses.

✦ Note that throughout the day, an athlete should be drinking about half of his/her body weight in ounces of water.

Nutrition during Exercise

When workouts last fewer than sixty minutes, hydration with just water is sufficient to fuel the activity. However, athletes need to replenish blood sugar and electrolytes during longer endurance sessions. While both liquid and solid carbohydrates are equally effective at raising blood sugar levels, most athletes prefer a sport beverage to get the job done.

✦ The ideal sport beverage should taste good to encourage hydration and should contain:
  • Around 15 grams of carbohydrates per 8 ounces of fluid
  • Combination of carbohydrate sources
  • Sodium: 110–220 mg /8 oz
  • Potassium: ~30 mg/8 oz
✦ A total of 30–60 grams of carbohydrates should be consumed for every hour of exercise
✦ Aim for 8 ounces of fluid at 15-20 minute intervals to stay hydrated

One of the most common questions clients and friends ask me is: "What's the best sports beverage?" The truth is that the answer is different for everyone. You need to find a drink that is palatable for you. Just because your buddy loves it doesn't mean that you will. The taste needs to encourage you hydrate! Then you need to consider your own needs. You may want to invest in a sports drink with extra sodium if you feel like your sweat losses are particularly intense. Or you may want a brand with extra carbo-

hydrates or one without any artificial dyes or colorings. Take the time to experiment with what works best for you. Gatorade, Clif, PowerBar, Cytomax, Accelerade, and Hammer Nutrition HEED are some of the most popular brands among athletes.

Hyponatremia

Hyponatremia is a condition that occurs when levels of sodium in the blood drop dangerously low. This can be caused by over-hydration when body fluids become too dilute. Most often, hyponatremia results from sweat losses of sodium that are not replenished during lengthy intense exercise sessions, especially in the heat. This is yet another reason why hydration and electrolyte maintenance is extremely important.

Post-Workout Nutrition

The goals of food and fluid intake after a workout are to restore muscle glycogen, provide protein for muscle repair, replace lost electrolytes, and rehydrate. The timing of recovery nutrition is critical. Carbohydrates and protein need to be eaten as soon as possible (no more than one hour after exercise). This time frame is when it's easiest for glycogen restoration, which means efficient recovery to prepare for the next session. Additionally, protein intake in this window allows for optimal muscle tissue repair. Complete protein (animal based) offers the full range of essential amino acids necessary for muscle needs. At least 10–20 grams of protein is recommended.

Recovery Foods
✦ ~10 grams protein
  • 1 ounce meat or tofu
  • 3 egg whites
  • 1 cup milk/yogurt or 1 ounce light cheese
  • ⅔ cup beans
  • ⅓ cup nuts or 2 tablespoons peanut butter
  • ½ cup 1% cottage cheese
  • 1 cup light Greek-style yogurt (~20 grams protein)
✦ Fruits with high carbohydrate/fluid content
  • Watermelon
  • Grapes
  • Melon
  • Oranges
✦ Starchy grains
  • Bagels
  • Bread
  • Crackers
  • Rice
  • Pasta
  • Oats

- Pretzels
✦ Simple Snack Ideas
  - 1 cup cottage cheese with ½ cup berries
  - 1 serving oatmeal with three egg whites
  - 1 cup yogurt with a small banana
  - ½ whole-grain bagel with 1 tablespoon peanut butter
  - Pretzels with 1 cup soy milk

Electrolyte Recovery

✦ The following foods offer essential electrolytes and should be incorporated into daily diet
  - Potatoes
  - Yogurt
  - Orange juice
  - Bananas
  - Soup
  - Cereals
  - Cheese
  - Breads

Guidelines for Replenishing Muscle Glycogen

Glycogen is the stored form of carbohydrate in muscle tissue. During intense workouts, the body's preferred source of fuel is blood sugar, but once blood sugar levels drop, glycogen is utilized to fuel the rest of the workout as a last resort. Recovering these carb stores is particularly important when an athlete plans to train again within four to six hours.

✦ Consume carbohydrate-rich foods within fifteen minutes post-workout, or as soon as it's tolerable to eat. Eating just a few grams of protein along with starchy foods is ideal.

✦ Food eaten at thirty-minute intervals will help to keep the hormone levels of insulin high for efficient glycogen restoration.

✦ Starchy carbs from bread, rice, and pasta are highly effective for glycogen recovery and should be eaten in addition to fruit.

Recovery Fluids

✦ Drink 2 cups of water for every pound lost during exercise.

✦ Stepping on a scale before and immediately after exercise is an easy way to assess hydration status.

✦ Remember to aim for no more than 2% of body weight loss from sweat.

IV. Top Ten Nutrition Tips to Improve Overall Health

Of course paying attention to all the little details that go into planning for a well-rounded nutrition plan is important for success. I know it can be a lot to incorporate a new regimen, so if you get stressed out, don't lose site of the big picture. You can always look back at the following tips as a general roadmap for smart nutrition choices. If you're new to healthy eating, starting with these pointers is a great way to dive into a healthier lifestyle.

1) At least half of grain intake should come from whole grains. These grains contain more fiber and nutrients because they are less processed. Look for food labels that say "100% whole grain," since products that simply say things like "multigrain" can have refined carbohydrates mixed in.

Top whole grains: oatmeal, brown rice, barley, rye, and whole wheat breads and pasta.

2) Eat a minimum of five to nine servings of fruits/vegetables daily. So what exactly is a serving?

Vegetables:
✦ ½ cup cooked vegetables (size of a baseball)
✦ 1 cup tossed salad (size of a closed fit)
✦ 1 medium potato
✦ ¾ cup vegetable juice
✦ ½ cup raw chopped vegetables (size of a baseball)

Fruits:
✦ 1 medium whole piece of fruit
✦ ¾ cup of fruit juice
✦ ½ cup canned fruit (size of a baseball)
✦ ¼ cup dried fruit

3) Eat colorful foods every day. Each color offers different antioxidants and phytochemicals to reduce the risk of disease and enhance recovery.

Red: strawberries, raspberries, tomatoes, watermelon, red peppers

Orange: oranges, mangoes, peaches, cantaloupe, sweet potato, carrots, pumpkin

Yellow: Pineapple, squash, corn

Green: Broccoli, spinach, Brussels sprouts, green peppers, beans, peas, kiwi, honeydew melon

Blue/Purple: blueberries, red grapes, beets, eggplant

White: Garlic, onions, pears, bananas

4) Include low fat dairy products like cheeses, yogurts, and milk in your diet. Choosing these reduced fat products will help lower saturated fat intake to help improve cardiovascular health. Additionally, these foods are excellent sources of calcium and vitamin D, which are essential for maintaining bone health. Low-fat dairy foods also contain complete protein to aid in recovery and growth of muscle tissue.

Top low-fat dairy products: yogurt, cottage cheese, ricotta cheese, string cheese, Greek-style yogurt, traditional yogurt, skim or 1% milk. (Many who are lactose intolerant are still able to enjoy cottage cheese and Greek-style yogurt).

5) Buy local foods when possible. Many small local farms employ organic practices but cannot afford the expensive certification. The less food has traveled, the fresher and more nutrient dense it is. Many major supermarkets are starting to showcase produce sections that are locally grown. Farmers' markets are also an option to buy produce directly from farmers in your own community. Please visit http://www.localharvest.org for more information about finding local food. When given a choice, becoming a "localvore" is the way to go.

6) If affordable, buy organic versions of favorite fruits and vegetables. The term "organic" refers to the growing practices that the farmers use. These practices are designed to be environmentally friendly to conserve water and soil all the while reducing pollution. Farmers who follow organic practices don't use chemical fertilizers or weed killers and do not give livestock any added hormones or antibiotics. There is much debate as to whether or not organic foods are more nutritious than conventional foods, but going organic when you're able to may help to reduce the amount of pesticides and hormones in the food you eat.

7) Eat fish rich in omega-3 fatty acids two or three times per week. Top sources include wild (not farm-raised) salmon, anchovies, sardines, and herring. A fish oil supplement kept refrigerated is an acceptable substitute. Avoid swordfish, shark, tilefish, and king mackerel to minimize mercury intake. Include other types of healthy unsaturated fats to support heart health too. When you cook, use a few teaspoons of extra-virgin olive oil and try to fit in ¼ cup of nuts daily.

8) Watch your alcohol consumption. While a glass of red wine does offer some heart-healthy antioxidants, there's no need to go overboard. Alcohol goes through the liver for detoxification. The liver is also the major organ involved in metabolizing the fats, carbs, and proteins in your diet, so keeping it in top condition should be a priority. Alcohol also has the ability to reduce the absorption of some essential vitamins. Nutritionists often refer to calories from alcohol as "empty," since they offer no real nutritional benefits.

9) Reduce your intake of red meat. It might be difficult to drive past Burger King (especially when dieting), but your body will thank you for it! Normally, farm-raised cows are fed antibiotics and the meat is high in artery-clogging saturated fat. Lean cuts of grass-fed beef like sirloin and tenderloin are better options but should still be limited to one or two times per week. Game meats like venison, bison, and ostrich that are not farm raised are the leanest of all meats and have no added hormones when they are wild caught. Active animals will always be leaner than those that sit around getting fattened up in small confined spaces.

10) Balance plant and animal protein sources. Animal protein, unlike plant protein, is metabolized in the body to an acidic precursor. There is some evidence that this increase in blood acidity may cause calcium to leach out of bones to act as a buffer. Try to plan for complete animal protein sources around a workout for muscle repairs and work in plant protein throughout the rest of the day.

Top lean animal protein sources: skinless chicken/turkey breast, chunk light tuna (avoid albacore), wild salmon, lean beef (sirloin, tenderloin, bison, ostrich, venison), eggs/egg whites, nonfat/low dairy (milk, cheese, yogurt).

Top plant protein sources: Beans (kidney, pinto, lentils), tofu, edamame, quinoa, and soymilk. (It's best to moderate intake of soy protein due to the potential for certain plant compounds to weakly mimic the hormone estrogen.)

V. Meal Planning Guidelines

✦ Eat breakfast every day. After a full night of fasting, eating within thirty minutes of waking up jump-starts metabolism and keeps the body out of the slow conservational "starvation" mode.

✦ Many athletes benefit from eating six to seven smaller meals/ snacks throughout the day (three to four hours apart) rather than two or three heavier meals. This strategy helps control appetite and distributes nutrients consistently to aid in recovery.

✦ Avoid "bottom-heavy" diets where most food is eaten in the evening hours post-workouts. Instead, aim to eat two-thirds of calorie intake before dinner. This will help to keep up mental focus and energy throughout the day.

✦ Meals should not be skipped, as this can decrease the levels of growth hormone and testosterone, which are important for muscle development and repair.

I'll never forget a frantic phone call from a fighter of mine who just couldn't control his appetite. He felt ravenous after every meal, and ended up significantly overeating in the evening hours after his last workout session. Finally, around 11:30 PM he felt full before heading to bed, only to wake up the next day and repeat this eating pattern. This cycle is unfortunately all too common. Meals and snacks need to be evenly spaced out to promote recovery throughout the day and to control appetite.

The first question I asked my client was about breakfast. He woke each morning still feeling pretty full from the night before and would work out in the mornings on an empty stomach. Without pre-workout fuel, his morning session suffered. Those big late-night eating sessions blunted his morning appetite and prevented him from getting the high-quality sleep he needed. Once we worked out a meal and snack schedule that was more spread out, his appetite shrank and his workouts became more energized.

Meal/Snack Suggestions

Cereal and Milk with fruit (400 calories)
1 cup any whole-grain cereal (look for a brand that has 120 calories or less per ¾ cup or 1 cup serving)
Serve with 1 cup of skim milk (or 1% milk, or soy milk)
Add 2 tablespoons of raisins, OR ½ cup of blueberries
Serve with 1 hard-boiled egg

Strawberry-Banana Cottage Cheese with Almonds (400 calories)
1 cup fat-free or 1% reduced-fat cottage cheese
Mix in ½ sliced banana
Mix in ½ cup sliced strawberries
Mix in 2 tablespoons of slivered almonds

Eggs with Turkey Bacon and Fruit (460 calories)
1 whole egg
3 egg whites
2 teaspoons extra-virgin olive oil
Any chopped vegetables (peppers, onions, spinach, tomato, etc.)
4 strips reduced-fat turkey bacon
1 orange.
Beat eggs and egg whites together. Heat the oil and panfry the eggs. Add the vegetables. Serve with turkey bacon and orange.

PB & J (400 calories)
1 toasted whole-grain English muffin
2 level teaspoons of peanut butter
2 level teaspoons of jam

Spread one side of the muffin with peanut butter, the other with jam. Serve with 1 pear

Oatmeal with Berries and Nuts (400 calories)
½ cup dry oatmeal prepared with hot water
2 tablespoons of slivered almonds
½ cup berries (sliced strawberries or blueberries)

Apple Slices with Peanut Butter (400 calories)
1 apple, sliced
Slice and serve with 3 level tablespoons of peanut butter

Strawberry-Kiwi Smoothie (320 calories)
1 cup skim milk
6 ounces fat-free vanilla yogurt
1 kiwi, peeled and cut into quarters
1 cup frozen strawberries
Puree ingredients in a blender

Banana-Blueberry Smoothie (280 calories)
½ large banana
½ cup frozen blueberries
½ cup skim milk (or light soymilk)
½ cup unsweetened apple juice
1 scoop of whey protein powder
Puree ingredients in a blender

Raspberry/Peach Smoothie (275 calories)
½ cup frozen raspberries
½ cup sliced peaches (fresh, or canned in very light syrup)
½ cup skim milk (or light soymilk)
½ cup unsweetened apple juice
1 scoop whey protein powder
Puree ingredients in a blender

Pumpkin Smoothie (210 calories)
½ cup canned pure pumpkin
½ cup light soymilk
6-ounce container of fat-free French vanilla yogurt
Dash of cinnamon/nutmeg
Puree ingredients in a blender

Greek Salad with Chicken and Feta (260 calories)
Lettuce, mixed greens, unlimited
2 ounces chicken breast (cooked), skinless
2 ounces low-fat feta cheese
10 pitted black olives
1 medium tomato, diced
½ small onion, sliced
2 teaspoons olive oil
¼ cup red wine vinegar
Dash of oregano
Top the salad greens with the chicken, feta cheese, olives, and vegetables. Add olive oil, vinegar, and oregano seasoning.

Chicken Teriyaki (320 calories)
6 ounces boneless, skinless chicken breast
3 tablespoons low-sodium teriyaki sauce
¼ teaspoon garlic powder
Dash of powdered ginger

Dash of ground black pepper
1 diced bell pepper (any color)
1 cup broccoli florets
Combine the teriyaki sauce, spices, vegetables, and chicken strips in a bowl (refrigerate for thirty minutes). Preheat a frying pan with 2 teaspoons extra-virgin olive oil. Add marinated chicken and vegetables to the pan and cook with medium heat until chicken and vegetables are thoroughly cooked (less than ten minutes).

Turkey/Avocado Sandwich (500 calories)
2 slices low-carb whole-grain bread
4 ounces sliced turkey breast
3 thin slices of avocado
Lettuce, tomato, onion slices
1 ounce reduced-fat or fat-free Swiss cheese (or Cheddar, Monterey Jack, etc.)
Optional: spicy mustard
Serve with 1 piece of fruit (apple, pear, or orange)

Veggie Tuna Salad (250 calories)
6 ounces chunk light tuna fish (packed in water), drained
½ carrot, diced and peeled
½ celery stalk, diced
¼ red pepper, diced
½ scallion stalk, minced
1 tablespoon reduced-fat mayonnaise
½ teaspoon lemon juice
In a medium bowl, combine tuna, vegetables, and lemon juice.

Baked Potato and Cheese (500 calories)
1 medium-size potato
1 ounce fat-free or reduced-fat Cheddar cheese
Optional: 2 tablespoons fat-free or reduced-fat sour cream and salsa
Prepare potato in the microwave by poking potato with a fork, covering with a damp paper towel, and heating on high for three minutes. Turn potato over and heat in microwave for another two minutes or until soft. Top cooked potato with cheese and optional sour cream and salsa. Serve with 1 cup steamed broccoli and 20 baby carrots.

Supplements

The number one question I hear is "what supplements should a fighter take?" This is a simple question with a very complicated answer. I only recommend certain supplements after meeting with a fighter and assessing his/her medical history, eating habits, and training schedule in order to determine if all nutritional needs are being met. If you're interested in supplementing your diet, here are a few things to keep in mind.

✦ Discuss the supplement with your doctor or the registered dietitian (RD) that you're working with. This way you'll be sure to go over any potential interactions with medications and side effects when considering your personal medical history.

✦ The whole is greater than the sum of its parts. The nutrients and healthy components of real food often work synergistically with other parts of the whole food. Isolating these compounds in supplement form does not always offer the same benefits.

✦ Ask yourself why you're taking the supplement. Can you get the same benefit from real food that has not been processed? There's always a risk of losing nutritional potency during heat and mechanical processing.

✦ Be aware that the government does NOT regulate the supplement industry (this is true of herbs as well). There is a potential for contamination with harmful or illegal substances.

✦ "Natural" does not mean safe! Just because something is found in nature does not mean that it is healthy for the body. Arsenic, for example, is a natural substance.

✦ More isn't always better. Certain vitamins and nutrients are healthy in small doses but can have negative effects when taken in higher doses. Skip supplements that contain greater than 100% of the daily recommended value of vitamins and minerals.

✦ Choose brands that are nationally recognized to reduce the risk of purchasing a contaminated supplement.

✦ Store your supplements in cool dry places and refrigerate when necessary. You should also use the product by the expiration date as indicated on the bottle.

✦ To minimize stomach upset, take your supplement with a meal or snack.

References

Clark, N. Sports Nutrition Guidebook, 3rd ed. Brookline, MA: Human Kinetics, 2003.

Dunford, M., and J. A. Doyle. Nutrition for Sport and Exercise. Belmont, CA: Thomson Wadsworth; 2008.

Hall, C. J., and A. M. Lane. Effects of rapid weight loss on mood and performance among amateur boxers. British Journal of Sports Medicine, 35(6): 390–95.

Koopman, R., W. H. M. Saris, A. J. M. Wagenmakers, and L. J. C. van Loon. (2007). Nutritional interventions to promote post-exercise muscle protein synthesis. Sports Medicine, 37(10): 895–906.

Koral, J., and F. Dosseville. Combination of gradual and rapid weight loss: Effects on physical performance and psychological state of elite judo athletes. Journal of Sports Sciences, 27(2): 115–20.

Rodriguez, N. R., N. M. DiMarco, S. Langley, S. Denny, M. H. Hager, M. M. Manore, et al. Nutrition and athletic performance. Medicine and Science in Sports and Exercise, 41(3): 709–31.

INTRODUCTION

To me, mixed martial arts is one of the most beautiful art forms. I think this is because it encompasses so many elements from the worlds of science, psychology, music and many other disciplines. Your journey through the martial arts is not just a journey of technique, but also a journey of understanding. All of the techniques in this book will stand on their own as basic ways of learning physical combat. But the idea I'd really like to impart is that the techniques also represent a way to train the conceptual themes underpinning our art.

Taking somebody to the ground and into a world of combat that they're unfamiliar with is great. However, if you keep looking for the armbar to finish the fight and fail to see the unprotected neck, then you're missing the big picture. Through learning these underlying concepts, you are planning for the second and third step throughout the fight. This is a formula that I've used to help train many world champions, police and military officers. After you learn the basic techniques, you discover through trial and error what works best for you, and this is the conceptual application of your art.

Some of the training imperatives to keep in mind are:

1. The mind is a muscle and needs to be exercised as one. Everyone knows that the body gets stronger by exceeding its limitations. Body builders lift extraordinary amounts of weight. When they do this, their muscles develop microscopic tears. The body repairs the damage, resulting in bigger muscles. The mind is no different. When you force your body to go further than you think it can, it breaks your muscles down physically, but it also breaks you down mentally. As your body gets stronger, your mind gets stronger.

You develop endurance, discipline and self-confidence. You establish a breaking point that gets harder and harder to reach. Everyone has a breaking point. You have to make yours so high that it is unreachable in a fight.

2. Fear is a normal reaction to any conflict. There's nothing wrong with being nervous, but you have to learn to control it.

3. Stay calm and stay hunting. It is essential that you stay focused on your opponent and what they are doing. You always want be in a "hunt them down" mentality.

4. Never let anger take control of you. It's great to fight with passion, but not with anger. Anger blinds reason and is the enemy of controlled violence.

5. Fall in love with winning, not the technique. Don't be so rigidly set in your ways that you can't adapt to changing circumstances. Don't chase down a particular technique, just because you are good at it; set it up and let it happen all by itself. Also, there may be a time when you have to jettison what you learn and do something outrageous to win a fight. Go for it. Fall in love with victory, not the means by which you achieve it.

Keeping all of these things in mind, I want to thank you for allowing me to share my passion for the craft of mixed martial arts in these pages. I invite you to accept the challenge to pursue your journey in the art to its fullest potential. Go hard!

CHAPTER ONE: THE FULL GUARD

While grappling on the mat, there are many different positions the fight can transition into. Out of all the possible positions, the full guard is likely the most important. In training it's the position that you should practice the most and is the position that you should feel the most comfortable in. However, the full guard is simply a defensive environment. Ideally, in a fight you should strive to acquire the top position. The full guard is like an insurance policy. If you fail to achieve a takedown and end up on the bottom, you should be fully confident that you can mount an effective attack from your back by properly structuring grips and angles.

While in pure grappling matches pulling guard can be a successful tactic, it rarely yields an advantage in an MMA match. When strikes are added into the mix, the fighter on top will have gravity working for him, and he will be much more dangerous in the top position than if strikes were disallowed. Therefore, in an MMA match, the guard should not be viewed simply as a platform for applying submissions, sweeps, and counterstrikes. Instead, one of the most important elements of the guard is escaping and getting back to your feet. This combination of structure and mobility is what will make your guard dangerous.

There's a core principle of my MMA strategy that you will find repeated in this book over and over again: don't let your opponent dictate the fight. I don't like being purely defensive or reactive and I don't believe in letting my opponent seize and retain the initiative. I prefer a proactive approach that involves initiating attacks and creating opportunities to finish the fight.

I am also an advocate of using deception whenever possible. Telegraphing movements and behaving in a predictable manner are sure ways to lose a fight. Throughout this book, you will see examples of feigning strikes and movements that allow you to change your angle of attack in an effort to deceive your opponent and achieve an advantage. This philosophy applies to the guard as well, but as mentioned before, the guard is not the best position from which to win a fight. If you have the best guard in the world, and win fights without ever using it, you have done your job well.

FULL GUARD BASIC POSITION

To be successful in the full guard, you must establish a grip on your opponent's upper body. Controlling the triceps is one effective way to establish a grip because it can limit your opponent's ability to grab, strike, reach down to break your guard, or reach up to grab your head. The triceps grip also puts your hands in a good position to transition into either wrist or neck control. A good grip also supplies you with the leverage necessary to mount an attack. As you develop your own guard, you will find opportunities to slide a hand down to the wrist or up to the neck to change your grip, but grasping both triceps is a great starting point to control your opponent's posture.

Your hands are not the only tool used to manipulate your opponent in guard, however. Using your legs is of critical importance as well. While your hands grip your opponent's upper body, your legs must control his hips. An open guard is offensive, while a closed guard is more defensive. Closing your guard can limit some of the avenues available to you, so when I attack, my guard is most often open.

Closed Guard: **The closed guard refers to crossing your feet behind your opponent to limit his movements.**

SUBMISSIONS

When a fight goes to the ground and you end up underneath your opponent, your four main options are a submission hold, striking, a sweep, or getting back to your feet. Of these four, a submission hold is usually your best option to immediately end the fight, as these holds can do serious damage to your opponent and can render him unconscious. As submissions are such powerful tools, many fighters seek to attack with a submission first and use that to open avenues for other attacks from the guard, such as sweeps and getting back to their feet.

Submissions from the full guard come from constant movement and persistent offensive attacks that keep your opponent off balance. Submissions can be secured when your opponent makes a mistake, but against a skilled fighter, submission opportunities must be created with complete control and dynamic movements. As mentioned before, you should never let your opponent dictate the action. Your plan should always involve setting up an attack. Don't lie on the ground in a defensive guard just reacting to your opponent's movements. Seize the initiative, control the pace, and keep the momentum moving in your direction.

NINETY-DEGREE CUT TO ARMBAR

The ninety-degree cut is a simple hip movement that can be used as an attack platform from the closed guard. By moving your body perpendicular to your opponent's body, you have the option of isolating his limbs and attacking his joints with a submission. However, the position is not only offensive. The ninety-degree cut can also be used to slip your head out of the way of punches, so long as you're maintaining proper control as you move. Unlike in gi-style grappling, in MMA your opponent cannot pin you as effectively from the top position, so we will use the ninety-degree cut several times in this book, and it's critical that you learn to execute this basic move properly. While there are many techniques that can be applied from the ninety-degree cut, in this technique I'm going to demonstrate how to apply an armbar.

Armbar: The armbar is one of the best submissions in MMA and one that you will learn from almost every position. It isolates the elbow joint and allows you to put the maximum amount of weight and pressure on it to hyperextend it, causing intense pain. If your opponent does not tap out, it will cause severe injury.

I am on my back with Joey in my full guard. I have established double triceps grips to control his upper body, and I'm using a closed guard to control his hips.

I reach across my body and grasp Joey's right triceps with my right hand, making sure to get my fingers behind his arm for control.

Now I bring my left hand across my body and grip Joey's left shoulder with it. This cross grip enables me to not only control Joey's posture, but also to control his arms. If Joey were to attempt to throw a punch with his left hand, it would be a simple matter for me to slide my grip down to his left triceps.

I unhook my feet to give me room to swivel my hips. If I kept my guard closed, it would be impossible to pivot enough to execute the move.

I cut to ninety degrees by contracting my oblique muscles and pulling my head toward my right side. This puts my torso perpendicular with Joey's torso, giving me a better angle of attack. Notice I still have both of my grips. I'm using my right grip to pull Joey's right arm across his body, and I'm using my left arm to control his posture.

Because of the ninety-degree cut, I'm able to easily clear my left leg around Joey's body and throw it over his head. At this point his arm is trapped between my legs, making an easy transition into the submission.

To complete the submission, I pinch my knees together, pressure down on his head and armpit by curling my legs downward, grab his right arm with both of my hands, and bridge my hips off the mat. This hyperextends his elbow joint, forcing him to tap out.

ARM DRAG TO ARMBAR

The arm drag position is a simple grip that can give you the leverage needed to move around your opponent's body, including moving to back control. However, if your opponent counters your movement and attempts to keep you flat on your back, which is quite common, it's a simple matter to transition into the armbar. By leaning into you to counter your arm drag movement, your opponent exposes his arm and gives you the opportunity to end the fight. The arm drag to armbar is a relatively low risk submission as well. After you initialize the arm drag position, your head moves away from your opponent's hands, making it difficult for him to counter with punches. As long as you secure your arm drag grip quickly, you will find yourself in little danger should the submission fail.

1 I am on my back with Joey in my full guard. I start with my standard triceps grip for control. To set up the arm drag grip, I slide my right hand down to Joey's left wrist.

2 After securing Joey's wrist, I now move my left arm across his body, hooking inside his left arm on the back of his triceps muscle. This gives me a two-on-one grip on his left arm, which provides me with a lot of leverage to pivot around his body.

3 Because Joey's right hand is now totally uncontrolled, I must immediately move away from his right side after securing the two-on-one grip. To do this, I pull Joey's left arm into my left arm pit, breaking his posture forward and moving him to my left side at the same time.

As I'm pulling Joey's arm into my armpit, I unlock my legs and move my hips out to my right, further increasing the distance between my head and Joey's right hand. This gives me a great angle to the side of Joey's body to take the back.

Joey, now realizing that he's in danger of losing his position, begins to drive back into me to take away my angle of attack. As his head and shoulders come forward, it becomes difficult for me to continue moving toward his back.

Rather than simply allowing him to stop my attack, I transition into a submission. Because Joey was forced to drive into me while our hips were perpendicular, he put himself into the armbar. After he drives his head forward, I simply need to throw my right leg over his head to secure his left arm and trap him in the armbar. To finish, I pinch my knees, curl my legs down, and bridge my hips up.

DOUBLE ARMBAR

Sometimes it's not possible to get a perfect ninety-degree cut while on the bottom. This next submission allows you to secure an armbar without angling your hips beforehand. By simply walking your legs up your opponent's body, you can secure both of his arms and submit him without utilizing the ninety-degree cut. The key to this technique is to move your legs up sequentially. Don't try to get both of your legs over his shoulders at once. By walking your legs up slowly, you prevent your opponent from escaping out the back door. This submission usually works best when your opponent has his hands on your shoulders and is driving his head forward, or when you are unable to move your hips underneath your opponent.

High Guard: The high guard is when you are able to secure your legs up around the shoulders of your opponent.

1

I am on my back with Joey in my full guard. I have one hand on his elbow to control his arm and the other on his head to control his posture. Because both of his hands are high on my torso, I decide to attempt the double armbar.

2

To begin, I open my guard and pressure down with my right leg to give me a slight angle to allow me to raise my left leg. At the same time, I drive Joey's right elbow toward the inside of his body using my left hand.

3

I now throw my left leg over Joey's right shoulder, making sure to control his triceps as my leg comes over his shoulder.

4

Now that my left leg is over his shoulder, I repeat the motion on the opposite side. I pressure down with my left leg in order to give me enough room to move my right leg.

5

I now bring my right leg up over his shoulder and lock my feet together in a high guard position. If you've controlled your opponent's upper body properly throughout the movement, his arms should be lying on your torso.

6

To complete the submission, I thrust my hips up and squeeze my knees together while pulling down on his wrists with my arms. This hyperextends his elbows, forcing him to tap out.

HIGH TO SINGLE ARMBAR

Although the double armbar can be a successful technique if all goes well, it can be difficult to hyperextend both of your opponent's arms at the same time. If your opponent tries to block the double armbar by driving his weight forward and stacking you, it often gives you the option to pivot your body, isolate one of his arms, and lock up a single armbar. It's a good backup plan when your primary attack is unsuccessful.

TECHNICAL NOTE: This is a core principle of Jackson's MMA. I strongly believe in flowing with the situation instead of going back to the guard. If you struggle to attain an advantage, such as a ninety-degree cut, don't give it up and go back to guard when your attack stalls. Don't retreat. Just continue to attack from a new angle. The double armbar is only one attack, and if it doesn't work out, then you must adapt and try a different angle. Don't go back to your comfort zone in the guard.

I am on my back with Joey in my full guard. I have one hand on his elbow to control his arm and the other on his head to control his posture. Because both of his hands are high on my torso, I decide to attempt the double armbar.

To begin I open my guard and pressure down with my right leg to give me a slight angle to allow me to raise my left leg. At the same time, I force his right elbow toward the inside of his body using my left hand.

I now throw my left leg over Joey's right shoulder, making sure to control his triceps as my leg comes over.

Now that my left leg is over his shoulder, I repeat the motion on the opposite side. I pressure down with my left leg in order to give me enough room to move my right leg.

I now bring my right leg up over Joey's shoulder and lock my feet together in a high guard position.

Joey blocks my double armbar attempt by lifting his head up, bending his arms, and driving into my body to prevent me from extending my hips.

To continue with my attack, I quickly pivot to a ninety-degree position by reaching underneath his left leg using my right hand. This allows me to pull my body to a ninety-degree angle while keeping his arms trapped my with high guard. I make sure to keep my left grip on his right triceps solid to prevent him from escaping.

Once in the ninety-degree position, I swing my left leg over his head while keeping his arm trapped and his leg hooked. This allows me to trap his arm between my legs in the armbar position.

To finish the armbar, I keep Joey's right arm trapped to my chest using my arms, pinch my knees together, curl my legs down, and bridge my hips up.

ARMBAR TO TRIANGLE

Many submissions chain together well with other submissions. Rather than simply attempting one submission and then abandoning your attack if it should fail, it's always a solid idea to have a backup plan. We've already seen two armbar submissions, so now we'll explore the options you have to continue attacking when your opponent extracts his arm and prevents you from applying the armbar. This reduces the risk of going for an armbar by providing you with a safety net in the event that your opponent is slippery or you don't have the strength to maintain a grip on his arm. If your opponent manages to escape the armbar, chances are he will give you an opening to attack with the triangle choke.

Triangle Choke: There are two types of chokes: blood chokes, which interrupt the flow of blood to the brain and cause the victim to lose consciousness, and airflow chokes, which disrupt the victim's breathing and often causes him to lose consciousness. The triangle choke is a blood choke that traps one of your opponent's arms and his head between your thighs. Your leg then forces his trapped arm against his neck and disrupts the flow of blood to his brain.

I will start from the armbar position with my hips at a ninety-degree cut and Joey's right arm trapped between my legs.

To defend the armbar, Joey rips his arm out. However, with his left arm isolated and both of my legs over his head, I'm still in a good position to transition to the triangle.

To apply the triangle choke, I need to secure his head and one of his arms between my legs. To accomplish this, I pass my left leg to the other side of his neck and reach up to control his head with my left hand. This prevents him from posturing up to escape my guard.

Now that I've repositioned my legs with Joey's head and left arm in between my guard, I now must rotate my body to the opposite side. I do this by curling my left leg down to pivot off Joey's upper body, and contracting my oblique muscles to move my torso.

I continue to pivot in a clockwise direction until I am ninety degrees perpendicular to Joey's torso, with my head closest to Joey's right leg. As I pivot, I make sure to keep my legs around Joey's neck and left arm, while controlling his head with my left hand.

I now raise my right leg up to bring it over the top of my left foot.

As my right leg comes up, I curl my left leg down.

As my left foot moves down, I place the crook of my right leg over my left foot.

As I lock my legs together and pinch my knees tight, I can release my grip on Joey's head. Because my legs are preventing him from posturing out of my guard, I now lace my left arm underneath his right armpit to prevent him from rotating or striking my head.

Now that Joey is secured in the triangle choke, and I'm protected from taking damage, I can finish the submission by curling my legs downward and pinching my knees together. This causes my left leg to press against his right carotid artery, and his own shoulder against his left carotid. This pressure reduces blood flow to his brain, forcing him to tap out or pass out.

ARMBAR TO OMOPLATA

As we've just seen, every submission attempt has a backup plan. In this sequence, I demonstrate another option should your opponent successfully defend against the armbar by freeing his trapped arm. Rather than controlling your opponent's head, this submission seeks to retain control over his opposite arm and move him into a shoulder lock called the omoplata. Like the armbar, the omoplata attacks the elbow and shoulder by isolating his arm and bending it in a way that puts your entire body weight on his shoulder joint. The omoplata is not a common submission in MMA because it's difficult to complete. However, it will always give you positional advantage and a great deal of control over your opponent, so it's a position that's worth attempting. Even if you are unable to end the fight with the omoplata, the omoplata position will usually create other attack opportunities.

I start from the single armbar position with my left leg over my opponent's head and his right arm trapped.

Joey postures up by pushing his left hand against my chest while lifting his right shoulder to get leverage. Next, he rips his arm out to avoid the armbar, but with his left arm isolated and both of my legs over his head, I'm still in a good position to transition to the omoplata.

The first thing I do to continue my attack is make sure I have control of his left arm. I grab his wrist with my left hand while sliding my right hand underneath his leg and hooking it behind his left thigh.

Using my right hook on Joey's left leg, I pull my body parallel with his body. At the same time, I drive my right leg down into his left shoulder, forcing his weight forward and his head toward the mat. Next, I hook the crook of my left leg over my right foot, trapping his shoulder in place. To secure the omoplata, I put my right ear up against his thigh and use my left hand to force his left hand upward, putting a tremendous amount of pressure on his left shoulder. It is important to notice that I keep my right hand on his left thigh to prevent him from escaping the submission by executing a forward roll. It is also important to mention that some fighters like to sit up from this position to add additional pressure to the submission. This is fine if your opponent doesn't tap, but make sure to maintain control of his lower body to prevent him from rolling forward.

NINETY-DEGREE CUT TO OMOPLATA

Now we'll use the ninety-degree cut to move directly into the omoplata to give you further submission options when you are in the full guard. Properly securing your opponent's wrist and leg will help you keep control as you are locking up the omoplata. This technique is best utilized when your opponent is posturing up. Instead of directly attacking his posture and breaking him down, you allow him to elevate his torso and merely rotate to the side and attack one of his flanks.

I am on my back with Joey in my full guard. I have both hands on his elbows to control his arms. Because I'm controlling his arms rather than his entire posture, Joey is able to elevate his upper body.

I reach across my body with my left hand and grasp Joey's left wrist to trap it.

This part of the technique has to be fast or Joey will be able throw elbow strikes with his left arm. I unhook my feet to get more mobility and make a ninety-degree cut with my upper body by turning onto my right side. Keeping my guard closed would make it impossible to pivot enough to execute the move.

I slide my right hand underneath Joey's left leg and hook it around his hamstring. This gives me leverage to continue pivoting in a counterclockwise direction.

I swing my left leg in front of Joey's head. As my left leg comes around, I creep my right leg up under his left armpit.

I continue to swing my left leg around Joey's head. Notice how I press my head against his left leg so he's unable to step over my head and escape. It is also important to notice that I've essentially spun 180 degrees at this point, facing the opposite direction from when the move started.

I bend my right leg over Joey's left shoulder so it's isolated and then press down on his armpit to force his body weight forward.

I hook the crook of my left leg over my right foot to secure Joey's arm.

I contract my abs to sit up while forcing my feet to the ground. Because of the lock on Joey's shoulder, this forces him to go face down into the mat. Notice I retain my hook on his left leg until the last possible moment. If he feels me release that control, he may attempt to do a front flip to escape the pressure.

I unhook my right arm from underneath Joey's thigh and put it over his back so he can't roll out. Now that he's secured, I can continue to sit forward to apply pressure to the submission.

I unhook my feet and move my left leg back. This allows me to continue leaning forward to rotate Joey's shoulder. His trapped arm is being bent over my right thigh in a way that it was not designed to and is very painful. If he doesn't tap, I am in a dominant position to transition to a rear mount.

I lean further over the top of Joey's body to apply additional downward pressure on his left shoulder. It is very important to notice that I still have his left hand trapped over the top of my right thigh. If you lose this control, your opponent can pull his arm out and escape the submission.

HEAD AND ARM CHOKE

Sometimes you must create your own openings for a submission, and sometimes your opponent will hand them to you on a silver platter. In this sequence, my opponent has become lazy and allows his arm to drift up high toward my head. This gives me a great opportunity to feed his arm across my torso and apply a head and arm choke, which is similar to the triangle choke because it traps one arm and presses it against your opponent's neck to disrupt the flow of blood to his brain. The head and arm choke can be easily accomplished from the guard, especially when your opponent allows his weight to drift too far forward, he leaves an arm outstretched, or he becomes too complacent and stagnant. It's quick and sneaky, and it sends a clear signal to your opponent that you have a lot of tools in your toolbox. Even if you're unsuccessful at completing it, there's very little risk in this move because if it doesn't work, you are still in the full guard, so you're not giving up anything to attempt it.

1) I am on my back with Brian in my full guard. I have one hand on the back of his head to prevent him from posturing up and the other hand on his elbow for control. **2)** I unhook my feet and scoot my hips out toward the same side that I'm controlling his arm (the right in this case) while pulling his head down with my left hand. **3)** As if I were slipping a punch, I push Brian's left arm past my head and pull his head all the way down to mine so we are ear to ear. I then wrap my left arm around his neck to secure his head in place. **4)** I fold my left arm over the back of his neck and place my left hand in the crook of my right elbow. **5)** With my grip in place, I fold my right arm over my left hand, squeeze my elbows together, and force my left ear into Brian's right ear. This cinches up the choke and cuts off the blood flow to Brian's brain. Should this submission fail, I still have a good angle to attack with armbars, arm drags, or I can take his back.

FORCED TRIANGLE (VERSION 1)

The previous technique showed a situation in which I waited for my opponent to make a mistake in order to set up a submission. The next two moves illustrate how you can force an unwilling opponent into a submission from the full guard by utilizing control and flexibility. Here I'm setting up a triangle from the closed guard on a resisting opponent. The aim of all triangle chokes is to retain one of your opponent's arms inside of your guard and force the other one out. This allows you to use your legs to choke off blood flow to his brain. However, against a resisting opponent it can be difficult to force his arm out of your guard. Here I'm utilizing a deep overhook to control his posture and wrist control to manipulate his arm. This allows me to attack his arm in a few different ways, always seeking to feed it out of my guard.

The key to this technique is a tight overhook. If he postures up while you have the overhook in place, he will be unable to fully elevate his torso. Because your overhook is pinning him to your body, he will only be able to create a small amount of space between your bodies, allowing you to slide your knee underneath his arm. However, if your overhook is loose he will likely posture up fully. At that point you should consider moving onto another submission.

1 I am on my back with Brian in my full guard. My left arm is overhooking his right arm to control his posture. My right hand is controlling his wrist, and my guard is closed to secure his hips.

2 I unhook my feet and scoot my hips to my left, allowing me to put my right hip on the mat. This creates the space I need to feed my leg under Brian's arm.

3 I push Brian's arm away from his body while bringing my right knee toward my chest.

4 I continue to draw my right knee up toward my chest. The goal is to bring my knee up high enough that my shin is pressing against Brian's biceps. This will create a barrier, preventing him from driving forward into me to eliminate the space I've created.

5 I now use my shin to force Brian's arm upward, creating ample space for me to draw my leg under his arm. Because his arm is so far away from his body, he will be unable to pin my leg down as it comes underneath his arm.

6

When there's enough room, I slip my leg completely underneath Brian's arm. To prevent him from driving forward to eliminate the space I've created, I keep his arm extended away from his body using my right hand and place my right foot on his biceps.

7

Now I slip my right leg under his arm and put it over his shoulder.

8

Releasing my right grip on Brian's left wrist, I underhook his left arm for leverage.

9

I use my right leg to drive his head down, controlling his posture. This will give me all the leverage I need to swing my other leg over and complete the submission.

10

I swing the back of my left knee over top of my right foot, while at the same time bringing my right hand across my body to control Brian's free arm.

11

Brian's head and arm are now trapped. I squeeze my knees together and curl my legs down to apply pressure to the choke and finish the submission.

FORCED TRIANGLE (VERSION 2)

Although the previous triangle can work great against a resisting opponent, he does have counters available to him. If he can drive his elbow in toward his body, it prevents you from achieving the space needed to slide your knee underneath his arm. This version of the forced triangle counters your opponent's counter. As he drives his elbow toward his body, you go with his energy and trap his arm to the inside of his body. While this makes it impossible to move your leg underneath of his arm, it allows you to move your leg over the top of his arm and setup the triangle. As with the previous triangle, a tight overhook is mandatory to secure this submission.

I am on my back with Brian in my full guard. I have my left arm overhooked on his right arm to immobilize it and I am controlling his head with my right arm to prevent him from posturing up.

I grab his left wrist with my right hand to start the forced triangle.

I unhook my feet and scoot my hips to my left while rolling onto my right hip. He senses the triangle coming and moves his left elbow toward his body to prevent me from sliding my right leg underneath his arm.

I counter by pushing his arm down below my hip while swinging my right leg out and over his trapped arm. Some people have a tendency to put their foot on their opponent's hip at this point, but I feel that it's easier to swing your leg out and over his shoulder.

My right leg comes up and over Brian's arm and presses against his left shoulder.

I let go of Brian's left wrist.

I underhook Brian's left arm for leverage. At the same time, I use my right leg to push him to my left side while rotating my upper torso to my right. This will give me all the angle I need to swing my other leg over and complete the submission.

Because of the perpendicular position of our torsos, it's now a simple matter to bring the crook of my left knee over my right foot, triangling my legs together. Brian's head and arm are now trapped. I squeeze my knees together to put all the pressure I can muster. With my right leg digging into the left side of his neck and my left leg forcing his trapped arm into the right side of his neck, blood flow is severed to his brain.

STRIKES

It's unlikely that you will knock your opponent out by striking from the bottom, but it's still an extremely useful tool that must be utilized to make your guard effective. When you have your opponent in your guard, strikes are best used to set up a submission attempt or get him to move in a way that's advantageous to you. An active guard is the best guard, so when all else fails, I advocate staying busy and using strikes from the bottom to set your opponent up for a maneuver.

This section will cover the basic strikes you have at your disposal when your opponent is in your full guard. However, instead of striving to use these strikes to KO your opponent, I show them in conjunction with submission finishes. The strikes shown in this section will cause an accumulation of damage should your opponent allow you to land repeatedly, but the real use of the strikes is to create a reaction that opens up a submission finish. I believe in keeping the arts open-minded instead of dictating to you what you should do in every situation. Practice these strikes and determine what you are comfortable following them up with. We'll look at a pair of strike-submission combinations, but then you play around with the moves you've learned and figure out what's best for you.

DOWNWARD ELBOW STRIKE

This strike maximizes the full leverage of the lower and upper body by pulling them together to deliver a devastating blow to the top of your opponent's head that can easily daze or cut him. It has to be thrown when your opponent's head is near to your hips or it won't be effective. By forcing your opponent's head down toward your hips, you gain more room to generate velocity for the strike. If your opponent keeps his head up next to yours, then this strike is not a good option.

The downward elbow is great for getting your opponent to make a mistake because it's hard to defend against and is so painful that he'll do anything to get away from it. Many times this strike will force your opponent to bring his hands up to protect his head or frustrate him enough to do something drastic, like posture up while leaving his arms on your chest where you can grab and attack them. This strike is great for creating openings for several of the submissions we looked at in the last section. Striking the back of the head is illegal in MMA, so you have to be careful to deliver this strike to the right place.

1 I am on my back with Julie in my full guard. Her head is pinned to my midsection and my hips are riding high on her torso.

2 Maintaining control of Julie's head with my left hand, I bring my other arm high above my head. I post my feet on the floor to allow me to bridge my hips off the ground. This will help me generate maximum power in the strike.

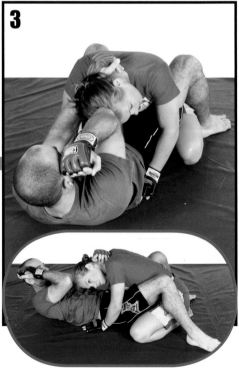

3 With one explosive movement, I contract my abdominal muscles and bring my elbow down on the top of Julie's head.

UPWARD ELBOW STRIKE

The upward elbow strike is a good tool to utilize when your opponent postures up and has stopped throwing punches. By trapping the back of the head you can stabilize your opponent's face, which allows you to throw accurate elbow strikes. There's a little risk when throwing this because your opponent can punch over your striking arm when it's extended. You can counter this by keeping your shoulder high to protect your chin. Remember, the goal is not to out-strike your opponent from your back, but rather to elicit a reaction.

1) I am on my back with Julie in my full guard. My right hand is controlling the back of her head to keep her face immobilized.

2) While pulling her head down with my right hand, I turn my left elbow upward, contract my abs, and rotate my shoulders in order to target her eye, temple, or chin. At this point, Julie could counterstrike over my elbow, but I am prepared for her reaction and will use it to my advantage.

UPWARD STRIKES

As I said before, striking at an opponent in your guard rarely results in a KO, but they're very useful in distracting him while you set up a submission or getting him to abandon a guard pass. Upward strikes are also useful when your opponent is postured up or is tired and doesn't have a real plan of attack. When your opponent lifts his head up and doesn't protect it, he is vulnerable. Take advantage of the situation with upward strikes and use the opportunity to create an opening for a submission or at least cause your opponent to rethink his course of action. Many times effective upward strikes will make your opponent protect his head by burying it in your chest, which allows you to trap it and strike it more.

1) I am on my back with Julie in my full guard. **2)** I reach my left arm over Julie's hands and grab her left wrist. By doing this, my forearm traps her right hand so both are immobilized. **3)** I draw my free hand back to strike up at her chin. The chin is the optimal contact point for strikes to the head. **4)** I strike upward with a cross-style punch while keeping Julie's wrists trapped so she can't defend against my strike. **5)** Using the momentum from the punch I bring my hand across my body to chamber it for a hammer fist. **6)** With Julie's wrists still trapped, I strike with the hammer fist to the side of her temple. Be sure to strike with the fleshy part of the hand and not the knuckles.

THE GROUND GAME

UPWARD STRIKES TO ARMBAR

In this sequence I demonstrate how to use the strikes we just learned to set yourself up for a fight-ending submission. A couple of hard strikes from the guard can really daze your opponent. When you finish a striking sequence with a hammer fist, it adds the momentum needed to pivot straight into an armbar. This technique combines the upward strikes and the ninety-degree cut to irritate your opponent, isolate an arm, and then attack it. There's little risk in this move because if your opponent rips his arm out before you can secure it, you're still in a good position to attempt a triangle or omoplata.

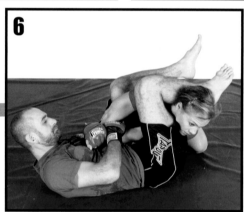

1) I am on my back with Julie in my full guard. To trap her arms in place, I reach my left arm over her hands and grab her left wrist. 2) I deliver a straight right punch to her chin. 3) As I recoil my arm, I move it across my body and chamber it for a hammer fist. 4) I strike across Julie's cheek with a hard hammer fist. In addition to causing damage, the strike gives me the leverage I need to make a ninety-degree cut and set up the armbar. 5) Having disrupted Julie's balance with the hammer fist, I turn onto my left hip and pivot my upper body ninety degrees by pushing off her head. It is important to notice that I have kept a tight hold on her left wrist and my feet are pointing toward my left side. 6) With Julie's left arm trapped to my chest, I apply the armbar by swinging my left leg over her head, pinching my knees together, driving my legs downward, and thrusting my hips upward into her left elbow.

ROUND KNUCKLE

Many times your opponent will bury his head in your chest to avoid strikes. In such a situation, the round knuckle is an excellent strike to employ because it allows you to continue to hit your opponent even though he is in a turtle-like position. Though I don't normally prefer a closed guard, you can keep your legs closed during this strike to make it harder for your opponent to pass as you punch.

1) I am on my back with Julie in my full guard. She has put her head on my chest to protect it, so I immediately place my left hand on the back of her head to trap it. Notice how I extend my right arm to get maximum velocity for a strike. 2) I turn my knuckles over and strike inward, aiming for the area just below Julie's ear. It is important to note that strikes to the back of the head are illegal, so if Julie turns her head away from the knuckle strike, I will switch my grip and strike with the other hand to avoid getting penalized.

ROUND KNUCKLE TO KIMURA

Now we'll expand on the round knuckle strike and learn how to use it to set up a submission. As you land repeated round knuckle strikes to your opponent's head, he will usually extend a hand to block them. Although this often allows him to defend against your strikes, it leaves him open for the kimura submission, which is where you attack his shoulder by rotating it backward.

1

I am on my back with Julie in my full guard. She has positioned her head low on my chest to prevent me from attacking her neck, so I use my left hand to pin her head down. At the same time, I extend my right arm to get maximum velocity for a strike.

2

I turn my knuckles over and strike inward, aiming for the area just below her ear.

3

When I retract my arm for another strike, Julie puts her left hand out to block my attack. This reaction has isolated her arm, which is precisely the reaction I was anticipating.

I quickly open my guard and sit up, coming onto my right hip. Simultaneously, I take my left hand off the back of her head and hook it over her outstretched arm to trap it.

With my right hand I grab Julie's left wrist for control. Since my left arm is already in place over Julie's left arm, it's a simple matter to grab my own wrist, totally immobilizing her left arm. Even if she were to block the submission from here, I'm still in a safe position because she can't reach across with her other arm and strike me. I'm also in a good position to try an omoplata should I lose my grip.

To complete the submission, I hook my right leg over Julie's body to prevent her from rolling out of my attack, rotate my shoulders toward my left side, turn onto my left hip, and crank her left arm toward her head using my grips. The combination of these actions places a tremendous amount of pressure on her left shoulder, causing her to tap in submission.

SWEEPS

Certainly there are situations in which fighters have won matches from the bottom position, but generally in a fight, you want to attempt to secure the top position. Sweeping your opponent allows you to move from a disadvantageous position into a beneficial situation. Sweeps can be achieved as a result of your opponent's mistakes or they can be deliberately created by manipulating your opponent's weight and employing strategic positioning. Always make sure you have enough room to accomplish a sweep before attempting it. If you want to roll your opponent over, but the cage is in your way, then obviously that sweep is not an option. If your chosen sweep is successful, it can change the scope of the fight and open up new opportunities.

LEG SWEEP

In this sequence I demonstrate an effective way to escape from underneath your opponent when an armbar submission fails. Although the leg sweep will put you in a position to execute a kneebar submission, it's important to keep in mind that this is not your objective. The leg sweep is just that—a sweep. The kneebar submission is so hard to secure from this position that I prefer to sweep my opponent all the way to his back, land in side mount, and then find a way to submit him. To nail the sweep, you must use your opponent's momentum and keep a firm grip on his leg throughout the technique.

1 I will start from the single armbar position. I am attacking Joey's right arm and attempting to finish an armbar.

2 Joey postures and pulls his right shoulder upward to get leverage. He rips his right arm out, but with his left arm isolated and both of my legs over his body, I'm still in a good position to sweep him. As we've seen before, this is a good opportunity to transition to an omoplata, but in case you cannot get full control of his left arm, the leg sweep is available.

3 I slide my right arm underneath Joey's left leg and hook it behind his thigh for leverage.

4 I bring my right knee to the ground to act as a pivot point for the rest of my body as I rotate.

5 My left leg moves around Joey's body and forms an X with my right leg. At the same time, I clasp my hands together behind his left hamstring. It's crucial that you keep your inside foot (the right one in this case) on your opponent's hip to maintain leverage. You'll need this foot to drive your opponent over.

6 I pull Joey's leg toward me while pivoting on my right knee.

Once Joey's leg is straight, he loses his balance and falls backward. I use my momentum to come up onto both knees.

I continue to roll Joey until he's flat on his back. When the roll is complete, I swing my right leg to the outside of his left leg and move my body to face him. Notice how I have maintained my left grip on his left leg to prevent him from escaping

I pivot and place my right hand underneath Joey's neck to gain positive control over him.

I follow through and land in side mount, cradling Joey's top leg with my left arm and his head with my right arm. Notice how I use my control to turn him onto his side and limit his escape options.

OMOPLATA SWEEP

The omoplata can be a difficult submission to lock in. The lack of friction between your legs and your opponent's arm often allows him to slip out. When attempting the omoplata you should anticipate the failure of the submission. However, if the submission fails, you're still in a great position to sweep your opponent. Having both his leg and arm trapped on the same side of his body allows you to sweep him with minimal effort. As soon as you realize the omoplata is going you fail, you must quickly adjust and transition into the sweep. If you allow your opponent to recognize the situation, he may find a way to escape both attacks and stay in the top position.

1) I start on my back in the omoplata submission position. I have my right arm hooked under Joey's left thigh and his left arm trapped between my legs. My left leg is hooked over my right foot to secure his limb. 2) I start by rolling onto my left hip, away from Joey. As my left foot drops to the mat, it stretches Joey's body out and weakens his base. It is important to mention that my left foot will be my main leverage point for the sweep. 3) As I continue to roll, I drive my body toward my left side using my left foot. This causes Joey to roll over my body. With his left arm and left leg trapped, he is unable to post on the mat and block the sweep. 4) Once Joey is on his back, I use the momentum from the roll to rotate to my knees. Notice I'm still trapping his left arm and leg. 5) I bring my head up and begin to turn into Joey's body. It is important to notice that I have maintained control of his left arm using my legs. 6) I rotate to side mount and change my hand position. My right arm goes under Joey's head and my left goes under his left leg. I protect my head by pinning it tight to his chest. 7) Rotating around so I am perpendicular to Joey, I now have full side mount and one arm trapped between my legs. It's unlikely that I'll be able to keep Joey's arm trapped, but even if he rips his arm out, I'll still be in a solid pinning position.

ARM DRAG SWEEP

As we saw in the first section of this chapter, the arm drag rips your opponent off balance and gives you an angle to attack him with various techniques such as an armbar submission, a transition to the back, or a sweep. There's little risk when executing these techniques once you've achieved your dominant angle. Even if your opponent recognizes your intentions and counters, you will simply end up back in guard, ready to attack once again. However, by chaining together several techniques from this position, the likelihood of succeeding with one of your attacks multiplies. In this sequence, I use the arm drag to take my opponent's back, he counters by driving his shoulder into me, and I use his counter to execute the arm drag sweep. Remember, if your initial attack doesn't work, build on it and keep attacking. Always dictate the fight.

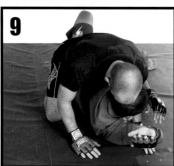

1) I am on my back with Joey in my full guard. Since he put a hand on my chest, I have moved my right hand down and grabbed his left wrist for control. **2)** With my left hand, I reach up and grab the back of Joey's left triceps, just above the elbow. There's a slight risk here that he will reach across and strike with his free hand. However, if I react quickly and move my body off-line he won't have time to land a power shot before I achieve a dominant angle. **3)** I push Joey's hand across my body using my right hand and drag his left arm toward my left armpit using my left hand. This causes him to lose his balance, forcing him to fall forward and to my left. At this point I unlock my guard to allow me to move my hips underneath Joey. **4)** I pass Joey's elbow completely across my body. Because Joey has lost his balance and is unable to put any weight on my hips, this enables me to move around underneath of his body. **5)** I sit up on my left elbow and reach across his back with my right arm to grab his lat muscle. In this position my first option would be to continue to move my hips right, escaping from underneath of Joey until I am able to take his back. **6)** As I'm attempting to take Joey's back, he counters my movement by driving his left shoulder into my body, stopping my movement and pinning me to the mat. Because my back transition has been stopped, I must move on to the sweep. To acquire the leverage needed to execute the sweep, I plant my right foot on the mat. Notice I keep his left arm secure with my left hand, maintain a tight grip on his lat with my right hand, and keep my chest close to his shoulder to prevent him from posturing. **7)** To initiate the sweep, I maintain my grip on Joey's lat and pull upward. At the same time, I post my right foot and roll onto my right hip. This is a simple movement, but because Joey is driving into me, he adds momentum to the sweep. With my right leg blocking his left leg, and with my left arm hooked around his right arm, it is very difficult for him to post out to block the sweep. **8)** When Joey's back hits the ground, I quickly throw my left leg over his torso to prevent him from rolling away. **9)** Using the momentum from the roll, I continue to rotate until I end up in the mount position with both my knees flat on the ground.

SCISSOR SWEEP

With the scissor sweep, you use one leg to push against your opponent's hips and your other leg to pull on his opposite leg. When done correctly, this scissor motion off-balances your opponent and forces him over to his back. It's especially useful when your opponent creates a little space between your torsos, but he doesn't quite posture all the way up. Like the arm drag, the scissor sweep is a versatile platform that gives you many options to attack. If the sweep doesn't work, it will usually create a couple of submission options that we'll cover later. Hip movement and abdominal strength are key to this technique because your lower torso will do most of the work.

1

I am on my back with Joey in my full guard. My right hand is on his neck to control his head and my left hand is just above his elbow. My feet are unhooked so I can rotate my hips and move my legs easily.

2

Maintaining a firm grip on Joey's head and arm to control his posture, I pivot my body until I'm resting on my left hip.

3

I bring my right knee between Joey's body and my own. I place my knee high on his chest, not on his stomach. The higher I bring my knee, the more leverage I will have to turn his body.

4

Now I start the sweep by pulling Joey's head lower and pulling his right arm into his body so he can't base out with it and block the sweep. This sweep will not work by simply pushing Joey over to one side. I have to pull his upper body toward me to take his weight off his hips. At the same time I pull Joey's head down, I drop my left leg down to the mat. The lower I drop my left leg, the more leverage I give myself to execute the sweep.

5

Now that Joey's head is down and his weight is off his knees, it's a simple matter to kick his legs out from underneath his body. By curling my left leg into his right leg and driving his upper body toward my left side using my right leg, he begins to tumble toward his back. Notice I'm still controlling his head with my right hand. It is also important to notice that his right arm and right leg are blocked, which prevents him from posting out and blocking the sweep.

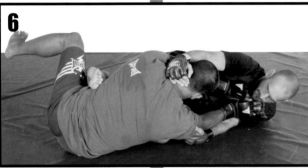

6

As the momentum builds, Joey and I continue to roll over.

7

As Joey rolls over and my left leg hits the ground, I drive off my left foot to add momentum to the roll. In some instances my head will also provide some leverage if it touches the mat.

8

Having executed the sweep properly, the momentum from the scissor motion carries me all the way to the mount.

9

I now secure a full mount position. Notice how both of my knees are flat on the mat.

SCISSOR SWEEP TO ARMBAR

In this sequence I demonstrate how to use the threat of a scissor sweep to set up an armbar submission. Many times a fighter will anticipate the scissor sweep and defend against it, when in fact your true intent is to attack with this armbar. The great part about this technique is that your opponent's counter to the scissor sweep moves him straight into the armbar, allowing you to catch him off guard. Personally, I find it very useful against overconfident opponents who assume they have figured out my guard game.

TECHNICAL NOTE: Deception is a major component of my fighting system. I believe in staying unpredictable.

I am on my back with my legs scissored on Joey's hips. My right hand is on his neck to control his head and my left hand is just above his right elbow.

As I try to sweep him over, Joey blocks the technique by posturing up. However, by fighting the sweep and driving his weight to his left, he has made it easy for me to switch directions and attack with the armbar.

I quickly switch my hips and rotate my upper torso back to my right side at a ninety-degree cut. Notice how this puts me in the perfect position to throw my left leg over his head for the armbar. However, it's absolutely critical that I maintain positive control of Joey's right triceps as I transition onto my right hip or I will lose the submission.

I swing my left leg over Joey's head, curl my legs down, and thrust my hips up to complete the armbar.

SCISSOR SWEEP TO TRIANGLE

This is another option you have when your opponent blocks the scissor sweep. By initiating your attack with a sweep, you often place your opponent into a situation where he must choose between relinquishing top control or opening up an opportunity for you to attack with a more threatening technique. Here my opponent stops my sweep, only to give me an easy path for a triangle choke.

I am on my back with Joey in my full guard. My right hand is on his neck to control his head and my left hand is positioned just above his elbow. My feet are unhooked so I can move my hips and use my legs easily.

Maintaining a firm grip on Joey's head and arm, I rotate onto my left hip and bring my right knee between our torsos.

As I scissor my legs in an effort to sweep Joey, he uses his right hand to base out and block the technique. Even though he's stopped the sweep, he's isolated his right arm away from his body. To utilize the space he's created, I switch the grip on my left hand to prevent Joey from moving his arm back toward his body. I must react quickly to his mistake or he will retract his arm and I will lose my opportunity.

I bring my left leg through the gap he's created and place it over his shoulder.

I now leverage my left leg down on the back of his neck. At the same time, I hip out to my right side. After my left leg is in position over his neck, I begin to move my right leg over the top of my left shin.

I continue to pivot my hips with my head moving toward Joey's right leg. Notice I'm still controlling his head with my right hand to prevent him from posturing as I adjust. It is also important to notice that I've underhooked his right arm using my left arm to prevent him from striking my head.

To complete the submission, I hook the crook of my right leg over the top of my left shin and squeeze my knees together, severing blood flow to his brain. I also clasp my hands together to trap his arm and prevent him from posturing.

DOUBLE-ANKLE PICK TO MOUNT

Many times your opponent will stand inside of your full guard to get more leverage behind his punches, which can be effective if he knows how to set his base and has solid defense. But if he is unstable and his weight is too far forward or back, employing the double-ankle pick is a great way to get him off his feet and transition to mount. Even if you fail to achieve the mount, this sweep can create several opportunities, such as a kneebar or heel hook. The biggest risk when attempting this move is your opponent dropping his weight to defend and then striking over the top of your defense. Any time you take your hands away from home it can create opportunities for your opponent to do damage, so be prepared to bring your guard back up high should your opponent begin to land strikes as you go for the sweep.

1

I am on my back with Julie in my full guard. My hands are on her elbows to control her arms and my guard is closed to control her hips.

2

Julie gets to her feet in order to throw strikes from the standing position. Notice how by rising up she has broken my guard open.

3

When she rears back to throw a strike, I grab both of her ankles and pinch my knees together in her midsection, which will give me more leverage to push her over backward.

Before Julie can throw a strike, I pull her feet toward my head. At the same time, I drive into her midsection with my knees. The combination of these actions causes her to fall backward.

As Julie is forced to her back, I use my hands to push myself up and past her legs. From here, I will transition to my knees one leg at a time. It is important to continue holding your opponent's ankles until you are passed his or her legs.

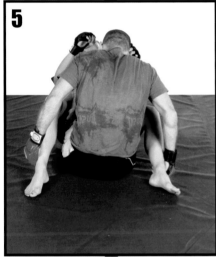

I end up in full mount on top of Julie with both knees flat on the mat.

TRANSITIONS

As I stated before it's imperative to keep an active guard and constantly look for any submissions opportunities that your opponent grants you, or to create those opportunities for yourself. Transitions are vital to opening up these opportunities. Being able to switch from one guard position to another is a critical aspect of the ground game. If you cease to be effective in one position, it's obvious that it's time to move on to your secondary plan of attack. Fighters who can transition from one guard to another are very dangerous. By continually moving they create openings that wouldn't have been available otherwise. Generally, transitions involve quick, explosive movements that take advantage of your opponent being off balance or unable to block your movement.

UNFORCED OCTOPUS TO REAR MOUNT

The movements in this upcoming series have the same goal—to transition from the full guard to the rear mount, which is an excellent position from which to finish the fight. The transition in this sequence, called the unforced octopus, is a simple movement that capitalizes on a mistake your opponent makes from inside your guard. The transition in the next sequence will demonstrate how to force your opponent into giving you the space needed to execute the octopus transition. Both moves rely on getting your upper body underneath your opponent's arm and then wrapping yourself around his upper torso to get his back. The technique shown below is useful when your opponent's strikes are slow or arc too far and create a lot of space for you to get under. The great thing about this move is the low-risk nature of the technique. If you fail to transition to your opponent's back, you're still momentarily protecting yourself from strikes. Anytime you can stall your opponent's offense and force him to defend your movement, you're dictating the pace of the fight.

I am on my back with Joey in my full guard. My guard is closed and my hands are on his elbows.

The transition starts when Joey reaches back to strike. By bringing his arm up high to throw a punch, he's created a large space for me to slide through. I quickly roll my torso to my right, not to block the strike, but to slip underneath it, giving me an angle to take his back. By raising my left arm I'm creating a ramp which Joey's punch will slide down, giving me access to his back. In case my timing or positioning is off and his punch manages to bypass my left arm, I'm also raising my right hand in front of my face to stop it.

As he strikes, the punch slides down my left arm while I slip underneath his right armpit. Notice I'm still protecting my head with my right hand.

The momentum from Joey's missed punch causes him to lean forward. At the same time, I wrap my left arm around his back and grab his lat muscle to use it for leverage. My right hand posts out on the ground to allow me to sit up and move my hips to the right.

Driving off my right foot, I rotate my upper body around to Joey's back and clasp my hands together under his right armpit.

Posting on my right foot, I draw my left leg out from underneath Joey and come to my knees. I am now on top of Joey with a positive control on his upper body.

7

With my left leg now free, I'm able to insert my left foot over the top of Joey's left leg. This leg hook gives me partial control over Joey's hips. After I insert my first hook, I move my hips over his back in order to place myself in a better position to insert my second hook.

8

I now slip my right foot in over top of Joey's right leg. This gives me complete control over Joey's hips, putting me in a great position to finish the fight.

FORCED OCTOPUS TO REAR MOUNT

This is the same move as the unforced octopus, but instead of taking advantage of your opponent being overextended, you initiate the move by controlling your opponent's arm and forcing it outward. This allows you to slip your head underneath his armpit and move toward his back. The end result is the same, but the forced octopus takes a little more effort than the unforced version. Controlling your opponent's arm and forcing him to make a mistake is more difficult than simply allowing him to botch up on his own. Unfortunately, you can't always rely upon your opponent to make a mistake, so actively forcing him into bad positions is sometimes the only path to winning a fight.

1

I am on my back with Joey in my full guard. My legs are closed to control his hips, while my right hand is controlling his left wrist and my left hand is controlling his right elbow.

2

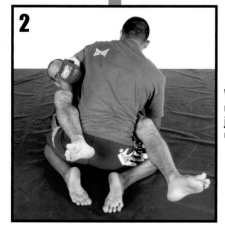

While maintaining control of his left wrist, I reach up with my left arm and grab his right arm just above the elbow, similar to an arm drag. I unhook my legs and move my hips out to my left.

With both hands, I pry Joey's left arm away from his body to create the opening I need to slide my torso underneath. This space is what allows me to continue forward.

I duck under Joey's left arm while maintaining control on his wrist with my right hand. Again I'm using my left arm as a ramp to guide my head underneath his armpit. With my left arm extended, it will be difficult for him to regain his position should I lose my grip on his wrist.

I wrap my left arm over Joey's back and grab his lat muscle on his opposite side for leverage. I post my right hand on the mat to assist me in sitting upright.

I continue to sit up and rotate my hips toward my right. If I need extra leverage I can push off of my right foot.

I reach across Joey's back with my right arm while slipping my left arm underneath his neck. Next, I clasp my hands together under his right armpit, which will prevent him from rolling out of my control.

Pushing off with my right leg, I continue rotating until I am able to lace my left leg over Joey's left leg.

I bring both of my heels over his thighs to get both hooks in and complete the transition.

ARM DRAG TO REAR MOUNT

We've seen how versatile and effective the arm drag is earlier in the book. In this variation you can use it to transition yourself to your opponent's back and secure a rear mount. It's similar to the octopus and is a good backup plan when your opponent sees the octopus coming and blocks it. As with any situation in which you've acquired a two-on-one grip on your opponent's arms, he'll have a free arm to strike your head. To prevent this you have to quickly move your hips out and grab your opponent's latissimus muscle. After you've achieved that control, you have many different sweeps, transitions, and submissions available to you. However, to put yourself in the proper position to employ those techniques, you must first secure the arm and move your hips out.

I am on my back with Joey in my full guard. My left hand is on his elbow and I have moved my right hand down to control his left wrist.

I release Joey's right arm with my left hand and reach across his body to grab his left triceps, just above the elbow. There's a slight risk here that he will reach across and strike with his free hand, so I must not hesitate in this position.

With my right hand I push Joey's arm across my body and prepare to drag him toward me until he's off balance.

With my left hand I pull Joey's left arm toward my left armpit. At the same time, I scoot my hips out to my right and push on his elbow to keep him off balance. After Joey is completely off balance, I post my right foot on the mat to give me leverage for the next step.

5

I sit up and post my left elbow on the mat. This elevates my torso, allowing me to grab his right lat muscle with my right hand. This gives me the leverage needed to move toward his back.

6

I continue to rotate my hips, using my right foot and left elbow as points of base to slide my left leg out from underneath Joey's body.

7

With my left leg now free, and my left knee on the mat as a point of base, I swing my right leg over Joey's back.

8

I slip my hooks in over his thighs to complete the transition.

TRANSITION TO FEET-ON-HIPS

The feet-on-hips guard, which is often referred to as spider guard, is a modified style of guard that allows you to create more separation between you and your opponent. It gives you an improved ability to push your opponent away, disrupt his attacks, and break away when you want to. Personally, I find it an effective position against wrestlers who like to drive forward. By placing your feet on his hips, you can create separation and escape the bottom position. The risk with the spider guard is that your opponent can back out from this position easier than he could if he were in your full guard. It's not a position that you should assume without thinking it out first. Giving up a full guard for a spider guard is something that should be planned for ahead of time after considering your opponent's strengths and weaknesses. Hand trapping and hip movement are the essential elements of this move.

1 I am on my back with Brian in my full guard. My right hand is on his left wrist and my left hand is cupped behind his head to immobilize it. Both of these hand positions are meant to keep my opponent from posturing up and striking while I perform the transition.

2 I break my guard and bring my right leg up until I can place my foot on his hip. Depending on the space between our hips, I may have to scoot my hips out in order to create the space needed.

3 I mimic the motion with my left leg while simultaneously slipping my left hand down from Brian's head to his right wrist.

4 The transition ends with both of my feet on Brian's hips and both of my hands on his wrists. This is the feet-on-hips guard.

TRANSITION TO BUTTERFLY GUARD

Similar to the feet-on-hips position, the butterfly guard is another position that requires you to place you legs between yourself and your opponent. However, instead of simply placing your feet on your opponent's hips to block his forward progress, you're using your entire shin as a barrier to create space. With your feet hooked underneath your opponent's thighs rather than placed on his hips, you not only have the ability to drive him away from you, you also have the leverage needed to elevate his body with your legs. This makes it a great position from which to initiate sweeps. It's harder to transition into the butterfly guard from the full guard than the feet-on-hips position, but depending on the situation, it can be worthwhile. Like the spider guard, the butterfly guard is not something you should transition to on a whim, because you have less control over your opponent's legs than you do in the full guard. If you're unworried about your opponent standing up and escaping your guard, then the butterfly position can be a great option.

I am on my back with Brian in my full guard. I have my right hand on his head and my left on his right arm, just above the elbow. This controls his upper torso and prevents him from posturing up and striking.

I open my guard and make a ninety-degree cut to my right.

The ninety-degree cut has created enough space to bring my left leg up and slip it to the inside of Brian's thigh. I place my left foot in between his legs with my knee facing up.

4

Now it's time to repeat the process on the other side. I execute a ninety-degree cut to the left by rotating my upper torso to my left.

5

I remove my right hand from Brian's head, hook it under his left arm, and then grab his shoulder for leverage.

6

Now I bring my right leg up and slip it to the inside of Brian's thigh, hooking my foot in between his legs. I now have both hooks inside his groin and am in a good position to push him up.

7

To complete the transition, I clasp my hands behind Brian's back and pull him close to me. The underhooks will make it difficult for him to reach down and push my knees toward the mat, which would make it easier for him to pass my guard.

ESCAPES

An escape is like hitting a reset button—it breaks the combatants away from each other and restarts the fight on a level playing field. You always have to maintain the ability to disengage from your opponent in case things go wrong. If your opponent is winning on the ground, an escape will allow you to negate his strength and transition the fight back to the standing position.

Oftentimes escaping relies on moving your hips and maneuvering an elbow underneath you to act as a post. That means one of your arms is unable to defend your head when escaping. To counter this vulnerability you have to make sure to do two things: create as much space as possible between you and your opponent and use your free hand to defend your head from strikes. After that, escaping is a question of maneuvering your hips until you can get to your feet and set your base. Speed is key when pulling your feet out from under your opponent because the last thing you want is for him to grab an ankle and put you on your back after all the work you did to get up.

Rather than simply escape back to my feet, in some of the upcoming techniques I actually use the escape to sweep my opponent to his back. I prefer to show these moves together instead of in different sections. Escapes can often be a great setup for sweeps. As I'm about to escape back to my feet, my opponent will often scramble desperately to keep me pinned to the mat. This can cause him to make a mistake, allowing me to turn him over. For this reason I've put combination sweeps and escapes into the same section.

TOILET PLUNGER

Deciding on which way to escape or get up often depends on the head position that your opponent chooses. If he keeps his head buried in your chest and his arms tight against your sides, like many wrestlers tend to do, then the toilet plunger is my preferred getaway. It's a fairly simple technique that works by pushing your opponent's head away from you and shrimping your hips out from underneath him until you can stand.

1

I am on my back with Brian in my full guard. Notice that Brian is low on my body with his elbows tight against my sides. His head is low on my chest and his arms are stationary.

2

I put my hands on the crown of Brian's head (one on top of the other). This will give me leverage to push his head down and make it very difficult for him to strike my head.

3

I push his head down, open my guard, and turn onto my left hip. I use my shoulder blades like little feet and gradually crawl away from him.

4

I roll back to my right and continue to shrimp away while pushing on Brian's head with my hands. Notice that I roll all the way over onto my sides for leverage. Don't just turn your upper body. Roll all the way over onto your hip.

5

When I get enough separation, I put my right elbow on the ground and raise my upper body so I can create more space for my right leg to move underneath my body.

6

I slide my left leg in front of Brian's torso and press my shin against his midsection. This braces him and prevents him from driving forward. I also base my right hand out behind me. Notice that I always keep my left hand on Brian's head so he can't lunge forward to block the escape.

7

Now it's time to act fast. I post on my right hand and left foot while pushing my left hand against Brian's head. This allows me to elevate my hips and gives me the space to bring my right leg out from underneath him and base it outside of his reach.

8

I quickly bring my left leg out while keeping a hand on his head so he can't lunge forward and grab an ankle. From here, I will turn and face Brian and get back into my fighting stance. If your opponent tries to get up and is within striking distance, it's a very good time to throw a punching combination, or if he returns fully to his feet, a knee strike to his head.

TOILET PLUNGER TO HIP HEIST SWEEP

This technique is the backup plan when your opponent blocks the toilet plunger escape. It may be the second option, but it often has a higher success rate than the toilet plunger. If your opponent blocks the escape by grabbing onto your legs, then you can use it to your advantage by raising your hips, rotating them strongly into his chest, and rolling him over into the full mount. The nice part about this technique is that as your opponent wraps his arms around your legs to prevent you from standing, he's effectively captured his own hands. This prevents him from blocking the sweep by posting his hands on the mat. From there, it's a simple matter to bump him over until you land in the mount position.

1

I am on my back with Brian in my full guard. Notice that Brian is low on my body with his elbows tight against my sides. His head is on my chest and his arms are stationary.

2

I put my hands on the crown of Brian's head (one on top of the other). This will give me leverage to push his head down and will make it very difficult for him to strike my head.

3

I push his head down, open my guard, and turn onto my left hip. I use my shoulder blades like little feet and gradually crawl away from him.

4

I roll back to my right and continue to shrimp away while pushing on his head with my hands. Notice that I roll all the way over onto my sides for leverage. Don't just turn your upper body. Roll all the way over onto your hip.

5

When I get enough separation, I post my right hand on the ground and raise my hips so I can create more space for my right leg to slide through.

At this point Brian grabs my legs to prevent me from escaping. I am now unable to pull my legs out, so I transition to the hip heist. Notice that my right foot is braced against his left knee. This will prevent him from basing his leg out to his side as I sweep him.

Posting off my right hand and my feet, I drive my hips into Brian's torso, rotating him to my right. At this point, driving his head down is no longer necessary, so I release his head with my left hand and place it on the back of his left triceps. This will prevent him from posting out with his left hand should he recognize the sweep and attempt to stop it.

I continue driving my hips into Brian, rotating him to his back. Because of the position of my legs, as we reverse positions I move straight to the mount. By holding onto my legs and refusing to let go, Brian has actually made it easier for me to roll him over.

I end the sweep in the full mount with both of my knees flat on the mat.

GRECO GET-UP

As mentioned before, your opponent's body position will somewhat dictate what escapes are available to you. When your opponent is ear to ear with you, then there's no room for the toilet plunger. In this scenario I prefer the Greco get-up. Greco-Roman wrestlers love to get underhooks to control their opponents. This move is a Greco-style technique that uses an underhook to create space and allows you to free your hips enough to get up. The underhook allows you to open a door and then your hips scurry through it. The first thing you have to do with the Greco get-up is decide which side you want to lift and escape through.

1

I am on my back with Brian in my full guard. He has his head up high next to my head. This prevents me from pushing his head straight down, so I must think of an alternate way to escape the bottom position.

2

I want to escape to my left, so I unclasp my hands and pummel my left arm in underneath Brian's right armpit.

3

I secure my underhook and hook my hand on Brian's right shoulder. This will give me the leverage I need to create space and move my hips out from underneath his body.

4

I plant my left foot to use as a base for the movement.

5

I then lift his right arm with my left arm, creating space between our torsos. I then push off with my left leg and slide my hips to my left.

6

I post up onto my left foot and my right elbow.

7

I now use my points of base, my left foot and my right elbow to elevate my hips off the mat. As my hips elevate, I begin to turn into Brian, which allows me to escape my leg from underneath his body. As my leg comes underneath, I post my right knee on the mat, giving me a strong base.

8

Now I raise my right knee off the mat and post my right foot well behind my body to widen my base. This will make it hard for Brian to drive into my hips and secure a takedown. To further prevent him from achieving a takedown, I remove my right elbow from the mat and place it on his head, creating a barrier between our bodies.

9

I step back quickly so Brian can't grab my legs and get into my fighting stance. If your opponent tries to get up and is within striking distance, it's a very good time to throw a combination or a knee since he won't have his guard up.

GRECO SWEEP

Like the toilet plunger, your opponent can block the Greco get-up demonstrated in the previous sequence by grabbing your legs. Although this defense prevents you from escaping up to your feet, it creates an opportunity to employ the Greco sweep and claim the full mount. It is important to mention that this technique requires more strength than the Greco get-up, and in order to be successful with it, you must be extremely fluid and powerful in your actions. The goal is to execute the sweep while your opponent is still defending against the Greco get-up. If you delay with the transition, he will remove his arm from your legs, which allows him to block your sweep by basing his hand on the mat.

1

I am on my back with Brian in my full guard. He has his head next to my head.

2

I want to escape to my left, so I unclasp my hands and pummel my left arm in underneath Brian's right armpit.

3

I secure my underhook and hook my hand on Brian's right shoulder. This will give me the leverage I need to create space and move my hips out from underneath his body.

4

I plant my left foot to use as a base for the move. Suddenly Brian moves his left arm down and grabs my right leg so I can't pull it free. This is fine because with both of his arms tied up, he won't be able to base out and I can easily sweep him over.

I get up on my right elbow and left foot for leverage.

I put my arm out as a base and try to get my hips as high as I can.

With as much strength as I can muster, I push off with my left leg, lift Brian's upper body with my left arm and blast my hips forward into his chest. This knocks him off balance and starts to roll him over.

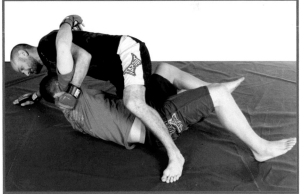

I continue the movement until Brian is on his back, and then throw my left leg over his torso to end up in the full mount.

I quickly get my weight down on him so he can't use the momentum to roll out of the position.

ESCAPES

BRACE GET-UP

We've looked at how to disengage from an opponent who keeps his head low and how to disengage from one who keeps his head high. Now we'll look at how to disengage from an opponent who keeps his distance and stays postured up. The brace get-up takes advantage of the space that is already between your opponent and you, keeps him from dropping his weight onto you, and allows you to escape back to your feet quickly. This is a favorite move of many MMA fighters because it not only allows you to escape to your feet while your opponent is down, but it also puts you in a great position to strike him as he gets up. There is a slight risk that your opponent will strike at your head while you execute this move, so keep your chin close in to your shoulder as you execute the escape.

1) I am on my back with Brian in my full guard. My hands are on the backs of his arms just above his elbows and my legs are unhooked so I can maneuver my hips easily and escape quickly. **2)** I place my left hand on Brian's right shoulder and push it away. My left hand will stay here throughout the move to ensure he doesn't lunge forward to block the escape. **3)** I move my right elbow behind me and plant it on the mat while rolling over onto my right hip. Notice how I have my chin tucked low into my left shoulder in case Brian tries to strike over my outstretched arm. **4)** I straighten my right arm to give me more leverage to lift my hips. **5)** I plant my left foot and right hand to secure my base, and then I lift my hips off the ground. **6)** With my hips off the mat, I'm able to easily pull my right leg underneath my body and plant it on the mat behind me. Notice my left hand is still on Brian's shoulder to create a barrier between our bodies. This prevents him from driving into me and taking away the space I just created. **7)** I back away and disengage. As you can see from the position we both end up in, I can deliver some hard strikes to Brian before he can get up or raise his arms for defense. If Brian lingers in this position, I can also drop down onto his back and attempt to take top position.

BRACE SWEEP

Like the toilet plunger and Greco get-ups, the brace get-up can be blocked if your opponent grabs your legs. Just like those other moves, you can use this to your advantage and sweep him into a full mount. The key here is to prevent him from driving your weight forward and dumping you back onto the ground. To do this you have to force your hips into him and blast forward before he has a chance to lift you up.

1 I am on my back with Brian in my full guard. My hands are on the backs of his arms just above his elbows and my legs are unhooked so I can maneuver my hips easier and escape quickly.

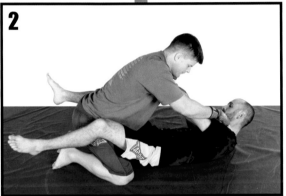

2 I place my left hand on Brian's right shoulder and push it away. My left hand will stay here throughout the move to ensure he doesn't lunge forward to block the escape.

3 I move my right elbow behind me and plant it on the mat while rolling over onto my right hip. Notice how I have my chin tucked low into my left shoulder in case Brian tries to strike over my outstretched arm.

4 I straighten my right arm to give me more leverage to lift my hips.

5

Brian suddenly realizes I'm attempting to stand up and wraps his arms around my legs to prevent my escape. At this point the escape will be difficult, so I decide to transition into the sweep. I quickly slide my left arm over his shoulder and wrap it around his left arm. This will prevent him from using it to stop my sweep.

6

Now I push off with my left leg and drive my hips into Brian's chest to throw him off balance and roll him over. It's important to execute this maneuver quickly and powerfully.

7

I land in the full mount.

8

I drop my weight onto his stomach to prevent him from using the momentum of the roll to escape.

UPWARD ELBOW STRIKE TO GET-UP

This is very similar to the brace get-up that we just looked at, but it adds a strike to create space, distract your opponent, and give you a better chance of success. The strike is not meant to cause much damage to your opponent, but it's a great way to disrupt him and disguise your true intent, which is to escape. Speed is more important than power when executing this move. Striking your opponent with an elbow will daze him, and you must take advantage of the time you have to move while your opponent is trying to get his bearings.

1 I am on my back with Julie in my full guard. I use my right hand to control the back of her head and prepare my left arm for an elbow strike.

2 I throw the upward elbow with my left arm while pulling her head into the strike with my right arm. Notice I'm keeping my left hand open and facing Julie as I throw the strike. This assists in defending my head as well as uncovering the bone of the elbow for a more damaging strike.

3 I use the momentum of the strike to put my left hand on Julie's shoulder. Like the brace get-up, my left hand will stay here throughout the move to control her upper body so she can't lunge into me and grab my legs. Simultaneously, I throw my right arm back to use as a base and rotate my hips, which will help me free my leg.

4 I get up on my right elbow, push off of Julie's shoulder, and quickly pull my right leg out from underneath her body.

5 I set my right leg behind me as a base while keeping a hand on her shoulder.

6 I back away and assume my fighting stance. As with other escapes, this is a good opportunity to throw strikes or secure the top position.

DOWNWARD ELBOW STRIKE TO GET-UP

As with the previous technique, this one uses the momentum of an elbow strike to create space and escape. It requires you to push on your opponent's head so you can pull your legs out, so your opponent's head positioning is key. The technique won't work if your opponent's head is up high, or ear-to-ear, with yours. If your opponent chooses to wrap his arms around you and hold on, you can easily transition to the hip heist sweep.

I am on my back with Julie in my full guard. Her head is in the middle of my chest—the perfect range for a downward elbow.

I unlock my guard and post both of my feet on the mat while bridging backward. This will allow me to generate maximum velocity with the strike. Notice I'm still controlling Julie's head with my left hand to prevent her from posturing up.

I throw a downward elbow on the top of Julie's head to stun her. Sometimes this will cause your opponent to defend the strikes by putting his hand on the top of his head, which will only make your escape easier to manage.

Reacting upon Julie's dazed state after the elbow strike, I force her head down and away from my torso using my right hand, post my left elbow on the mat, plant my right foot on the ground, and lift my hips off the floor.

As I post up on my left elbow and right foot, I turn my hips into Julie, causing my left leg to move out from underneath her body. As my leg moves under my hips, I plant my left knee on the ground to increase my base.

I post my left foot out and stand to complete the escape. I back away and assume my fighting stance. As with other escapes, this is a good opportunity to strike.

INSIDE THE FULL GUARD

Until now we've studied what options you have available when your opponent is in your full guard. Now we'll flip the coin and look at what to do when you are inside your opponent's guard. My overall philosophy is to stay busy. Use punch-pass combinations to constantly strike while looking for a way to pass your opponent's guard. Always use your punches to set up the pass. If your opponent blocks your pass, go back to punching. You should be thinking, "Hit, hit, hit, try to pass." Conversely if your opponent uses his hands to stop the pass, it will open him up to more punches. Keep going back and forth between punching and passing until one succeeds. If you attempt to use only one without the other, your opponent can easily shut you down.

STRIKES

When striking from inside of the guard, it is important to establish your posture first. The best method for creating posture is to put one hand on each of your opponent's shoulders and use them as a base from which to push yourself up. If you place your hands on your opponent's biceps or wrists, he can still strike over your hands with his. With most of your strikes delivered from the guard, you want to keep your torso at a forty-five-degree angle to the ground. Try to strike when and wherever his guard is absent and alternate your attacks—changing from low to high, left to right, head to body, and so on. Changing the location of your strikes will allow you to cause more damage to your opponent.

STRAIGHT PUNCH

I begin inside of Tom's closed guard with my hands on his shoulders to control his torso.

I pull my right arm back, elbow up high, to generate power for the punch.

I extend my right elbow, bringing a straight punch down on Tom's chin. When throwing straight punches from the guard, you should always twist at the hips and utilize your full body weight to deliver the strike.

HAMMER FIST

The hammer fist is a great way to break through an opponent's defense as it's very difficult to block. To deliver the strike, I contract my right elbow, raising my right hand up to my ear. This will allow me to generate maximum force with the punch.

Unlike other punches, the hammer fist has a straight trajectory. I simply extend my right elbow, allowing my right fist to crash into Tom's face. Because of the straight up-and-down path of the strike, it's not necessary to twist your hips while throwing a hammer fist.

ELBOW TO HEAD

To deliver an elbow strike from inside of the guard, I must first elevate my elbow and turn my palm outward. This gives me plenty of room to generate momentum with the elbow.

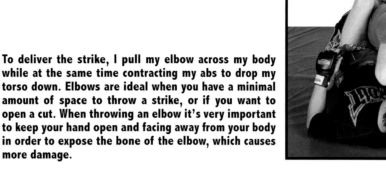

To deliver the strike, I pull my elbow across my body while at the same time contracting my abs to drop my torso down. Elbows are ideal when you have a minimal amount of space to throw a strike, or if you want to open a cut. When throwing an elbow it's very important to keep your hand open and facing away from your body in order to expose the bone of the elbow, which causes more damage.

ROUND KNUCKLE

This strike is great for getting around a defense and adds a unique angle of attack to your arsenal. If your opponent covers his face with both arms then the round knuckle is the most effective way to strike his head around his hands. I bring my elbow up high to get more velocity behind the strike.

To deliver the punch, I rotate my torso, forcing my hand to move toward the side of his head. This allows the strike to move in from the flank, sneaking past Tom's guard.

STRAIGHT TO THE BODY

Attacking the head repeatedly gets predictable. By punching your opponent's body, you can mix up the strikes and get him to drop his hands. I like to vary the strikes between the head and body to keep him guessing. Here I'm throwing a straight punch to the body. To initiate the strike, I raise my right elbow high from a postured position while controlling Tom's upper body with my left hand.

Similar to other punches thrown from the guard, I twist my shoulders and force my right hand into Tom's abdomen while dropping my body weight into the strike. This allows me to deliver the punch with maximum force.

ROUND KNUCKLE TO BODY

Just as you used the round knuckle to attack your opponent's head, you can use it to attack his body from an angle. Power shots to the ribs and liver hurt bad and will force your opponent to lower his guard. Again, I initiate this attack by raising my right elbow high to generate momentum for the punch.

To deliver the strike, I rotate my torso and target the right side of my opponent's rib cage. Shots to the body such as this will force my opponent to defend low.

HAMMER FIST TO BODY

The hammer fist is great for splitting a defense as we've seen before. It can also be used to deceive your opponent. Like the other body shots, it will force him to drop his defenses and leave his head open for a follow-up shot.

Like all hammer strikes, the hammer fist to the body is done with a simple extension of the arm. With no twisting action involved it causes less damage, but it is a safer, quicker punch to throw to the body.

ELBOW TO RIBS

This is another strike that can deceive your opponent. If he sees it coming and covers his head, his torso will be exposed and he will absorb the full force with his ribs. To throw the strike, I raise my elbow high in order to generate momentum for the strike.

To deliver the elbow, I rotate my torso and pull my arm across my body, the same as an elbow strike to the head. However, I pull my right arm lower as the strike is incoming, targeting my opponent's rib cage. While there's no chance of cutting your opponent by elbowing his ribs, by alternating your targeting you can fool your opponent into lowering his guard the next time you throw a side elbow.

ELBOW TO STERNUM

1

2

This is a very painful strike. A hard elbow to the sternum can interrupt your opponent's breathing and make him drop his hands out of instinct. The setup is the same as other elbows. By raising your elbow high, you allow yourself to generate momentum without giving away the trajectory of the strike.

To deliver the elbow, I bring my hand up high, point my elbow toward my opponent's torso, and contract my abs to bring my body weight down onto the point of my elbow. An added benefit of this strike is that the right side of your head is protected by your hand, making this a very safe strike.

HEEL HOOK PASS

The heel hook pass is a great way to pass the guard if your opponent is not actively attacking your posture. It can also hide a great punch when you fake reaching for your opponent's legs and then switch to a strike. The crux of the move is discovering which of your opponent's legs is on top of the other, which you can do by feel or by a quick visual check. Remember not to reach your arm under the legs, but under the heel, as reaching under the legs will create the opportunity for your opponent to secure a triangle.

1

I am in Tom's guard with my hands on his shoulders to prevent him from moving or throwing strikes. His guard is closed so before I can advance, I must open his legs.

2

I rise up and fade my head back to make it difficult for Tom to land strikes to my face. I keep my hands on his torso to prevent him from sitting up.

3

I reach back with my right hand and grab Tom's top ankle while keeping my left hand on his torso. This gives me control over his body and would allow me to push him flat to the mat should he sit up.

4

I break his guard by prying his left ankle away from his right ankle. This is done by hooking the back of his left heel and pulling upward with my right arm. Because my right arm is so close to my body, my arm will be stronger than Tom's leg in this scenario.

5

I lift Tom's left leg up to my shoulder. This forces the right side of his body upward, which causes him to roll.

6

I pass his leg over my head to continue to roll him and expose his back. I also walk my hips out to my right to increase the angle I have on his back. Notice that I do not pull my left hand out from between his legs.

7

I throw Tom's leg to my left and roll him to his side. I quickly drop my weight and drive my knees up against his back to prevent him from rolling onto his back and pulling guard. I also like to get my right arm over top of his left arm so he has less chance of pulling guard.

8

I end the pass cradling Tom's top leg with my left arm and his head with my right arm.

KNEE SPLIT PASS (CROSS SIDE)

You have many different options to pass your opponent's guard. With the next two passes, I demonstrate a style of pass that involves driving your knee straight through the center of your opponent's legs. There are two types of knee split passes: one that goes across the body and one that goes to the same side. In this sequence, I show the cross side knee split pass, which involves driving your knee through your opponent's guard, across your body toward your other leg, and landing in side mount. In both this pass and the next, hip and arm control will lead the way though his guard. Use your knee to trap your opponent's thigh and your arm to trap his body. This control will give you the opening you need to bring your other leg through and pass. Like any guard pass, it is important to keep a solid base and your hips low so that you don't get rolled while in transition.

1 I am in Tom's guard with my hands on his shoulders so he can't sit up to block the move or deliver strikes to my head. I can't do this pass if I'm chest to chest with him, so I must posture up slightly to create space between our bodies.

2 I bring my right knee up to my chest and post my foot underneath my hips. It's important to keep pressure on his right shoulder with my left hand so he can't strike or push my knee back into his guard.

3 I put my right knee on his right thigh and pin it to the ground. At the same time I slip my right arm underneath his left armpit to control his torso.

4 I drop my right shoulder and upper-body weight onto his left shoulder to pin him down. At the same time, I continue to bring my right knee over his thigh until it touches the ground. At this point, Tom is effectively pinned to the mat.

With his leg trapped, it's time to bring my left leg through his guard and plant it on the ground out wide as a base. Notice I'm still pinning his shoulders with my underhook and I'm pinning his hips with my right leg.

I slide my left arm underneath his head to gain complete control over his upper body.

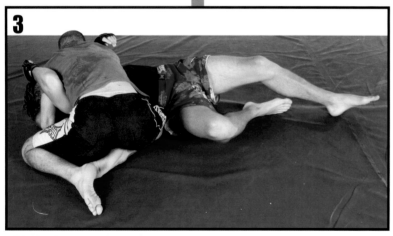 

With his shoulders pinned flat, I pop my right foot out from his guard, giving me side mount.

KNEE SPLIT PASS (SAME SIDE)

This is the same basic pass, but now you will slide your knee through your opponent's guard to the opposite side of your other leg. This allows you to pass straight to mount rather than to side mount. This move also depends on controlling your opponent's lower body through the entire technique. Should you lose control of your opponent, he will likely end up placing you in half guard.

1 I am in Tom's guard with my hands on his shoulders so he can't sit up to block the move or deliver strikes to my head. I can't do this pass if I'm chest to chest with him, so I must posture up slightly to create space between our bodies.

2 I bring my right knee up to my chest and post my foot underneath my hips. It's important to keep pressure on his right shoulder with my left hand so he can't strike or push my knee back into his guard.

3 I put my right knee over his left thigh and pin it to the ground. At the same time, I control Tom's head with my right arm to prevent him from rolling.

4 With Tom's guard open, I slip my left foot over his leg to prepare to pass over his guard. This is a critical point in the pass, because if I fail to bring my left leg out before I release my right leg, Tom will simply secure me in his half guard.

5 This step has to be done quickly. I roll my weight over to my right hip. At the same time, I keep Tom's upper body pinned and grab his right leg underneath the knee. This prevents him from rolling into me and closing his guard.

I slide my left arm underneath Tom's right armpit and swing my left leg over his body.

I step my left leg over Tom's body. Next, I force my knees up into his armpits and end the pass in the full mount.

DOUBLE UNDER PASS

The double under pass is a great move if you can sneak both of your hands under your opponent's legs. Once you have control of his lower body it can be easy to get his hips high in the air, allowing you to attack his guard from the flank. The main risk is your opponent attacking your head. Since your head is low and isolated away from your arms, it will be difficult to stop any incoming attacks to your head or neck. To prevent this scenario, keep your chin tucked and move quickly until you've elevated your opponent's hips.

I am in Tom's guard with my hands on his shoulders to control his upper body.

I posture up and pummel my hands underneath Tom's legs. This must be done quickly and simultaneously. If you move one arm under at a time, you will undoubtedly get stuck in a triangle choke.

3

I wrap my hands around Tom's legs and grip his thighs. Speed is key here because at this point my head is exposed and my guard is down. If I linger in this position, Tom can attack my head with strikes or my neck with chokes.

4

I posture up, lifting my head and maintaining a tight grip on Tom's legs. This elevates his hips off the ground until the only parts of his body making contact with the mat are his shoulders.

5

I throw Tom's legs to my left side, pulling my head back to allow his legs to slide past my shoulders.

6

I quickly crash my weight back down onto Tom's abdomen before he can roll away or recapture me in guard. I end the pass in side mount with Tom in the cradle position.

TARANTULA PASS

This is a variation of the double under pass, but uses a quick and unexpected move to gain rear control instead of side mount. As your elevate your opponent's hips, he will typically expect the double under pass and may try to roll away from you to avoid it, exposing his back in the process. However, it's riskier than the double under pass because you will momentarily release all control that you have in order to achieve a more dominant position behind your opponent. For that reason, quickness is key.

1

I am in Tom's guard with my hands on his shoulders so he can't sit up or deliver strikes to my head.

2

I posture up and pummel my hands underneath Tom's legs.

3

I wrap my hands around Tom's legs and grip his thighs. Speed is key here because at this point my head is exposed and my guard is down. If I linger in this position, Tom can attack my head with strikes or my neck with chokes.

I posture up, lifting my head and maintaining a tight grip on Tom's legs. This elevates his hips off the ground until the only parts of his body making contact with the mat are his shoulders.

I throw Tom's legs to my left side, pulling my head back to allow his legs to slide past my shoulders.

This next step has to be done quickly. Instead of following his momentum and falling into side mount, I rotate my torso, placing my shoulders on the mat parallel with Tom's shoulders. This gives me chest to back contact with Tom, which will allow me to pursue further back control.

I raise my left foot over his left thigh and secure underhooks with my left and right arms.

To secure my second foot hook, I raise my right foot and drop it over top of Tom's right thigh. This gives me positive control of Tom's back, allowing me continue with several different attacking options.

LEG LACE (VERSION 1)

The leg lace is one of my favorite ways to pass my opponent's guard, but there are several different variations on this single pass. This variation moves you to the front of your opponent's body, placing you in scarf hold. As the name implies, the leg lace works by lacing your arm underneath one of your opponent's legs and over his other leg. That arm eliminates any leverage he may have below his waist, preventing him from rolling over and attempting a sweep. With his legs effectively neutralized you can then pass them by leading with your knee in a similar fashion to the knee split pass. The two keys to this move are maintaining control of your opponent's legs with your arm and using your head to push his upper torso into the ground so he can't sit up or roll.

I am in Tom's guard with my hands on his shoulders so he can't sit up or deliver strikes to my head.

2

I posture up and slide my left hand down to control Tom's right wrist. Next, I underhook his left leg using my right arm.

3

I drive my head into the center of Tom's chest and drive forward to keep him down. My right arm then weaves over his right leg. Now that my right arm is laced under Tom's left leg and over his right leg, his hips are pinned to the mat.

4

My head now becomes the main pivot point for my guard pass. I drive my head into Tom's chest for a point of base while stepping my left leg out to the side. This widens my base and makes it extremely difficult for Tom to halt my movement. Notice I'm still maintaining wrist control on Tom's right arm.

5

I now pull Tom's left (upper) leg to the ground and begin moving my right knee through his guard. At this point it's extremely critical that I keep Tom's shoulders pinned down using my body weight, driving through my head. Also if Tom frees his wrist at this point, it will be very difficult for me to continue the pass.

6

I bring my right knee through Tom's guard. Next, I turn both of my hips toward his hips, walking away from his legs to prevent him from placing me back in his guard.

7

I am now past Tom's guard. I straighten my left leg out to establish a base so he can't sweep me. His best bet is to roll into me, but with my leg based out and my weight still on his chest it will be extremely difficult.

8

With side mount secured, I release Tom's wrist. From here, I have several options for launching submission attacks.

LEG LACE (VERSION 2)

This is similar to the first leg lace version, but instead of transitioning toward the front of your opponent's body, you transition to his back. This can be a useful option if your opponent attempts to roll into you to prevent you from moving in front of his body. As with the first leg lace option, you lace one arm through your opponent's legs for control. Note, it is important to keep your head close to your opponent's chest to protect it.

I am in Julie's guard with my hands on her arms so she can't sit up or deliver strikes to my head. I have already created the space I need for the move by backing away and letting Julie bring her knees up high on my chest.

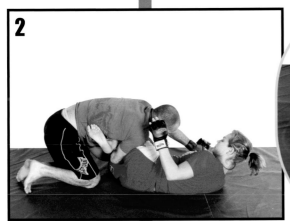  

I secure control over Julie's right arm by sliding my left hand down to her right wrist. At the same time, I wrap my right arm under her left leg and weave it over her right leg while rolling her over to her right hip.

I roll Julie all the way over to her right hip, driving my head into her chest and pressing my weight into her legs to prevent her from moving her hips. At the same time, I base my left foot to the outside of my body.

4

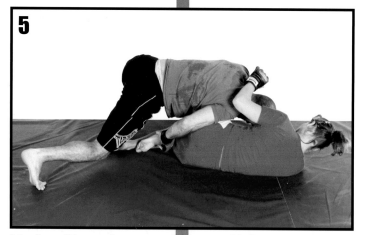

If Julie presents too much resistance by rolling toward her belly, or if I'm unable to clear her left shin, I will be unable to move to the front of her body. However, this makes it much easier for me to move toward her back. To move to Julie's back, I unlace my right arm and place it on the back of her left heel.

5

I begin walking my legs to my right, toward Julie's back. Notice I'm still controlling her right arm to prevent her from turning into me, and controlling her left leg to prevent her from extending it and trapping me back in guard.

6

As I continue walking toward my right, I release Julie's right arm. From here, I will wrap my right arm around her head, hook my left arm under her left leg, and secure a cradle position from side mount.

KNEE SPLIT TO HEEL HOOK

The knee split pass works on the premise that raising your knee through your opponent's guard isolates his legs, allowing you to pass each individual limb one at a time. Isolating your opponent's limbs not only opens passing opportunities, but submission opportunities as well. The knee split to heel hook starts out similar to the knee split pass but then changes directions and transitions into a powerful submission. This is a useful transition when your opponent blocks the pass by pushing on your knee to prevent your leg from sliding through his guard. Rather than being persistent with the pass, you will simply secure your opponent's leg and fall back for a leg lock submission.

I am in Tom's guard with my hands on his shoulders so he can't sit up. Tom's guard is open, and I've decided to attempt the knee split pass.

I post up on my right foot, bringing my right knee up to my chest. This splits Tom's guard and allows me to elevate my head safely. It's critical that I maintain pressure on Tom's right shoulder with my left hand so he can't initiate an offensive attack.

Tom posts on my knee as I attempt the knee slide pass, preventing me from moving through his guard. Rather than abandon my attack, I transition into the heel hook submission. To do this, I post up on my left foot, trapping my opponent's right leg with my left hip. Now that I've isolated his leg and balanced on both feet, I simply need to fall to my hip to initiate the submission.

4

I fall onto my right hip and immediately wrap my left leg over Tom's right leg. By digging my right heel into Tom's hip, I can control his body and prevent him from sitting up. By squeezing my knees together as well as pinching my left elbow into his right leg, I have totally isolated his limb from his body.

5

To attack his isolated limb, I raise my left arm and move it over top of Tom's right leg.

6

To finish the submission, I hook Tom's right heel with the bony part of my left wrist. Now I lock my hands together to firmly to secure his heel. To apply pressure to Tom's leg, I push his hip away with my left leg while arching my back and pulling his heel toward my head. This moves his leg in opposite directions and twists his knee, causing immense pain and extreme damage to the ligaments in his knee. Notice how I use my right foot to elevate his left leg during the submission. This hinders him from rolling and escaping my attack.

KNEE SPLIT TO FOOT LOCK

Much like the previous series, in this technique I'm opening my attack with a knee split guard pass. However, rather than continue all the way through with the pass, I decide mid-attack to spin into my opponent's leg and finish him with a foot lock. Speed is key with this move, as you don't want to expose your back any longer than necessary. Although the pictures show each step in stop motion, this is a continuous movement around your opponent's leg that does not stop until you are facing his knee. The move is a great option if your opponent fails to realize you've isolated his leg as you're passing his guard, and it can be a quick way to end the match. Unlike the previous technique, which requires your opponent to stop the guard pass, in this movement your knee must be free to drive through your opponent's guard and spin through for the submission.

I am in Tom's guard with my hands on his shoulders, which will prevent him from blocking the move or throwing strikes at my head.

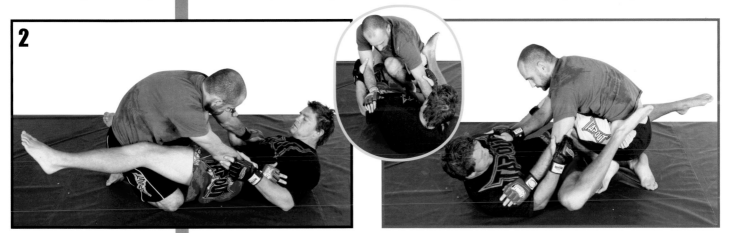

I post up on my left foot and bring my left knee up to my chest. This splits Tom's guard and allows me to elevate my head safely. It's critical to maintain pressure on your opponent's right shoulder during this step so he can't initiate an offensive attack.

Because Tom's left leg is extended as I begin the knee split pass, I decide to attack his leg land attempt to finish the fight. To do this, I pivot on my right knee and spin around his left leg. It is important to mention that this step must be performed quickly to prevent your opponent from freeing his leg. To initiate the spin, I pivot on my right knee and drive my left shin across Tom's hip. At the same time, I turn my hips away from his head, toward his legs. This allows me to isolate his left leg as I spin around.

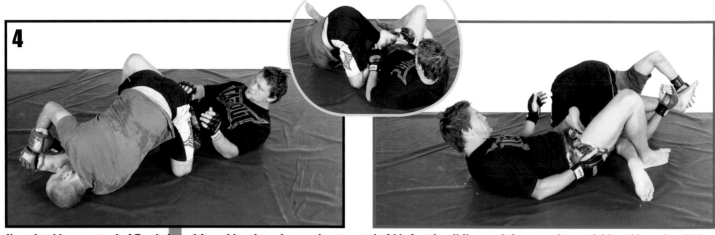

4

Now that I have control of Tom's leg with my hips, I reach up and get control of his foot by sliding my left arm underneath his ankle and grabbing his foot with my right hand. It is important to mention that I am pinching my knees together here to prevent his escape. My left foot is hooked on his thigh and my right leg is underneath his right leg.

5

I continue to spin around to give me more leverage to finish the submission. I'm still pinching my knees together tightly to control his leg. My right leg is laced underneath his right knee to further restrict his movement.

6

To finish the submission, I lean forward and press on Tom's foot with my right hand. This leverages his ankle over my left forearm, hyperextending the ligaments in his foot. Unable to escape due to my control, he quickly taps in submission.

INSIDE FULL GUARD: STANDING

There's no hard-and-fast rule that commands you to stay on your knees while passing your opponent's guard. In fact, standing inside of your opponent's guard can afford you several very powerful avenues of attack, such as throwing downward strikes. With gravity on your side, these strikes are much more powerful than your opponent's. However, standing adds risk. By climbing to your feet you elevate your hips, which increases the chance you will be swept to your back. In addition, standing generally creates space between you and your opponent, which can allow him to execute an escape or throw a powerful upward strike, such as an upkick. That being said, the benefits of standing inside of the guard often outweigh the risks, and the position should be practiced thoroughly.

BASIC STANDING GUARD PASS

While the heel hook guard pass shown earlier can work perfectly fine from the knees, standing can make the move more powerful. Climbing to your feet gives you more leverage and puts more pressure on your opponent's ankles, making it easier to break open his guard. Just as with other techniques, setting up the pass with strikes will dramatically increase your effectiveness. As you posture up and rid your opponent of his control, you gain more leverage to deliver powerful downward punches. As he attempts to defend against those punches, you execute the pass.

I am in Julie's guard with my hands on her shoulders to keep her from sitting up.

As I rise to my feet, I must ensure my knees are up high to close off space between our hips. If I fail to close off the space between our hips, Julie will have enough space to escape back to her feet. Once I have closed off that space, I obtain control over Julie's right arm by sliding my left hand down her arm to her right wrist. This grip prevents her from hooking my leg to interfere with my guard pass.

To stand, I post up on one foot at a time, starting with my left foot. It's important to steady your base before trying to break the guard, so I split my legs to increase my balance. Notice that because I am controlling her right arm, I position my left leg forward. If I were controlling her left arm, I would stand with my right leg forward. This positioning increases my base and helps prevent her from sweeping me backward.

While controlling Julie's right hand, I stand up fully, take my right hand off of her shoulder, and dig my right hand underneath her left leg. Notice how I slide my hand in between her ankles to break them apart. With the majority of her body weight being supported by her feet, it takes very little pressure from my right arm to pry her ankles apart. It is also important to notice that even though I'm fully standing, I'm still controlling her right wrist.

As Julie's guard breaks, I quickly grab her left leg and move it in front of my body.

I throw Julie's leg to my left and drop my weight onto her hips.

As I move into side mount, I keep Julie's left leg hooked and roll her hips away from me. At the same time, I feed her right hand to my left hand, allowing me to control her left leg and right arm with the same hand.

I now overhook Julie's head with my right arm and pull my arms together. This squeezes her chest to her knee, leaving me with a very strong cradle pin.

LION'S MOUTH TO BELLY BUMP PASS

The lion's mouth to belly bump pass is actually two movements combined into one fluid guard pass. The lion's mouth is the initial position, in which you control your opponent's hips and deliver strikes. This is an ideal position from which to damage your opponent because it offers great control of your opponent's hips while keeping your hands free to rain down punishment. The next portion is the belly bump pass, which is used to clear your opponent's legs out of your way in order to allow you to move past his hips. The key to this combo is to press your knees together. The lion's mouth is so effective in controlling your opponent's hips that your opponent will often use drastic measures to escape. Often he will lower his hands and try to hook your legs to regain control. This is the perfect opportunity to drive your hips forward and execute the belly bump pass.

I am in Julie's guard with my hands on her shoulders so she can't sit up or strike my head.

In one fluid motion, I pop up to my feet and drive my hips forward, closing off all space between our legs.

With Julie's legs still raised high between my thighs, I pinch my knees together to trap her hips. My toes are pointed out to increase my base and my weight is dropped down to immobilize her hips.

4

I'm now in the lion's mouth position, so called because my thighs are biting into Julie's legs to prevent her from moving. From this standing position it's easy to throw effective punches. Because I'm elevated and lined up directly over Julie's head, each punch I throw can be a devastating blow. I mix up my punching attack, striking up, down, left, and right, trying to catch Julie off guard.

5

As I continue punching, I try to land strikes to the unprotected parts of Julie's body. If she guards her head, I'll punch to the body, and vice versa.

6

As long as I can maintain this position, it's a good idea to continue throwing punches and deliver as much damage as possible.

7

Notice that as I strike, I keep my weight down on her legs to restrict her movement.

8

Eventually Julie has no option but to try an escape. She hooks my right leg with her left arm, but this just opens her up to the belly bump pass. To begin this pass, I grab her ankles and force her hips forward.

9

I throw Julie's ankles to the ground while sliding my belly across her legs. As her legs move across my body, my belly bumps them out of the way, clearing a path for my hips. As Julie's legs clear my body and end up on the mat, she can force a scramble. At this point I need to react quickly and secure a pin, or else risk losing the position.

GOAL POSTS TO BELLY BUMP PASS

This is another way to use strikes to set up a pass. Just like the lion's mouth sets up the belly bump from a fully erect position, the goal posts move will set up the belly bump from a crouched position. Being in a crouched position makes it easier to establish your base and keep yourself steady, but it's not as conducive to throwing hard strikes because of the close proximity to your opponent. To increase your effectiveness, you want to use strikes that are effective from short range. That's why the elbow is perfect for this move. Again, the pass is the same. The only difference with the goal posts is that it allows you to initiate the pass from a lower position.

I am in Julie's guard with my hands on her shoulders so she can't sit up or strike my head. I have already snuck my knees up close to her thighs to close off all space between our hips.

I stack my body forward to get closer to Julie's head and slip my hands behind her neck. I cradle her head with my hands and pull it toward my chest.

From here I must act quickly, as my arms are exposed. As soon as I grasp Julie's head, I immediately pop up to both feet, elevating my hips.

With my left hand behind Julie's neck to control her head, I raise my right elbow to strike.

I bring my right elbow down on Julie's head.

With Julie stunned from my elbow strike, she momentarily opens her guard. To initiate the pass, I quickly reestablish my right-handed grip on the back of her neck.

Before Julie can close her guard, I quickly elevate my torso. However, I make sure to retain the pressure with my hips, closing off all space between our legs.

I grab Julie's ankles and rotate my hips to my right to execute the pass.

I throw Julie's legs to my right and drop my weight on top of her hips.

Now that I've passed Julie's guard, I hook her head with my left arm and cradle her body, capturing her in side mount.

MATADOR PASS

When you stand up in your opponent's guard, a lot of times he will place his feet on your hips. This gives him the ability to drive your body away from him, which will sometimes allow him to make a quick escape to his feet. Placing his feet on your hips also gives him the ability to deliver an upkick to your face. The matador pass is an excellent way to deal with this position. All it entails is obtaining control of your opponent's ankles, moving his feet to the side of your body like a matador moves his cape, and then dropping down into side mount. The most essential part of this technique is speed. It can be difficult to maintain control of your opponent's ankles for a prolonged period of time, and if you stall in the position, there is a good chance that he will free one of his legs and then either execute a sweep by kicking out one of your legs or delivering an upkick to your face.

I am in Julie's guard with my hands on her shoulders.

I push off Julie's shoulders and pop up to my feet. My ankles are out wide so she can't grab them and try a double-ankle pick sweep. It's important to keep your hands on your opponent's shoulders so he can't sit up or deliver strikes.

Julie counters by putting her feet on my hips and grabbing my wrists.

I wrench my wrists free from Julie's grasp in order to gain positive control of her legs.

To control Julie's legs, I slide my hands up and grip her ankles. Notice I'm still leaning into Julie to prevent her from kicking me.

Once I secure control of Julie's ankles, I back away and elevate my torso. This will prevent her from executing a sweep or delivering an upkick to my head.

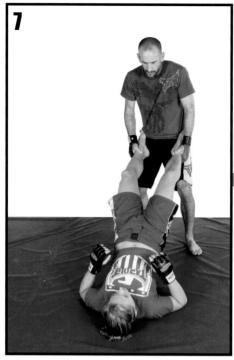

7

I continue to back away, pulling Julie's legs out until they're fully extended.

8

Now comes the part where I utilize the momentum of Julie's legs to toss them out of my way. To begin, I move her legs toward my left side.

9

Julie forces her legs toward her left side to prevent me from moving them toward her right side. Instead of resisting this pressure, I go with it by throwing her legs toward her right side. The key to this step is being unpredictable. If your opponent anticipates the direction in which you're going to throw his or her legs, the move will be much more difficult to achieve.

10

Using the momentum generated by the rocking motion, I throw Julie's legs to the mat.

11

Now that Julie's legs are no longer an obstacle between our bodies, I drop a full-power right-hand punch to the side of her head. In a real fight, if this strike should fail to KO your opponent, you can simply drop your hips to his or her side and attain side mount.

AXE KICK PASS

When there is a considerable amount of distance between you and a downed opponent, the axe kick pass can be a great option to close the distance. The axe kick pass uses a bit of deception to strike through your opponent's guard. It's especially useful when you have an opponent who refuses to come forward or stand up from the guard position. The traditional way of dealing with an opponent like this is to kick his thighs in order to inflict some damage when you would otherwise be inactive. By throwing a kick to your opponent's thighs, you create an expectation in your opponent's mind that you intend to remain standing and will not actively try to pass his guard. So, as you chamber your leg for the second strike and come over top of his guard with an axe kick, it will often catch your opponent off guard and allow you to advance into a dominant position.

I am standing a few feet from Julie, who is on her back with her guard up.

I want to initiate my attack by peppering her leg with some kicks, so I begin to pivot on my left foot to throw a right round kick.

I chamber my right leg for a kick to Julie's thigh.

I strike Julie's outer thigh and quickly retract my leg before she can grab a hold of it.

Now Julie is fully expecting another round kick to her thighs, thinking that I am choosing not to engage.

I chamber my right leg as if I am intending to throw another round kick at her thigh.

At the last second I change the direction of the strike and elevate my knee up high, which prepares me to throw an axe kick through her guard.

I drive the heel of my right foot straight down into Julie's sternum. At this point there is some risk of her grabbing my leg and attempting a submission, so I have to act fast.

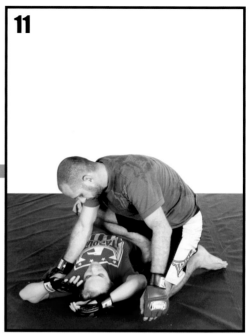

After the strike I put my right foot on the ground next to Julie's right hip. This split's Julie's guard, allowing me to slide through her legs. Julie is likely still stunned from the strike and will have a difficult time reacting to any upcoming movements.

I bring my left leg over Julie's guard and rotate my upper body so I'm perpendicular to her torso.

I end the pass in side mount with my right knee on Julie's belly and my right hand controlling her left arm.

SPINNING PASS

Like the axe kick pass, the spinning pass tricks your opponent into thinking that your intention is to strike rather than engage on the ground. As your opponent prepares to defend against your leg kicks, he leaves an opening for you to pass his guard. If you look at the photos below, you'll notice that this technique capitalizes on the momentum from a leg strike to step around your opponent and pass his guard. Explosive power and speed are the keys for this move. You need to kick your opponent's thigh hard enough that you can step in and then spin quickly around his legs. Like the previous two passes, you have to drop your weight quickly before your opponent can roll away or pull guard again. It is important to note that whenever you turn your back on your opponent there's an added risk. In the split second that your back is turned, your opponent can change direction, roll, stand, or execute any number of offensive actions. Your spin has to be quick to reduce the amount of time that your opponent is out of sight, so trying this move late in a fight when you're tired might not yield the best results.

1 I am standing a few feet from Julie, who is on her back with her guard up.

2 I want to initiate my attack by peppering Julie's leg with some kicks, so I begin to pivot on my left foot to throw a right round kick to her left thigh.

3 After the strike, I plant my right foot on the mat and swing my left leg around in a counterclockwise direction. This causes me to spin away from Julie and to the left of her guard.

4 I plant my left leg, transfer my weight to it, and keep turning in the same direction.

5 My spin continues until I am facing Julie, at which point I drop my weight. I shoot my left arm down to prevent her from rolling into me or away from me.

6 I continue to drop my weight down on Julie's torso.

7 Because of my powerful spinning motion, I land high on Julie's body, prompting me to move into the north-south position. From here I can launch a variety of attacks.

REVERSE HEEL HOOK

When standing over your opponent, you have a number of options. As you have already learned, you can land damaging strikes to his legs or body, and you can control his legs to set up a pass. However, it's also possible to use the control over your opponent's legs to lock in a submission and end the fight immediately. With this move, you control your opponent's legs in order to lock in a reverse heel hook. It is important to note that when you apply the heel hook, one of your legs will be exposed, which will prompt many inexperienced fighters into attempting to lock in a heel hook of their own. As long as you anticipate this submission and your opponent's movements, you'll be able to lock in your submission before he can lock in his.

1) I am standing over Julie and controlling her ankles with my hands.

2) I step around Julie's right leg and squat down, isolating her leg between my thighs. At the same time, I cup her knee with my left hand to prevent her from twisting out of my grasp.

3) I fall to my hip and pull Julie's right knee toward me with my left hand. Maintaining a firm grip during this step is critical. If you fall to your back and don't have control of your opponent's knee, then the move fails.

4) To secure Julie's leg, I triangle my legs together with my left foot behind my right knee. I dig my right heel into Julie's thigh to prevent her escape, but this also baits her into attempting a foot lock of her own.

5) As Julie contemplates attacking my foot, I complete the submission by wrapping my right arm under her heel, clasping my hands together, and extending my back to pull her knees apart. This is an extremely powerful submission, and will likely cause pain only once it causes damage. You must continue extending your back until your opponent submits. However, due to the violent nature of this submission, you want to go easy with it during grappling practice.

ACHILLES LOCK

The Achilles lock is a great submission that attacks the Achilles tendon of your opponent. Like all submissions, you must first isolate the limb you wish to attack. By driving your knee into your downed opponent's guard, you create a great opportunity to isolate his leg and execute the Achilles lock. This is a great technique to use against an opponent who extends his legs and does not keep them actively moving or kicking. There's some risk in this move because you have to give up your standing position and fall back to the mat, as we saw in the reverse heel hook. If you don't have a firm grip on his ankle, then you'll end up giving up your dominant position with no return. There's potential for deception with this move—you can fake throwing your opponent's legs to one side as in the matador pass and then go through his legs for the Achilles lock instead. However, once you decide to attack with the Achilles lock, you must move forward quickly in order to secure the submission.

1

I am standing over Julie and controlling her ankles with my hands.

2

Because Julie's legs are inactive, I feel safe in moving forward into her guard. I drive my left knee forward and use it to apply downward pressure on her right thigh.

3

I now wrap my right arm around Julie's left ankle. This secures the leg and isolates it from her body. Notice that I keep my left hand on her right foot in case she suddenly decides to become offensive and throw an upkick toward my head.

4

Making sure I have a firm grip on Julie's left ankle, I fall back on my left hip and swing my right leg over her hip. At this point, I'm still controlling her right leg to prevent her from escaping.

5

I roll onto my left hip to increase the power I can apply to the submission hold. Notice that I keep my right leg on Julie's hip to prevent her from sitting up and stealing the top position.

6

I figure four my hands with my right wrist laced underneath Julie's Achilles tendon. Notice how my right hand is grasping my left wrist, and my left hand is gripping her right shin. To finish the submission I extend my back. This drives my wrist into her Achilles tendon. With her leg immobilized, it causes immense pain and forces her to tap out.

CHAPTER TWO: GUARD VARIATIONS

While the basic closed guard affords you several methods to dominate the fight from your back, there are many advanced guard variations as well. This chapter will focus on four modified guards—the butterfly guard, spider guard, half guard, and downed guard—and explore the ways to use each one's unique properties to your advantage. Each guard has a different purpose and is designed to achieve different goals. For example, the spider guard is very effective against wrestlers who like to drive into you and close off space, and the downed guard is a great method to attack an opponent who refuses to engage you on the mat.

Much like the basic guard, the advanced guard variations shown in this chapter should be a strong point in your game. Being able to transition into many different guards allows you to be offensive without the risk of losing position. Knowing which guard to use in each situation is critical to winning a fight from your back. That being said, you should almost always try to avoid the guard, because more often than not, your opponent will have an advantage in striking you from the top position. Trading strikes with a fighter in your guard will lead to unnecessary damage, and could prevent you from winning the fight.

I always advocate taking an aggressive strategy and attacking no matter what position you're in, so we'll explore submission strategies from each modified guard. We'll also look at striking options, transitions to new positions, and full escapes from each guard. Knowing each individual guard system will make you a better-rounded fighter off your back, giving you options no matter what game plan your opponent pursues.

BUTTERFLY GUARD

The butterfly guard is a modified bottom position that differs from the full guard by the position of the legs and feet, which are hooked underneath your opponent's groin to control his lower body. The premise of the butterfly guard is to use your shins pressed against your opponent's hips to drive him away, and then use your feet hooked under his legs to lift him up. Because the butterfly guard makes it so difficult for your opponent to drive into you, it is the perfect tool for keeping a fighter away from your hips. Because of your leg position, if your opponent chooses to posture up and strike, it will be relatively easy to elevate his hips and sweep him to his back. However, as mentioned earlier in the chapter, the butterfly guard is situational. While it is fantastic for shutting down a wrestler who likes to drive into your guard, posture up, and throw punches, it is almost useless for keeping a fighter trapped in your guard. If you're matched up against a striker who will look for any opportunity to stand and escape back to his feet, the butterfly guard will be ineffective.

You should not transition to the butterfly guard on a whim. Although it's a great addition to your toolbox, it's not a position that you will land in accidentally. It's a guard that should be planned for ahead of time by studying your opponent and figuring out if he's vulnerable to it. The butterfly guard is a comfortable position to be in for some fighters. If you're fighting a stronger grappler with great balance and good guard passing skills and who doesn't often throw strikes from the guard, it's not a tool that will be very effective. The butterfly guard is a position that takes time to master, so this section will concentrate on the fundamentals of the butterfly guard and the advantages it affords you.

BASIC BUTTERFLY GUARD POSITION

In the basic butterfly guard position you're on your back with your legs bent and your shins pressed against your opponent's thighs. This allows you to extend your legs to create pressure against your opponent's hips, driving him backward. This also enables you to hook your feet underneath your opponent's thighs, allowing you to elevate his hips when the opportunity arises. To control his upper body, you have one overhook and one underhook. This position is like a spring. With your opponent's base extended, he's unable to sit up. And because you have control over his upper and lower body, at any moment you can extend your hips and spring into an offensive attack.

This is the basic butterfly guard position. I'm controlling Julie's hips by inserting my feet between her thighs, and I have my legs flexed. I'm controlling her upper body by overhooking her left arm and underhooking her right arm. By pulling down with my upper body controls and slightly extending my legs, I extend Julie's base, making it very difficult for her to sit up. This is an excellent defensive position for me, as Julie is unable to move in any direction without the risk of being swept. It's also a great offensive position, as a simple extension of the legs will allow me to create space and attack with a sweep or submission.

SITTING UP IN BUTTERFLY GUARD

The butterfly guard is extremely useful against fighters who try to posture inside of your guard, but to execute submissions and sweeps, you will need to secure your opponent's upper body. In this series of pictures, Julie is postured up and I have already slipped my leg hooks in between her thighs. To secure control of her body and break her posture back down, I must sit up and obtain my over/under hook arm position. This will allow me the greatest variety of offensive movements while still keeping me very defensively sound.

I am lying on my back with my feet inserted between Julie's thighs. My knees are bent and I'm lying flat on my back. However, Julie has broken away from my grip and managed to sit straight up.

If I were to linger flat on my back, Julie could easily strike or attempt to pass my legs. To avoid this, I quickly sit up, obtaining an underhook with my left arm and grabbing her left elbow with my right hand.

Now that my torso is fully upright, I clasp my hands together behind her back, establishing double underhooks. This will prevent her from driving my torso away from her torso. With the combination of my double underhook bodylock and my legs hooked under Julie's thighs, I have a multitude of offensive options.

BUTTERFLY GUARD SUBMISSIONS

Many fighters will use the butterfly guard simply as a platform for attempting sweeps from the bottom position. While this is a solid strategy, many submissions are available from the butterfly guard as well. However, because your feet are tucked inside of your opponent's thighs, you must extract your legs quickly in order to secure upper-body submissions. On the other hand, lower-body submissions will become more available because your legs are already separating your opponent's legs. Whatever offensive route you decide to take, attempting submissions will make your butterfly guard more dangerous and effective.

ARMBAR

The armbar from the butterfly guard is very similar to the armbar from the full guard. It relies on a simultaneous two-part movement to spin your body ninety-degrees underneath your opponent and isolate an arm for the submission. Leg placement is key for a successful execution. In order to create enough leverage to apply the armbar, you must free your far leg from under your opponent's leg and swing it over his head. This requires space, hip movement, and good timing. Because it's easy to isolate your opponent's arm and swivel your hips from the butterfly guard, this can be a very high-percentage submission. However, this move has some risk. When you slip your leg under your opponent's stomach, he will have a greater chance of passing over that leg. Fortunately, if you have the proper control, this will not become an issue.

1

I am on my back with Julie in my butterfly guard. My left arm is underhooked under her right arm and my left hand is wrapped over her right triceps.

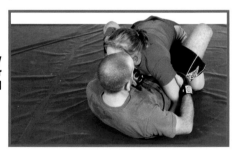

2

I slip my left leg under Julie's stomach. This will create space and give me the leverage needed to move my hips farther. My upper body bends to my left to put me in a position for the cut.

3

Pushing my left leg off Julie's hip and pulling on her shoulder with my left arm, I rotate my hips ninety degrees to my left. I still have my right arm on Julie's left triceps to prevent her from ripping her arm away to defend the submission. As my leg comes around, I throw it over Julie's head to control her upper body and give me leverage to apply the armbar. At this point Julie could hop over my left leg and pass my guard since my knee is so low, so I keep my left forearm pressed against her torso for control.

4

I complete the submission by curling my right leg down to control her posture, and driving my hips up to hyperextend her left elbow.

TRIANGLE

While many submissions from the butterfly guard can be accomplished with your shoulders low, others require your torso to be elevated. This move starts from the sit-up variation of the butterfly guard and uses a quick off-balancing movement to force your opponent to post a hand on the mat for balance. This creates enough space to slide your leg underneath your opponent's arm and lock in a triangle. Keeping your opponent's arm isolated is the key to this move. If your opponent brings his arm back, he can block your knee as it slides underneath. Once his arm is posted on the mat, you need to ensure it remains there. This move can take some hip flexibility as you bring your leg up high to lock in the triangle. As we talked about in the strategy section, you need to know your own strengths and weaknesses. If your hip flexibility is lacking, then this submission may not be a go-to move for you.

1

I'm in the sit-up version of the butterfly guard. My left arm is underhooked under Julie's right arm and my right hand is gripping her triceps.

2

I quickly move my hips forward and roll back onto my right hip. As I rock back, my left leg hook elevates Julie's hips, lifting her to her left. Julie is forced to post her right hand on the mat to prevent me from sweeping her to her back. Now that her arm is isolated from her body, I need to capitalize. I slide my right arm down from her triceps to her right wrist. This is a critical part of the move. If I fail to seize the opportunity to brace her arm and prevent it from moving back toward her body, she'll not only prevent the sweep, but also any follow-up submission attempts.

3

Julie's momentum continues carrying her to my right. Because she posted out, she has prevented the sweep. But because her hips are now very high, and her arm is isolated from her body, she's opened herself for submissions. When I feel she is extended enough to give me the room needed, I lean back and pull my right knee up to my chest, feeding it underneath her right arm.

4

While maintaining control of Julie with my left underhook and leg hook, I pass my leg through the space under her left arm and throw it over top of her left shoulder.

5

Now it's time to pivot. I rotate my body ninety degrees to the right by sliding my right hand from Julie's wrist to her shoulder, giving me an underhook. I use this to pull my upper body to my right, giving me the ninety-degree cut needed to finish the triangle. Notice my left hand is still underhooked under Julie's right arm so she doesn't pull it out before I can finish the strangle.

6

To complete the submission I bring my left leg up and hook it over my right foot. I squeeze my thighs together until Julie taps, all the while controlling her left arm at the shoulder to prevent from landing damaging punches to my head as I lock in the submission.

KIMURA

The most important distinction of the butterfly guard from other guard systems is that it allows you to elevate your opponent's hips, altering his balance almost at will. You can hook your feet under your opponent's thighs to lift his legs and toss his weight around, opening up both sweeps and submissions. With his hips elevated, your opponent's most common method of regaining his base will be to post his hand on the mat. This gives you a great opportunity to reverse your momentum and attack his arm with the kimura.

The great thing about this move is that it's low risk. If you make a mistake and lose the submission, there are many backup attacks available from the kimura. You can roll into an omoplata, sweep, or trap the elbow for a straight armbar. This move illustrates two of the core philosophies of Jackson's MMA: no movement is meant as an individual attack, as there are always backup moves if your primary plan goes awry; and deception should be used to attack your opponent at the point where he's most vulnerable.

1 I'm in the sit-up version of the butterfly guard. My left arm is underhooked under Julie's right arm and my right hand is cupping her left triceps.

2 I quickly move my hips forward, and then rock back onto my left hip. As I rock back, my right hook elevates Julie's hips, lifting her to her right. She counters by posting her right arm out to regain her base.

3 With Julie's right arm isolated away from her body, she will anticipate me attacking that limb and be prepared to defend. However, due to my deception, her left arm is completely defenseless. To capitalize, I quickly reverse direction by turning my shoulders to my right and seizing her left arm. To secure the grip, my right hand slides down to her wrist and I throw my left arm over her head and wrap it around her left arm. Notice how I grab my right wrist with my left hand.

4

My right leg comes up and hooks over Julie's back, giving me leverage to move my hips as well as prevent her from rolling forward to escape the submission. My left foot stays hooked under her groin to keep her off balance.

5

I lean back and roll my shoulders to my left. My grip must remain tight, keeping Julie's arm tight to my chest. My left hand supports my right hand, preventing Julie from hammering her arm straight.

6

To finish the submission, I continue rolling my shoulders to my left and cranking Julie's arm upward. Notice how my right leg stays on her back to prevent her from rolling out, and I keep her arm pinned to my chest.

GUILLOTINE

The guillotine choke is a good backup move when the kimura from the butterfly guard fails. If your opponent keeps his arms tight around your waist or fails to protect his neck, you can transition to the guillotine by throwing an arm over his neck and seizing control of his head. This gives you the opportunity to drive your forearm into your opponent's throat, crushing his windpipe and forcing him to submit. Even if your opponent keeps his head in tight, the guillotine can still be effective. You will simply need to drive his hips away by extending your legs. This will stretch his neck and force your forearm underneath his throat, forcing him to tap. The guillotine from the butterfly is useful against an opponent who stays low on your torso and refuses to release your midsection. There's little risk in the move because if you can't secure the guillotine, you are still in a solid butterfly guard position.

I'm in the butterfly guard with my back on the mat. Julie is lower on my torso than the previous technique so my hands are clasped behind her head instead of underhooked or controlling her arms.

I sit up, put my right elbow on the ground as a point of base, and throw my left arm over her back. This prevents Julie from posturing up if she senses the move coming, and puts me in the perfect position to attack her arm or her neck.

I push Julie's hips away from me by extending my legs and driving my shins into her thighs. This allows me to scoot my hips back, affording me more room to slide my arm around her head and under her neck. As I wrap both arms around Julie's neck, I clasp my hands together under her throat. The key to this step is placing your left hand directly on your opponent's throat, allowing you to cut off airflow.

I slip my left foot across Julie's stomach and hook it over her left thigh. This will allow me to move my hips out to my right, as well as give me a point of leverage to drive her hips away from me as I finish the submission.

To finish the guillotine, I roll back onto my left hip and throw my right leg over Julie's back to prevent her from rolling over to escape. My arms are pulling up into her throat to cut off her air, and I'm pushing her away with my left leg to straighten out her torso, putting more pressure on her neck.

ANKLE LOCK

As mentioned earlier, lower-body attacks are ideal for when you're in the butterfly guard. Because your legs are already between your opponent's legs separating them, it's a simple matter to spin and isolate one of his legs with a leg lock. Submissions from the butterfly guard start when you lean back and off-balance your opponent, and the ankle lock is no exception. To block your initial sweep your opponent can base out with both hands to prevent you from rolling him over. This submission is a good countermeasure to use against that defense. By throwing his arms out wide and spreading his weight, he gives you the ability to create the space you need to rotate underneath of him and lock in an ankle lock submission. This move carries risk because you have to release your upper body controls and rotate quickly around to your opponent's leg and secure it before he scrambles away. But if executed properly, there's a very strong possibility of ending the fight with this move.

I'm in the sit-up version of the butterfly guard. I've established double underhooks and have clasped my hands together in the center of Julie's back.

2

I quickly lean back, rocking Julie forward and elevating her hips. With her hips elevated, she posts both of her hands on the mat to prevent me from rolling her to either side.

3

With the sweep blocked, I un-clasp my hands and slide both of them underneath Julie's arm-pits, digging my thumbs in deep for leverage. I intend to use my hands to push Julie's entire body weight upward, so I make sure to get as secure a grip as possible.

4

I extend both arms and both legs, elevating both Julie's upper and lower body at the same rate. This creates the space I need to rotate underneath of her.

5

In a split second, I rotate my torso to my right and kick my left leg straight. As Julie drops back to the ground, I press her to my left by driving my right hand into her armpit. Julie spreads her legs wide to increase her base, but with my right leg now between her legs, this only helps me iso-late her leg and begin my attack.

6

I isolate her left leg by wrapping my right leg and right arm over top of it. My left arm is extended, pressing Julie away by the armpit, while my left foot is pressing against her right knee and my right foot is hooked into her hip. These movements will prevent Julie from turning back into me to escape the submission.

7

With her left leg isolated, it's time to complete the submission. To do so, I trap Julie's left toes under my armpit and clasp my hands together, placing my right wrist on her heel. By extending my back and driving her away with my legs, it twists her leg at the knee joint, forcing her to tap out. Notice my right foot still hooked over her thigh. This prevents Julie from rolling to escape, and is crucial to the completion of this submission.

BUTTERFLY GUARD SWEEPS

With your feet hooked inside of your opponent's legs, the butterfly guard affords you more control over your opponent's lower body than the full guard. Your leg position not only allows you to drive your opponent's hips away, but it also allows you to elevate his legs individually, making sweeps an extremely accessible move from butterfly guard. A sweep can be a simple matter of elevating your opponent's hips unevenly, disrupting his base and forcing him to his back. Just like a three-legged table, he'll become wobbly and easy to sweep. Another big advantage of the butterfly guard is its versatility. From within this guard you can sweep your opponent in five directions—forward, backward, left, right, and at a forty-five-degree angle. This gives you the ability to sweep an opponent regardless of how he resists. Even if you're up against a cage, you can use one of these sweeps to roll your opponent away from the wall and into the open space of the fighting arena.

There are two common aspects to all of these sweeps that stay consistent regardless of which technique you are attempting—upper-body control and lower-body manipulation. In all sweeps from the butterfly guard, you will lock down your opponent's upper body while simultaneously leveraging his legs into the air, raising his center of gravity, eliminating his ability to post out, and then sending him to his back.

BASIC SWEEP

The basic butterfly guard sweep uses your body as a fulcrum to upset your opponent's balance, throw him toward you, and then reverse direction to blast him the other way. This creates the momentum you need to quickly sit up, push him over backward, and roll through into the mount. This move requires power, speed, and strength—you need power to lift him up over top of you, speed to create momentum and get your legs underneath you before he can block the sweep, and strength to hold his upper body tight so he can't escape and so you have something to pull yourself up from.

The risk in this move is low in the first few steps, but it increases when you pull one foot out to push your opponent over. In the beginning of the sweep, he can block the sweep by basing his legs out, but you will still be in an advantageous position with your feet hooked inside his legs so you can immediately go back to the butterfly guard. In other words, you're not giving up anything to attempt this move. If he stands before you can pull a foot out and push him over, though, you will have to stand too. However, this doesn't matter as long as you maintain a tight grip with your arms wrapped around his upper body because you'll be in a standing Greco-Roman wrestling hold with double underhooks.

1

I am on my back with Brian in my butterfly guard. Both of my arms are underhooked and wrapped around his back with my hands clasped together at his shoulder blades.

2

While gripping his upper body tight, I lean back, muster up power in my legs, and throw them in the air. I'm careful to get his legs off the ground, but not too far so he goes over my head. Also, if I raise him up too high, he can spread his legs and pass my guard, so I only lift him up about forty-five degrees. Brian's natural response is to base both of his hands out behind my head to prevent him from going all the way over.

3

Brian naturally forces his legs down, doing some of my work for me. As we roll I use his momentum to bring myself up. This is where a firm grip is important.

4

We reach the apex of the roll and the point of no return for this sweep. If I have not generated enough momentum to continue the sweep, I don't want to retract my leg and try to push him over. Instead I would look for a way to sweep him to one side or the other, since his balance is probably upset. If I have generated sufficient momentum for the basic sweep, then I keep going.

5

I do two things simultaneously—slip my head down into his chest so I can use it to push him, and get my legs underneath me. My head and right leg will be the two points of contact that will allow me to complete the sweep. Notice that I have my right shin and left foot underneath me instead of being on my toes. It's easier for Brian to knock me backward if I'm on my toes.

6

I push off with my right shin and my head until he topples backward.

7

I continue to drive forward until Brian is on his back. I quickly throw my left leg over his legs to pass his guard.

8

I finish the sweep in the full mount.

DOUBLE-ANKLE PICK

This is a contingency plan that you can use when your opponent blocks the basic sweep by basing his legs out. We saw how to execute a double-ankle pick in the previous chapter, so now we'll take that knowledge and use it as a backup plan when the basic butterfly guard sweep goes awry. The key to this move is momentum and continual movement. Some fighters might panic when they try the basic sweep and suddenly find their opponent blocking it by standing up. Don't hesitate. Keep rocking backward and then forward just as you were planning on doing with the basic sweep. If you hesitate and stop your momentum, your opponent will have a dominant position on you.

1 I am on my back with Julie in my butterfly guard. Both of my arms are underhooked and wrapped around her back with my hands clasped together at her shoulder blades.

2 As before I grip her upper body tight, lean back, muster up power in my legs, and throw them in the air.

3 Instead of trying to force her legs down, Julie quickly puts her feet on the ground.

4 Without hesitating, I let go of her upper torso and bring my hands down to grab her ankles. It's critical that I keep my feet hooked under her legs so I have something to push her back with.

5 As she stands up to strike me, I push her backward with my knees and pull her ankles forward.

6 Julie has no choice but to fall backward. As she does, I sit up and prepare to follow her over.

7 I get up on my toes and use the momentum of the roll to come forward. When she hits her back my head is exposed and vulnerable to a strike, so I keep it down.

8 I get my knees over her thighs to pass her guard and put both hands behind her head. You can also place your hands on your opponent's shoulders to prevent him from rolling, sitting up, or striking.

9 I bring my feet over her legs to complete the sweep.

ELEVATOR SWEEP

As I said earlier, the butterfly sweep affords you the option of going in any direction you want to. We just saw how to sweep your opponent to your front by throwing his lower body. Now we'll look at sweeping him to your right and then we'll look at a sweep to the left. The elevator sweep is a quick move that elevates one side of your opponent's body while trapping the other side so he can't block it. You then use the momentum to roll to one side and end up in the side mount. This move is versatile enough that it's useful against any opponent in any situation, but it's particularly efficient against a tired opponent who can't mount a defense. Speed and technique are more important than strength. This is not a move that relies on muscling your opponent over.

I'm on my back with Julie in my butterfly guard. My left arm is underhooked under her right arm and my right hand is on her left triceps. Before I even start the sweep I make sure my grip on her left triceps is tight because I want it trapped.

In one swift move, I pull her left arm toward me to upset her balance, pull my hips out, and lift her right side with my left leg and left arm.

As we roll over, I get my left shoulder into hers to push on her while my right leg comes to the ground. I will transfer my weight to this leg and use my right knee as my base.

4

As Julie's back hits the mat, I bring my left leg all the way over to the floor and chop down her leg to prevent her from pulling guard. I also pull my right knee out wide to prevent her from pulling guard and prepare to spin into side mount. Notice that my right foot is still over top of her left leg so I can push it down when I transition to side mount.

5

I hold down her left leg with my right foot and bring my left leg over it until my knee hits the ground next to her ribs. I then pivot my upper body counterclockwise to get into side mount and slip my right arm under her head.

6

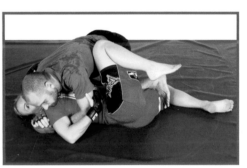

My right knee comes out and gets snug next to her armpit to prevent her from escaping. I end the move in side mount.

TEETER TOTTER SWEEP

This sweep combines the power of your legs with one arm to throw your opponent to one side. It's useful when your opponent has an arm overhooked on one side because that arm will not be able to block the leg-grab portion of the sweep. This sweep maximizes the amount of leverage you have over your opponent by isolating and lifting one leg high enough that it's nearly impossible to block, even if your opponent bases a hand out to stop the roll. There is some risk with the teeter-totter because your arm will be somewhat trapped under your opponent's leg as you roll over. During this step of the sweep he can strike your head without you being able to mount a defense. That's why speed is important once you get control of his leg.

1 I'm in the sit-up version of the butterfly guard. Both of my arms are underhooked under Julie's arms and my hands are clasped together behind her back. She has her left arm loosely overhooked on my right arm, so that's the leg I am going to grab.

2 I lean back and pull her toward me so she's off balance.

3 With my right foot, I lift her left leg up and then hook my right hand underneath her leg. At this point she could strike my head with her left arm, so I have to act quickly.

4 I lift her left leg up high to make it hard for her to take it back. The crook of my right arm is all the way up behind her knee. To prepare for the sweep, I have my right foot on the ground to push off of and my left foot still underneath her leg so she can't put it down and block the sweep.

5 In one quick move, I get Julie in the air by lifting her left leg with my right arm and lifting her right leg with my left foot.

6

To sweep her, I have to pull forward with my left arm that's still underhooked under her right arm. This will get her weight moving forward and trap her arm so she can't base it out to block the sweep. I also push off with my right foot, which is where all my power is coming from. My right arm and left leg roll her over to my left side.

7

I continue to roll Julie over by pushing off with my right foot.

8

Once she is on her back, I shift my hips out to my left so I can keep my legs outside of her guard.

9

I release Julie's left leg, slide my left arm under her head, and clasp my hands together over her left shoulder. I end in side mount with my knees tight against her side.

JAPANESE WHIZZER

This technique capitalizes on the overhook (sometimes called a whizzer) you have on your opponent when in the sit-up guard position. It involves dragging him forward, extending his body so he is not in a position to block the sweep, and then pushing him over using your legs. It's similar to many throws in judo because it concentrates both of your arms and upper body on one of your opponent's arms and throws him to one side. We've seen sweeps that go forward, left, and right. This one goes off to the side, but is at a forty-five-degree angle instead of ninety-degrees, so it adds another angle for you to attack from. You could easily end this sweep in the side mount, but I prefer to use the momentum of the sweep to go all the way into the north-south head control position because it's unexpected and opens a new array of attacks that your opponent may not be ready for. All fighters train on how to defend themselves while in side mount, but not many train to defend against north-south control.

I'm in the sit-up version of the butterfly guard with one arm underhooked under Julie's arm and one arm on the back of her triceps.

I want to drag her forward to upset her balance, so I let go with my left arm and bring it across her body to grab her left arm. I now have both hands grabbing her left arm—one is overhooked and one is underhooked. I lean back and drag her.

With Julie off balance, I start the sweep by rotating my upper body and lifting her up with my left leg. I keep her from basing out with her left hand by maintaining a firm grip on it.

4

At this point she can do nothing to block the sweep. I keep rolling her and use the momentum to get myself into a dominant position.

5

As her back hits the ground, I get my shoulder into her chest to control her upper body and keep her from escaping. It doesn't do any good to continue pushing with my legs, so I get them underneath me to prevent her from pulling guard. I keep my left leg on her left leg to trap it and base out with my right leg.

6

At this point I pivot to side mount and get my right arm over her head and arm. I could stop here and stay in side mount, but I like to stay unpredictable and do things my opponent wouldn't expect.

7

I continue to pass all the way to north-south head control. As I do this, I throw Julie's right arm over to the left side of my head so she can't grab at it.

BUTTERFLY GUARD TRANSITIONS

The difference between a sweep and a transition is the ending position of your opponent. In the previous moves I swept my opponents so they always ended up on their backs with me in a dominant top position. A transition changes your position without changing your opponent's. Instead of throwing your opponent or using your strength to move him in a different direction, a transition moves your body around his, so he ends up in the same position he started in but with you in a dominant position.

ARM DRAG

We've already seen several moves that start with the arm drag. It's an effective way to pull your opponent toward you and off balance so you can get around to his back or start a submission. This version of the arm drag starts the same way as the Japanese whizzer, by using both of your hands to grab your opponent's arm and pulling him forward. Only this time you're going to pull your opponent to the inside of your guard instead of the outside. The risk with this move is low because if the arm drag fails, you are still in the butterfly guard and can easily transition to the Japanese whizzer, since you have both of your hands on one of your opponent's arms.

I'm in the sit-up version of the butterfly guard with one arm underhooked under Julie's arm and one arm on the back of her triceps.

I want to drag her forward to upset her balance, so I let go with my left arm and bring it across her body to grab her left arm underneath her triceps. I now have both hands grabbing her left arm. Next, I quickly slide my right hand down to her left wrist and trap it. At the same time I slide my hips out to the rear to create space for the move.

With my legs still hooked underneath hers, I force her left arm across my body to my left side and push it away.

4

I then pull on Julie's left arm with my right hand to bring her toward me and off balance. This exposes her back so I can rotate myself around her.

5

To keep her from escaping, I wrap my hands around her head and right arm before continuing to the next step. This will prevent her from rolling away or sweeping me. My right leg is out at this point to prepare for the rotation around to her back.

6

Now it's time to rotate to her back. I push off with my right leg and get up on my left knee. Notice that I didn't pull my left leg out from inside hers. Since the beginning of the transition, my left leg has stayed connected with her inner thigh. Now that I have her back, I get my left hook in. As you can see in these photos, you may have to let go of your grip and use your arms to push off the ground to make the transition work.

7

To complete the transition, I swing my right leg over and get my other hook in. From here I can roll over to my back, attempt a rear naked choke, or flatten her out and strike her head.

BUTTERFLY GUARD ESCAPES

You always have to retain the ability to escape from whatever guard you're in. Whether it's a deliberate escape to get the fight back to standing where you have an advantage, or an escape to get out of a bad situation, the ability to disengage is something that has to be trained and is a skill that is too often overlooked.

GET-UP

This method of getting up from the butterfly guard takes advantage of the leverage you have with your feet in your opponent's groin and the bent position of your legs. Both of these act like springs and give you the opportunity to push off, base a leg behind you, and disengage from your opponent. Controlling your opponent's upper-body weight is the key to this escape. You want to drag his upper body toward you and off balance in the same fashion as the arm drag and Japanese whizzer so he can't strike or grab your legs as you back out of the butterfly guard. The risk associated with this move is medium. Since your goal is to disengage completely, it's hard to get caught in a bad position, but it is possible. It's critical that you maintain control of your opponent's upper body so he can't grab your legs as you escape. It's also important to keep your head up so you don't get caught in a guillotine choke.

I'm in the sit-up version of the butterfly guard with one arm underhooked under Julie's arm and one arm on the back of her triceps.

I lean back and pull Julie toward me to get her off balance. I also lift up with my left arm (still underhooked) to get her rotating to my right.

I rotate my upper body to my right and place my right elbow on the ground. Notice that I do not let go with my right hand. I want to keep control of her left arm so she doesn't strike or use it to grab my legs. At this point my left foot is on the ground because I will use it to push off with soon.

With my left foot on the ground and both hands still controlling her upper body and arms, I pull my right leg out and get it behind me as a base.

I slide my right hand up to Julie's head to prevent her from getting up or lunging at me. My left leg stays inside her groin until the last second to prevent her from standing up. From here, I can safely stand up and back away.

BUTTERFLY GUARD PASSES

We've looked at several options you have when your opponent is in your butterfly guard, so now we'll turn the tables and look at options you have when you are in your opponent's butterfly guard. It is important to mention up front that submissions and strikes are not your best courses of action. As we learned with the previous moves, the butterfly guard gives you leverage, so now that the shoe is on the other foot, your opponent has that leverage advantage. That's why I prefer to pass the butterfly guard first and then look for submissions. Since your opponent's feet are not wrapped around your torso, there are two basic ways to pass a butterfly guard—over it and around it.

FOOT DRAG PASS

This is a safe way to pass the butterfly guard. After this we'll look at the riskier ways of passing it, but for now we'll explore the traditional way of going around the butterfly guard before going over it. It's accomplished in steps. First you have to get one leg free of the butterfly before moving on to trapping your opponent's leg and passing over it. This is a useful way to pass against an opponent who is inexperienced with the butterfly guard or is inflexible. The risk in this move is your opponent getting his hips out and rolling away just as you pass, because you won't have any far-side control of his upper body. If your opponent is successful with his escape, it will most likely bring the fight up to the feet, so it's not a huge risk.

I am in Julie's butterfly guard. Her butterfly hooks are in and she has established a left overhook and a right underhook.

2

The first thing I want to do is pull my right leg out of her butterfly guard and get it inside her legs, which will provide me the leverage I need for the pass. To set this up, I reach back and wrap my right arm around her left leg to trap it.

3

I pull Julie's left leg outward using my right arm. This creates the space I need to straighten my right leg and get it off of her foot.

4

I bring my right leg into her guard and get it tight up against Julie's thigh so she can't get her foot back in and reestablish the butterfly guard. Notice how I am still controlling her left leg using my right arm.

5

Now I want to pass her other leg. To begin this process, I place my left hand on her right knee and drive her leg toward the mat. This will trap her leg to the floor, which will make it difficult for her to pull full guard and block my pass.

In one swift movement, I push Julie's right knee to the mat using my left hand. Once accomplished, I grab the top of her right foot using my right hand. Notice how this traps her leg to her body, making it difficult for her to pull full guard. With a clear escape route, I kick out and slide my hips over her right leg to pass her guard. Notice that I keep my head buried in her chest to protect it throughout the move.

Now I bring both of my knees in on her side and keep in tight so she can't roll away.

I rotate my upper body, let go of Julie's foot, wrap my left arm around her head, and clasp my hands together under her left shoulder to complete the pass.

KNEE HOP PASS

This pass is a timing move. It involves a hop and a slap that has to be timed right or you could find yourself being kicked or thrown across the ring. You will have to slap your opponent's knees down as soon as your feet get up in the air to pass over his legs. Speed is important, but not as much as timing the hop and slap right. There's significant risk in this move because you will be completely in the air at one point and will briefly give up all control that you have over your opponent.

1

I am in Julie's butterfly guard. Her butterfly hooks are in and her arms are underhooked under mine with her hands clasped behind my back.

2

The first thing I want to do is break her grip, so I bring my right arm up and place it in her throat.

3

Supporting my right arm with my left arm, I push both arms into her throat. Her natural instinct is to protect her airway, so she breaks her grip to defend her neck.

4

As soon as I feel her hands unclasp, I slide my hands to her shoulders so she can't sit up or roll away. Since my hands are on her shoulders, they're also in a good position to push off of when I bring my legs up in the next step.

5

I bring my legs up and prepare to jump over her legs. My hands are still on her shoulders at this point. If you prefer to throw a strike or two before moving on to the hop, then that's fine. Just be careful not to spend too much time in this standing position or your opponent could pull you into his full guard.

6

This is the critical step. I simultaneously hop up high enough to get over Julie's knees and slap them down so she can't extend her legs and kick me off.

7

I land on Julie's upper body and quickly get a hold of her hands so she can't strike me.

8

I end the pass in the full mount with my knees up against Julie's armpits. From here I can execute ground and pound or go for a submission, such as a roll-off armbar.

CARTWHEEL PASS

Like the knee hop pass, the cartwheel pass goes over the top of your opponent's guard and starts by forcing him to break his hand grip. The first part of the two passes is so similar that you could use one as a backup plan for the other. If the knee hop isn't there, then you can drop your weight down and use the cartwheel as a second option. This is a fancy move and one that carries a lot of risk with it because you are vulnerable for a few moments while your body is in the air. To reduce the risk, keep your hands firmly clasped together behind your opponent's buttocks so he can't roll to block the pass.

1 I am in Julie's butterfly guard. Her butterfly hooks are in and her arms are underhooked under mine with her hands clasped behind my back.

2 The first thing I want to do is break Julie's grip, so I bring my right arm up, place it in her throat, and push down. Her natural instinct is to protect her airway, so she breaks her grip to defend her neck. In this instance I did not have to use both hands to get her to break her grip.

3 As soon as I feel her hands unclasp, I slide my hands to her shoulders so she can't sit up or roll away. At this point I can do either the knee hop or the cartwheel passes.

4 I quickly drop my weight and clasp my hands together behind Julie's buttocks. At this point I could eat a few round knuckle shots from her right hand so I want to protect my head by keeping it tight against her side.

5

Now comes the acrobatic part. I push off with my toes and flip my body up and over her legs. At this point Julie could bring her arms up and wrap them around my torso, which would probably give her an advantage, so I have to flip fast.

6

I land with both feet over her head and off to one side. I still have a grip on her legs to prevent her from rolling into me and getting my back.

7

Obviously I can't stay on top of Julie on my back, so I have to turn over fast and establish control. I let go with my hands and turn to my right quickly. I don't turn toward her head because that would make it easy for her to throw me over her head and escape.

8

I get my knees up against her side and slide my right arm under her head to finish the pass in side mount.

SPIDER GUARD

Unlike in the full guard where you wrap your legs around your opponent, or the butterfly guard where you hook your feet to the inside of his legs, the spider guard is a modified guard where you place your feet on your opponent's hips. In contrast to the butterfly guard, which gives you the ability to lift your opponent up, the spider guard gives you an improved ability to push your opponent away, which can be used to disrupt his attacks or disengage completely. The spider guard is great for keeping separation between you and your opponent, so if you're fighting someone you don't want to get close to, this guard is effective. The spider guard is also very effective against wrestlers who like to drive in, because you can use your feet to push off and frustrate their attacks. It also creates submission opportunities because your legs are in a higher position on your opponent than they are with the butterfly and full guards. However, the spider guard is slightly riskier because it's easier to pass than the full guard or the butterfly guard. With your ankles within easy reach, a competent grappler can create a pass by isolating or controlling one or both of them.

BASIC SPIDER GUARD POSITION

My feet are on Brian's hips with my heels on his pelvis and my toes hooked over his hipbones. This makes it harder for him to pass my feet. My own hips are somewhat elevated since my feet are pushing on him. It's unnatural to underhook or overhook his arms, since the spider guard's specialty is maintaining some distance between the two combatants, so I just grab his wrists to control them and prevent him from striking. Some grappling styles advocate grabbing the backs of your opponent's arms and squeezing them against your knees to control them, but this is too defensive for me and defeats the purpose of keeping your opponent at a distance. All that technique does is tie up both of you in a mutual body lock and limit your options.

SPIDER GUARD SUBMISSIONS

When your feet are on your opponent's hips, the counterpressure that he provides can actually help with your attacks. This counterpressure affords you excellent mobility in your own hips and can increase the ease with which you transition into different submission holds and positions. And with the spider guard allowing you to create space between you and your opponent, it's also an excellent position from which to escape to your feet. We will only look at two submissions from the spider guard: the armbar and the triangle. However, the omoplata can be used as a backup plan as we're about to learn.

ARMBAR

The armbar from the spider guard is great to use against an opponent who leaves his arms extended or postures up frequently. It combines the ninety-degree cut that we've already used in several other moves with wrist control to trap his arm before he even realizes what's happening. Even if your opponent blocks the move by ripping his arm free, you can easily transition to an omoplata the same way we learned from the full guard, so there's little risk in this submission.

1) I am on my back with Brian in my spider guard. My feet are on his hips and my hands are controlling his wrists. 2) I take my right leg off of his hip and bring it out wide. Many times this will fool an opponent into thinking you intend to kick him with your heel. 3) Using my legs as leverage, I execute a ninety-degree cut by spinning to my right. This has to be a fast move that I snap into before he has a chance to block it or pull his arm out. 4) I complete the submission by bringing my left leg over his head, curling my legs downward, pinching my knees together, and elevating my hips to hyperextend his elbow.

TRIANGLE

As with the armbar, the triangle is easier from the spider guard because your feet and hips are already higher up on your opponent than they would be in the full or butterfly guards. Therefore, your feet have less distance to travel to get around your opponent's head. To set up the triangle from this position, you want to trap one of your opponent's wrists, move it out to the side, and slip your leg through the space you've created. Once you get your leg through and over his shoulder, it's just a matter of locking your feet together and squeezing until he taps.

1) I am on my back with Brian in my spider guard. My feet are on his hips and my hands are controlling his wrists. 2) I slide my hips out to my left and push him away just enough to give my right leg some maneuver space. 3) In one motion I force Brian's left hand out to the right and bring my right leg up through the space I've created. Controlling his wrists is critical at this point. If he gets them free he could block the submission, grab my legs, and pass my guard. 4) I extend my right leg so it's as far over his shoulder as possible. I want to get the back of my right knee completely over his neck. 5) With my right hand I pull Brian down and wrap my right arm around his left arm to trap it against my head. I continue to control his right hand with my left so he doesn't pull it out. 6) To complete the submission I lock my left leg over my right and squeeze his head and arm together until he taps. I also wrap both hands around the back of his left arm so he can't escape.

SPIDER GUARD SWEEPS

There aren't many sweeps from the spider guard because your feet aren't in an advantageous position to trap your opponent's legs or roll him to one side. However, there's one sweep from the spider guard that I think anyone can do and should be part of everyone's skill set.

BASIC SWEEP

The spider guard sweep begins by driving your opponent away from you. In order for the sweep to be successful, your opponent must react to this pressure by driving back into you, which is often the case. As your opponent rebounds, you move into his hips before he can get his arms into the position needed to hold your body at bay. The goal is to gain control of both of your opponent's legs, but even if you are only able to gain control of one, you will usually be left in a position that has attack options. However, this move is slightly risky. You have to completely release all control you have over your opponent, and there's a possibility that he'll sprawl his legs away so you can't grab them. There's also the possibility that he'll anticipate the move and get his arms down and around your head as you lunge for his legs, which allows him to apply a guillotine choke. For these reasons, it's important to get your head and arms around his legs as quickly as possible.

1

I am on my back with Brian in my spider guard. My feet are on his hips and my hands are controlling his wrists.

2

I raise my hips up to create the space I need to sneak my right leg out from underneath Brian's body. Although the move is broken down into steps in the following photos, it's a fast move that happens in one motion.

3

While keeping my left leg on Brian's hip, I throw my right leg across his body and outside his guard. This creates the momentum I need to lunge forward for his legs.

4

I take my left foot off of Brian's hip, let go of his wrists, and sit up quickly. My right elbow and right leg provide the base that I push off of. My head has to duck underneath his chest, so it might be necessary to throw his hands up just enough to get under him.

5

I lunge into Brian's hips and wrap my arms around his legs. It's hard to see in the pictures, but my head is well protected up against his hip.

6

With my hands around his legs and my head in his stomach, I push him off balance and onto his back to complete the sweep.

SPIDER GUARD ESCAPES

The spider guard is probably the best guard position for disengaging from an opponent. With your feet on his hips, it's much easier to push him away and create space for the escape than in any other guard, and there's minimal risk since your goal is to just get away. As with any escape, though, there's always a chance of having your feet get caught as you push away, so you have to move your legs with purpose.

BAIL OUT

This is a great way to disengage completely from the spider guard. One of the purposes of the spider guard is to control your opponent's wrists, so if you can't and he manages to rip an arm out, you can combine his backward momentum with the pushing action of your feet to get away. This doesn't mean you should escape whenever your opponent gets an arm free while you have him in the spider guard, but if you choose to escape this is the best time to. When you roll away from him, it's important to roll off to one side and over your shoulder instead of straight back. If you go straight back then your roll will be slower and you risk injuring your neck. You also need to move your feet quickly so they don't get caught.

1) I am on my back with Brian in my spider guard. My feet are on his hips and my hands are controlling his wrists. **2)** Brian raises his right arm up to strike. **3)** I am unable to control his wrist and he gets his arm free. At this point, I decide it's best to escape and start to bridge by lifting my hips and pushing Brian away with my feet. **4)** I let go of his wrist with my right hand and push him away with both feet. My left arm comes down to the ground so I can roll over my left shoulder. Notice that I do not kick off and go straight back over my head. **5)** Once I've pushed off of Brian's hips and started the roll, I retract my feet quickly so he can't grab them. My right arm is out so it can make first contact with the ground once I roll over. **6)** I get my hands onto the ground and continue to roll. **7)** Once the roll is complete, I quickly get my feet underneath me and bring my head up to spot Brian to see if he's striking. **8)** I get my feet underneath me and establish my base. I let the momentum of the roll carry my upper body backward over my feet and quickly get my guard up in case Brian decides to strike. From here, I will stand back up and reestablish my fighting stance.

GET-UP

This move is also a way to disengage when you're in the spider guard, but it's different from the previous escape in a few ways. This technique doesn't lose sight of your opponent and is a good backup plan when you try the other escape but your opponent manages to get a hold of one of your legs. It is important to mention that this technique represents one of the underlying themes of Jackson's MMA—every move has a backup plan. You will probably also have noticed by now that many moves have similar aspects to them. This escape is similar to the brace get-up from the previous chapter because you push off of your opponent's shoulder while bracing yourself up.

I am on my back with Brian in my spider guard. My feet are on his hips and my hands are controlling his wrists.

I have already decided to get away from Brian, so I extend my legs and push away from him.

I put my right elbow on the ground to establish a base to stand, but Brian sees it coming and grabs my ankles to pull me back in.

He leans forward to pass my guard, so I stop him by putting my left hand on his shoulder so he can't continue coming forward.

I rip my right leg away from him, turn my torso, and base my leg behind me. I keep my left hand on his shoulder to prevent him from lunging at my legs and taking me down.

I use my based-out right leg and my left hand to rip my left leg free and place it far enough away that he can't grab it. I have to step quickly to get out of his reach and get back into my fighting stance facing him.

SPIDER GUARD PASSES

Up until now we've explored the options you have when controlling your opponent with spider guard. Now we'll turn the tables and look at the options you have when your opponent places you in spider guard. Once your opponent gets into the spider guard position, you need to change your offensive strategy. If you attempt to drive forward you will be stopped short. To be effective from the top, you must strip your opponent's feet off your hips and pass the spider guard.

HIP DROP PASS

It is often very difficult to move aggressively when you are in a fighter's spider guard. Striking in particular is limited because your opponent can push your hips away anytime you attempt a meaningful strike. One method of taking the initiative back is the hip drop pass, which will get you back into your opponent's full guard, neutralizing his advantage. While this doesn't pass you into a dominant position, it allows you to move back into a full guard, which for most MMA fighters, will be much more familiar territory

1

I am in Julie's spider guard. She has her feet on my hips and is controlling my wrists.

2

I quickly extend my right leg and drop my right hip. This rotation action of my hips forces Julie's left foot to slip off my hip.

3

I repeat the move on the opposite side by extending my left leg and dropping my left hip while turning my upper torso to the right. This forces both of Julie's feet off my hips, eliminating her ability to maintain the spider guard.

4

I end the pass by bringing my knees up and getting into her full guard. This eliminates Julie's hard work in attempting to secure the spider guard and takes away any game plan she may have had to attack from the spider guard position.

STANDING BELLY BUMP PASS

The goal of this move is to completely pass your opponent's guard instead of simply dropping into his full guard. The technique is similar to the previous belly bump pass from the full guard as well as the matador pass. The most important aspect of this pass is that you control your opponent's ankles before you try to stand. If you don't have control of his ankles, your opponent can kick your hips away and rise to the standing position. Additionally, your opponent can also kick your knees and cause a lot of damage, so be sure to control his ankles before attempting this pass.

I am in Julie's spider guard. She has her feet on my hips and is controlling my wrists.

The first thing I want to do is free my hands so I can get control of her ankles for the pass. I simply posture up and pull my hands away from Julie.

I reach down and grab Julie's ankles. As I said before, this is the critical part of the pass, so I make sure to get a firm grip on each one.

I get to my feet, lean forward, and bend at the knees. I do this to protect my legs so if I lose control of one ankle and she kicks my knee, it won't hyperextend.

I simultaneously push my belly forward to prevent Julie from hooking my hips while tossing her feet to my right. Notice that I keep my weight low and my knees bent so I'm protected throughout the pass.

I drop my weight quickly onto Julie's hips so she can neither pull guard nor roll away and escape. I also slide my knees into her back to prevent her from shrimping her hips back into me.

I let go of Julie's ankles and wrap my left arm under her head to control her upper body. From here I can take her back and attempt a submission or trap her top leg and move into mount. I also have the option of isolating her arm and locking up a kimura from side mount.

SIT-UP GUARD

The sit up guard is a great attack platform that affords you many more options than your opponent has from the top position. When you rise up into a sit-up position your opponent cannot strike your head, while you have several submissions and sweeps at your disposal. From the full guard we looked at the armbar, double armbar, omoplata, triangle, and head and arm choke. From the sit-up guard we will look at two different submissions—the kimura and the guillotine choke, both of which are more effective from the sit-up guard than the full guard. We'll also explore new sweeps and variations of a sweep that we saw earlier in the book—the hip heist. The beauty with the sit-up guard is that it complements the full guard very well. The two are mutually supporting, so if one doesn't work for you, the other can be used as a backup plan.

BASIC SIT-UP GUARD POSITION

To achieve the basic sit-up guard, I first start in a regular guard with my hands behind Brian's head to control his posture.

I quickly unhook my feet, turn my torso to the right, and use my abdominal muscles to sit up. I push Brian's head to my left with my right hand to give me the space I need to bring my left arm over his head.

My left foot posts on the ground for leverage, while I sit up and continue turning my shoulders to my right. I get up on my right elbow and brace it underneath my shoulders. Once I plant my elbow, it's very hard for Brian to push me back down or strike me, while I have plenty of options available to attack.

SIT-UP GUARD SUBMISSIONS

Your options for submitting your opponent from the sit-up guard are different from your options from a basic full guard position. Your opponent's arms and head are closer and easier to reach from the sit-up guard than they would be if you were lying flat on your back in the full guard. By sitting up, you can easily isolate your opponent's arm or neck and lock it up, forcing him to tap out.

KIMURA

The kimura is one of my favorite guard submissions for an MMA match. The reason being that it's an extremely powerful submission hold, and it's extremely simple to finish once you lock it into position. However, if your opponent defends the kimura after you've secured the grip, you're still in a great spot. By sitting up and isolating his arm, it makes it impossible for him to land strikes to your head. If he makes one simple mistake, you can be back on the offensive, only seconds away from finishing the match. Once you've sat up and grabbed your opponent's arm, his options are very limited, while yours are many, so the risk in this move is low. If he doesn't immediately protect his arm, all you have to do is lean back and put pressure on the shoulder to end the fight. The critical part of this move is wrapping your legs around your opponent's waist so he does not roll forward to escape the submission. If you execute the move properly, it will put your opponent in a very bad situation.

I am in the basic sit-up guard position with my torso turned to the right and my right elbow bracing me up against the ground. My left foot is on the ground to provide leverage for my hips. Brian's left arm is unprotected, so I am going to attack it.

With my right hand, I grab Brian's left wrist. I then wrap my left arm around his left arm and bring it down to grab my own wrist. This secures my figure-four grip, locking up Brian's arm. Even if Brian defends at this point, I'm in a very safe position on my back.

Now I'm going to turn my body to put pressure on his arm. I plant my right leg on the mat to get leverage and push off of my left leg to scoot my hips out to my right and rotate my upper torso to the left. I must move my hips toward Brian's trapped arm to enable me to put leverage on the arm.

I lean back to the mat at a ninety-degree angle to Brian's body. This makes it hard for him to escape and will enable me to put maximum pressure on his shoulder. My right leg comes up and over his back to prevent him from rolling forward.

I scoot my hips out to the right again to gain more leverage on the submission. To finish, I roll onto my left shoulder. Because Brian's body is trapped with my right leg, this action cranks his shoulder, forcing him to tap out.

GUILLOTINE (ARM-IN)

While the guillotine is an extremely high-percentage submission, often you're unable to secure the traditional grip. The optimal guillotine choke is when both of your arms are wrapped around your opponent's neck, which is called an "arm-out" guillotine. You can still accomplish the submission when he has an arm in, but the dynamics of the submission change. Often from the sit-up guard, you're unable to secure the traditional arm-out guillotine, which makes attacking with an arm-in guillotine your best option. The arm-in variation can be more difficult to work, as your supporting arm has to travel farther to assist in the choke. However, if you manage to secure your hands in the proper position, it can still be an effective submission. To make the technique work, you have to create some space between you and your opponent. If you're too close, then you won't be able to get the proper grip on his neck.

I am in the sit-up guard with my left arm over Brian's back. Instead of planting my elbow on the mat, I have my right arm extended to establish my base on my right hand. My left foot is on the ground to allow my hips to remain mobile.

Because Brian is driving his head underneath my armpit in an attempt to push me flat, I bring my left arm over top of his head to trap it.

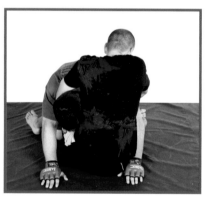

I wrap my left arm all the way around Brian's throat.

Brian blocks the full guillotine by forcing his left shoulder into my chest as he's pushing me flat. This forces me to transition into the arm-in guillotine. I slide my right arm underneath Brian's right armpit and grab my left wrist with my right hand. My grip is critical here—my left arm must be inserted deep underneath Brian's neck to apply pressure to the choke.

5

As I lean back onto my left hip, I bring my legs up to secure Brian's hips and prevent him from escaping.

6

To complete the submission I wrap my legs around Brian's back and hook them together to prevent him from rolling or escaping. I apply pressure to the choke by pushing Brian's hips away with my legs while pulling up with my arms, forcing them into his neck. This drives my left forearm deep into Brian's throat, which chokes him and forces him to tap out.

GUILLOTINE (ARM-OUT)

As mentioned before, the guillotine can be completed in two different ways. In this technique I'm going to demonstrate how to apply the guillotine choke with both arms clasped around your opponent's head. This choke can be more powerful than the "arm-in" variation as both hands are gripped directly underneath your opponent's neck with no interference. With this version, you will use a different grip than with the arm-in guillotine. With the arm-out you clasp your hands together rather than grabbing your wrist. As before, the key element is to shoot your hips back to create enough space to complete the submission.

1

I am in the sit-up guard with my left arm over Brian's back. My left foot is on the ground to allow my hips to remain mobile.

2

Because Brian is driving his head underneath my armpit in an attempt to push me flat, I come up onto my right hand and rotate my body in clockwise direction with the goal of trapping his head.

3

I begin wrapping my left arm over the back of Brian's neck.

4

I wrap my left arm all the way around Brian's throat. He doesn't defend the choke, so I wrap my right hand underneath his throat and clasp my hands together.

5

I lift my right elbow up high to cinch down on his neck.

I fall back to my left hip. To finish the submission, I lock my feet together, push Brian's hips away with my legs, pull my hands up into my armpit, and lever my right elbow down onto Brian's left shoulder.

6

SWEEPS

While sweep-specific bottom positions like the butterfly guard make forcing your opponent to his back extremely simple, a specialty guard such as the sit-up guard has many options for sweeping as well. In an MMA fight your opponent will often try to posture from within your guard in order to deliver powerful punches. By following your opponent's momentum, you can often drive your hips into his torso and easily throw him backward. However, if such a method of attack fails, this guard also puts you in a great position to isolate your opponent's arms, making it extremely easy to steal his points of base away and send him to his back without any resistance. These factors make the sit-up guard an excellent platform for not only attacking your opponent's arms, but also isolating his arms and putting him on his back.

LEG HOOK SWEEP

When I'm in the guard, my first priority is always to look for a submission. In the sit-up guard the highest-percentage submission is the kimura, but if your opponent feels it coming, he can defend very easily by locking his hands together behind your back. However, with the kimura, like all techniques I teach, I have a backup plan to counter his counter. With your opponent's hands clasped together behind your back, he won't be in a position to base out and stop a sweep. In fact, he has almost no options when in this defensive mode. You can generate a tremendous amount of leverage with this move, so even if your opponent is bigger or has better wrestling, you can successfully sweep him. The key is a realistic attack with the kimura. You must threaten your opponent's arms to convince him to grab his hands together and take away his own base.

I have Brian in my sit-up guard. My shoulders are turned to my right and I'm sitting up on my right elbow. I reach over Brian's head with my left arm to attack his left arm with a kimura.

Brian senses the kimura coming and blocks it by clasping his hands together behind my back. I can't get enough leverage on his arm to pop it out for the submission, so I decide to transfer to the leg hook sweep.

I reach across Brian's back, grab my right ankle with my left hand, and pull my right leg up tight to Brian's ribs. This helps me anchor my torso in position to prevent Brian from driving me flat.

4

I slide my right arm under Brian's left leg and cup my hand on the back of his hamstring. This is where the previous step comes into play. Taking my right elbow out from underneath my torso would make it very difficult to remain in a sit-up position without my left hand hooking my leg.

5

Now it's time to sweep my opponent. I begin the movement by twisting my upper torso to my left. I simultaneously lift Brian's left leg with my right arm and pull on my own right leg to force him over. I also post my left foot on the ground and drive upward to assist with the rolling movement.

6

As we begin to roll, I release my left grip on my right leg. Once my back hits the mat, there's no longer a need to sit up, so I eliminate the anchor and release my left hand to prevent it from becoming trapped as I roll.

7

I keep rolling Brian over and post my left arm underneath me, which will allow me to rise up onto my elbow.

8

As Brian lands on his back, I release his left leg, post my hands out wide, and secure a low mount.

HIP HEIST SWEEP

This sweep works by trapping both of your opponent's limbs on one side of his body and driving him in that direction using your hips. Like the previous sweep, this one is great when you can't isolate his arm for the kimura. But instead of grabbing your leg and going to your left, you can use this and go to your right. In many situations this sweep will be extremely easy to execute, as it eliminates your opponent's ability to post with either his arm or his leg, giving him all the balance of a two-legged table. The hip heist sweep gives you another reversal option in situations when there is limited maneuvering space, like when up against a cage wall. By having two directions in which you can sweep your opponent, you make yourself more threatening in all situations. This move has a very low risk factor because, as we'll see later, there are several backup moves if your opponent counters.

1

I have Brian in my sit-up guard. Posting up on my right elbow, I reach over Brian's head to grab his left arm and attempt a kimura.

2

Brian senses the kimura coming and blocks it by clasping his hands together behind my back. I can't get enough leverage to free his arm and attempt the submission, so I decide to transfer to a sweep instead. However, this time I will go to my right instead of my left. Immediately as Brian defends, I base my right foot on the mat while cupping the back of his left triceps with my left hand.

3

I quickly extend my right arm in order to post my right hand on the mat. This allows me to elevate my shoulders. At the same time, I extend my left leg, which elevates my hips.

4

With my torso elevated, it's now a simple matter to drive my hips into Brian. Notice how I still have his left arm trapped with my left hand. His left leg is also trapped by my right leg, which eliminates any possibility for him to post out to his left and stop the sweep.

5

I continue to drive my hips into Brian, allowing momentum to drive him to his back.

6

Now I have successfully swept Brian and landed in the full mount position.

7

I pull my left arm out from underneath Brian in order to attain my base from the full mount and complete the technique.

HIP HEIST SWEEP (COUNTER LEG BASE)

This is a contingency plan for the hip heist sweep that I demonstrated in the previous sequence. While the hip heist is a great technique, sometimes your opponent will resist the sweep by posting his leg out wide. With his leg based out, it will be all but impossible to roll him to his side. However, by simply maintaining your handgrip and kicking out his leg, you will again topple his foundation and force him to roll to his side. Just like a bicycle without a kickstand, your opponent will fall over and allow you to steal away the top position.

I have Brian in my sit-up guard. I am posting on my right elbow, which allows me to elevate my shoulders. I reach across to grab his left arm and attempt a kimura.

Brian senses the kimura coming and blocks it by clasping his hands together behind my back. I can't get enough leverage to free his arm and attempt the submission, so I decide to transfer to the hip heist sweep instead. As before, I extend my right arm and left leg to elevate my hips and prepare me for the attack.

Despite my right leg hooking Brian's left leg, he manages to kick his left leg out to block the sweep. With his base now extremely wide, I am unable to sweep him to my right.

I keep my right arm and left leg extended to elevate my hips off the mat while I retract my right knee in toward my stomach. This allows me the space to place my right foot on Brian's left thigh, just above the knee.

I extend my right leg, kicking Brian's left leg out from underneath him. Notice that I kick it away just far enough to maintain contact between my foot and his knee.

With Brian's sole point of base eliminated, he begins to roll to his left as I kick his knee out. To assist his rotation, I drive my hips into his torso and roll my shoulders to my right.

I roll Brian all the way over until his back is on the ground, giving me the full mount.

HIP HEIST TO KIMURA

This move is sneaky and is a great example of how complicated grappling can be. The hip heist and the kimura work so great together because the defense for one move puts your opponent in danger for the other. With this technique, I go back and forth between the two attacks. This allows me to get one step ahead of my opponent, and finally lock in the kimura. If you look at the photos below, you'll notice that instead of blocking the hip heist sweep by posting his leg out to his side, as my opponent did in the previous sequence, he defends by positioning his hand on the mat. Instead of eliminating his base and continuing the sweep, I attack his unguarded arm and secure a kimura. This brings us full circle—the series starts and ends with the kimura. As always, all techniques in Jackson's MMA have a backup plan. In a series such as this, even the backup plan has a backup plan.

1

I have Brian in my sit-up guard. I post my right elbow on the mat to allow me to elevate my shoulders. I reach over Brian's head with my left arm and hook it over his left shoulder.

2

Like before, Brian senses the kimura coming and blocks the submission by clasping his hands together behind my back. I decide to counter with the hip heist sweep. To initiate the reversal, I hook my left hand on the back of Brian's left triceps.

3

As I drive my hips into Brian, he attempts to block the sweep by hammering his left arm free of my grip and posting his left hand out wide. While this prevents me from executing the sweep, it opens his arm back up and allows me to attempt the kimura once again.

I quickly pounce on the opportunity to isolate Brian's unprotected arm. To trap Brian's arm I grab his left wrist with my right hand while hooking my left arm over the top of his arm and grabbing my right wrist with my left hand.

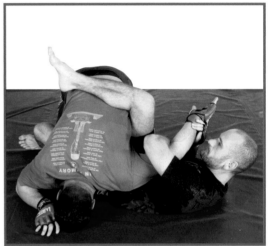

Just like the kimura submission earlier in this section, I lean back at a ninety-degree angle and pin his arm to my chest with my figure-four grip. My right leg comes over Brian's back to prevent him from rolling forward. This makes it hard for him to escape and puts maximum pressure on his elbow.

I scoot my hips out to the right and roll my shoulders to my left. This rotates Brian's left shoulder. To apply the submission, I drive his left hand toward his right shoulder, forcing him to tap.

HEAD AND ARM ISOLATION SWEEP

This sweep is a great contingency plan for when your opponent prevents you from establishing the sit-up guard by driving his head into your chest, which keeps your shoulders pinned to the mat. However, you're still going to utilize the sit-up guard philosophy to sweep him to his back. By taking away your opponent's points of base on one side of his body, you can roll him in that direction with little to no resistance. The key to this technique is using deception. When you make your move, an inexperienced grappler might be fooled into thinking your intention is a head and arm choke. As he becomes preoccupied with defeating your grip to defend his neck, he'll likely forget about his legs. By the time he realizes he's in danger of losing position, you're already on top.

1

I am on my back with Brian in full guard. Instead of posturing up, he's driving his head into my chest to prevent me from sitting up. To tie him up, I clasp my hands together behind his neck, which prevents him from raising his head up.

2

I decide I'm going to sweep Brian to the left, so I slip my left arm underneath his right armpit while maintaining head control with my right hand. This allows me to isolate his right arm.

3

I now clasp my hands together and squeeze my elbows together. This traps Brian's right arm and head. From this position, Brian will likely think I'm attempting to attack his neck and will forget to defend his legs.

4

I open my guard and put my left foot on Brian's right hip. Like the spider guard, my toes stay hooked over his hip, giving me maximum leverage of his lower body.

5

I move my hips out to my right and pull Brian's head and arm toward my head. This takes his weight off his knees, which will make it easier for me to sweep him in the next step.

6

I slide my left foot down to Brian's right knee and prepare to push it away.

7

I extend my left leg, kicking Brian's right knee out from underneath his hips. This drops Brian's hips, forcing him to roll to his right. Notice I maintain my grip on his head and arm to prevent him from posting out with his right hand to stop the roll.

8

I drive off the mat with my right foot, continuing Brian's roll to his right. With his left arm trapped and his left leg kicked straight back, he is unable to defend the sweep.

9

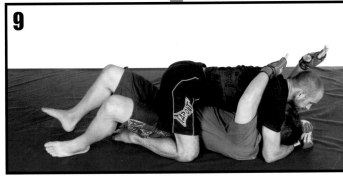

As Brian rolls all the way to his back, I hook my legs underneath his hips and end the technique in the full mount.

SIT UP GUARD TRANSITIONS

Transitioning from the sit-up is often not thought of as a primary attack, but more of a situational technique. As I've mentioned, the sit-up guard affords you many opportunities to finish your opponent while remaining in an excellent defensive position. Leaving the safety of the sit-up guard should only be considered after exhausting all your other offensive options. My favorite technique for transition out of the sit-up guard is executing a switch to the rear mount. My philosophy is that the sit-up guard is such a great position, there's little advantage to be gained by leaving it and entering another neutral position. Unless I can take the back or mount, I will generally just opt to stay in the sit-up guard and continue attacking.

SWITCH TO REAR MOUNT

The primary reason the sit-up guard affords so many submission opportunities is because it presents the ability to isolate your opponent's arm. While this makes it easier to attack the arm and the neck, it's also exactly the quality needed to execute a switch from the bottom. Similar to a switch in wrestling, the technique shown below is applied by sitting forward, keeping your shoulders off the mat, and hooking your opponent's inside leg. With that leg hook you can pull your opponent forward and off-balance him, which allows you to rotate around his hips in order to take his back. This is a great move because it transitions so freely from the sit-up guard submissions; you can attempt a kimura, fail, and easily transition to the switch and take your opponent's back. This keeps your opponent on the defensive, allowing you to impose your game plan.

I have Brian in my sit-up guard. I have my left arm over top of his head, resting on his left shoulder, and I'm posting my right arm on the mat to assist me in sitting up.

I extend my left arm, reaching over top of Brian's left arm. With my left arm fully extended, I slide my hand in between his thighs and hook the inside of his left leg.

I lean back and to my left, pulling Brian toward me. At the same time, I post my right foot on the mat and scoot my hips out to my right, giving me an advantageous angle to move to Brian's back.

I post my right foot and left hand on the mat, lift my hips off the ground, and turn my torso to my left. As my hips turn, my left leg stays in place in between Brian's legs. At the same time, I reach over Brian's back with my right arm to hook his right arm. This control will prevent Brian from escaping.

I swing my right leg over Brian's back and slide my right foot over his right leg, establishing my second hook and giving me optimal control of the back position.

With both leg hooks sunk in, I have completed the transition. From here, I can flatten Brian out by extending my legs, start attacking with ground and pound, or go for a chokehold.

THE DOWNED GUARD

When your average MMA competitor talks about the guard, he is often referring to the position where you are on your back, controlling your opponent with your legs. However, the downed guard is more of a temporary condition than a true guard position. The downed guard often arises when you get knocked to your back and your opponent stands over you. Since you're not controlling his body using your legs, it's not a true guard position, but that doesn't mean you can't get offensive. To attack from the downed guard, you need to control the space between you and your opponent. If you're able to maintain space between your bodies, it provides you with an opportunity to stand back up, and if you are able to close off the space between your bodies, it gives you the ability to execute a reversal. In this section, I will demonstrate both options.

SWING TO SINGLE LEG

As in all situations, I recommend attempting to use the downed guard offensively. Even if your opponent just dropped you with a punch, you can still close of the space between your bodies and initiate a reversal. Personally, I've found one of the best ways to accomplish that is to utilize the swing to single leg demonstrated in the sequence below. Like the basic sweep from the spider guard, to initiate this technique you move rapidly forward and secure your opponent's leg. Once you have that control, you can quickly take your opponent to the mat and secure a dominant position. However, when shooting in to your opponent's leg, it's important to turn the corner quickly and protect your head by keeping it to the inside of his body. If you allow your opponent to push your head to the outside of his hip, he can grip your neck and attempt a guillotine choke.

1) I am on my back while Julie is standing over me. I have my legs in the air with my feet positioned in front of her knees to prevent her from throwing kicks to my thighs. I also have my left hand up to prevent her from kicking over my legs and landing strikes to my head.

2) I quickly sit up, fold my left leg underneath me, and roll forward to my left knee. As I come up, my right foot lands outside Julie's lead leg, so my momentum carries me off to her side.

3) I wrap both arms around Julie's lead leg and stand up to both feet. My head is tight against her stomach so she can't attempt a guillotine choke.

4) To eliminate Julie's ability to post on her left foot, I pull my arms up, elevating her leg and taking away her base. From here, I can take her down by sweeping her other foot out from under her, rotate around to her back for a standing rear naked choke, or simply disengage and return the fight to the standing position.

LEG KICK GET-UP

Although I advocate being offensive in all positions, oftentimes your opponent will refuse to come forward into your downed guard. While this may prevent you from rolling forward and seizing control of his leg, the space enables you to disengage and transition back into the standing position. The leg kick get up is a simple way to freeze your opponent in place and give you the window you need to escape back to your feet. Even though this might seem like a simple move, it should be a part of everyone's toolbox. Not only does it allow you to disengage from a fighter standing over top of you, but it's also a safe and efficient movement that can be executed even when stunned or tired.

I am on my back with Julie standing over me. My legs and arms are up to defend against any strikes she may throw.

I simultaneously base my right hand behind me, plant my left foot, and kick Julie's lead knee with my right foot. This stops her forward momentum and momentarily shifts her onto the defensive, which creates a window of opportunity for me to escape.

After kicking Julie's leg, I reverse the direction of my right leg and plant my right foot on the mat behind me for base. Notice that I still have my left hand raised high to prevent Julie from landing an unobstructed punch or kick to my head.

I raise my torso and back away into my fighting stance.

HEAD KICK GET-UP

The previous technique is useful for halting your opponent's forward momentum and giving you a small window of opportunity to escape. However, if your kick to his lead leg misses or fails to stop his forward momentum, a good option can be following up with a head kick. Not only can throwing a head kick cause a tremendous amount of damage when you land it clean, but it can also act as a feint. If your opponent sees the head kick coming, which is likely, he will most likely lean back to avoid contact. This halts his forward momentum, giving you the space you need to escape.

1) I am on my back with Julie standing over me. My legs and arms are up to defend against any strikes she may throw. 2) I simultaneously base my right hand behind me, plant my left foot, and kick at Julie's knee with my right leg. However, I've missed the knee and she continues coming forward. 3) I bring my right leg down and plant it on the mat as a point of base. 4) I extend my right arm and right leg to give me leverage to kick upward at Julie's head with my left leg. 5) My left foot plants on the ground. I still have my left arm up to defend any strikes Julie may throw as I'm transitioning into the standing position. 6) I plant my right foot behind me, elevate my torso, and back away into my fighting stance.

THE HALF GUARD

The half guard is a very interesting position, as it's often thought of solely as a transition—halfway to passing the guard or halfway to achieving full guard, depending on your perspective. While these things are very true, it is also a platform from which you can launch attacks. I advocate being offensive from all positions, and the half guard is no exception. With the proper controls, it's possible to execute sweeps, transitions, and submissions from the half guard. Maintaining good control is very important and can make the difference between success and failure in these maneuvers.

There are two bottom half guard position variations we'll look at—the underhook and the overhook. The difference between the two is where your top arm is in relation to your opponent, as we will see. Both methods can be used to execute specific techniques. If you have the underhook from the bottom position, one set of maneuvers will be available to you, while if you have the overhook, another set of movements will be possible to execute. Each variation has its advantages, so it's best to learn when to utilize each set of techniques. This section will prepare you to attack from the half guard regardless of which control position you're able to achieve.

OVERHOOK HALF GUARD

If your opponent is on top of you with his outside arm hooked tightly under your armpit, then it's often best to attempt to secure a tight overhook to counter his control. The overhook half guard relies on a tight whizzer on the outside arm to pin down your opponent's torso. This prevents him from posturing or basing on his outside hand. However, the overhook alone is useless without bringing your outside knee in between your bodies and driving your shin into your opponent's belly. The combination of these two actions allows you to not only keep your opponent's posture low, but also prevent him from driving into you and flattening you out. If your opponent begins striking with his free hand, use your free hand to protect your head until it's time to mount an attack. In the half guard, there's always a risk of your opponent slipping around your foot and gaining side mount, so it's important to keep your legs locked tight to prevent him from easily sliding past your guard and gaining a dominant position.

ESTABLISHING THE OVERHOOK HALF GUARD

The traditional half guard requires you to wrap both of your legs around one of your opponent's legs so he cannot pass to side mount. This is a common position to land in when a fight transitions to the ground if you are unable to pull your opponent into your full guard. However, this is an extremely defensive position, and it's only a matter of time until your opponent passes this type of half guard. I prefer to take a more active approach and establish a half guard position that allows me to mount attacks and sweeps. To establish the overhook half guard position, you must unlock your opponent's leg, slip your hips out, and force your top leg to the inside of your opponent's torso. This gives you leverage to push him away and mount an attack while keeping him from passing or mounting you.

I'm on my back with Julie in a traditional half guard position. I have both of my legs wrapped around her right leg with my right foot hooked under my left knee to prevent her from sliding to side mount. Julie has her right arm underhooked under my left arm and has her hands clasped together behind my back. For this reason I have decided to transition to an overhook half guard.

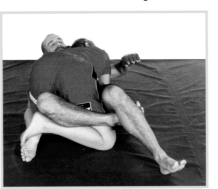

My first goal is to isolate and control her right arm, so I prepare to hook my left arm over her right shoulder. This must be done quickly, or she will capitalize on my now extended left arm.

3

I force my left hand under Julie's right armpit, drive it deep between our bodies, and pinch my elbow down to lock in a whizzer grip. At the same time, I unhook my legs and base my left leg wide to give me leverage to move my hips.

4

I drive off my left foot, move my hips out, and turn onto my right hip. This creates enough space for me to bring my knee in between our bodies.

5

I force my left knee between our bodies, driving my shin against her stomach. I'm now in an overhook half guard.

OMOPLATA

All submissions from the overhook half guard rely on isolating your opponent's arm, moving your hips underneath his body, and then using the space created to lock in a submission. Here I demonstrate an omoplata from the half guard. While it may seem difficult to execute the omoplata from this position, because my hips are already off-line with my opponent, this move becomes a very high-percentage attack. The key to this technique is isolating and controlling your opponent's arm throughout the move. If you fail to secure a tight whizzer grip, your opponent will likely rip his arm free, posture up, and slide past your legs.

1

I am on my right hip with Julie in my half guard. My left arm is over-hooked on Julie's right arm and my left knee is pressing into her mid-section.

2

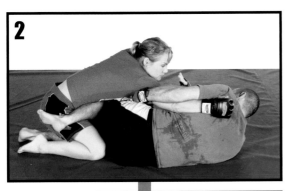

I pull my right leg up and brace it against her left knee. This will give me the leverage I need to rotate my body for the submission.

3

I slide my left leg off of Julie's midsection and swing it over her head. My right hand pushes her head away to create the space I need to toss my leg over her head. This will also prevent her from driving her head back toward my body to counter the submission.

4

I swing my shoulders to my left as I bring my left leg over Julie's head. When my leg gets completely over her shoulder, I let go of the overhook with my left arm and hook my foot under her chin to completely isolate her arm. However, it is important to notice that I still have her right hand trapped in my left armpit.

5

I roll onto my left hip, which gives me the space needed to free my right leg and hook it over my left foot. This locks Julie's arm in between my legs, which puts me in great position to finish my attack. From here, I can control Julie's hips and sit forward to finish the shoulder lock, or simply allow her to roll to her back and land a reversal.

TRIANGLE

The triangle submission can be difficult from the half guard due to the distance your leg must travel before it can go over your opponent's shoulder. As a result, you must create more space than the half guard typically affords, which requires good hip movement as well as good flexibility. It is also important to retain a tight overhook to prevent your opponent from posturing out of the submission. If you fail to secure your opponent's upper body, you will lose the triangle even if you succeed in locking your legs into position.

1

I am on my right hip with Julie in my half guard. My left arm is over-hooked on her right arm and my left knee is pressing into her mid-section. My free hand is on her free hand to prevent her from landing strikes to my head.

2

To create the space to pull my right leg out from underneath Julie's body, I drive my left shin into her midsection. This gives me a point of leverage to move my hips to my left. I roll onto my right shoulder to afford me maximum space to extract my right leg from underneath Julie's hips.

3

I drop my right hip to the mat to the outside of Julie's body. Having created space between us, I quickly slide my right leg out from underneath her body. While controlling Julie's right arm with my overhook, I push her left arm out to create space. Next, I bring my right leg underneath Julie's left armpit, and as it clears, I force my leg over her shoulder.

4

Once my leg is hooked over Julie's shoulder on her neck, I turn my tor-so to the right so I have the angle I need to complete the submission. Although I have bailed on the over-hook, I am still controlling Julie's arms to prevent her from attaining posture.

5

I let go of Julie's right arm and rotate my torso to my right at a ninety-degree angle to her body. As I attain this ninety-degree-cut position, I overhook Julie's left arm and bring my legs up to prepare to lock them together in a triangle.

6

As I wrap both of my arms over Julie's left arm, I hook the crook of my left leg over my right foot to secure the triangle. To finish the submission, I squeeze my knees together.

OVERHOOK SWEEP

In a fight, your opponent can often determine the techniques available to you. By instituting certain controls or movements, he gives you certain options while taking other options away. The technique demonstrated in this sequence is only available to you when your opponent drives forward into your hips in an attempt to pass your half guard. With his weight propped up onto your shin, it's easy to lift his hips, pull on his overhooked arm, and roll him over to his back. Like many sweeps, this one requires equal amounts of control and timing. If you do not wait for your opponent to drive forward, or your overlook or leg positioning is not precise, the technique will most likely fail.

I am on my right hip with Julie in my half guard. My left arm is overhooked on her right arm and my left knee pressing into her midsection. My free hand is on her free hand to prevent her from landing strikes to my head. I can feel Julie driving her weight forward to pass my guard. This is my trigger to execute the overhook sweep.

To initiate the sweep, I flatten my right leg against the mat to act as a pivot point and simultaneously drive my left shin upwards. Because Julie was driving her weight forward, this elevates her hips and begins a rolling movement. To prevent her from basing her arm out and blocking the sweep, I maintain my left overhook on her right arm.

With Julie off balance I continue to roll her over toward her back. If I need more leverage, I push her left shoulder away with my right hand as we roll.

As Julie's back hits the ground, I slide my right hand to her knee for control. My left knee is still on her stomach and I'm lying on my left hip.

I now switch my knees, sliding my right knee over top of my left knee. Notice I'm still on my hip and haven't firmly established side mount yet, so this step needs to be executed quickly.

I rotate my hips so I am on top of Julie in a knee-on-belly position. From here I can mount either a striking or submission attacks.

GET-UP

As I stated before, the half guard is not a place you want to wait for your opponent to make a move. If he successfully blocks your submission attempts and sweeps, then it's time to disengage and try another avenue of attack. To accomplish this, you have to create the space to free your bottom leg and then base it out behind you so you can get the fight to a standing position. Because of the angle of your hips while controlling your opponent from the overhook half guard, this can actually be a fairly easy option to execute from the bottom. If you fail at your submission attempts, your hips will be positioned far enough off to the side to allow you to extract your bottom leg and stand up into your fighting stance.

1

I am on my right hip with Julie in my half guard. My left arm is over-hooked on her right arm and my left knee is pressing into her midsection. My free hand is on her free hand to prevent her from landing strikes to my head.

2

I release my control of Julie's right arm so I can post on my right elbow. Because Julie's hand is now free, I must move quickly from this point or else risk taking damage from Julie's left hand.

3

I push off of Julie's midsection with my left knee. With my weight being carried on my right elbow and my left knee, I am free to pull my right leg out from underneath Julie's body and plant my right knee on the mat.

4

I extend my right arm and left leg, allowing me to elevate my torso. My left arm is still creating downward pressure on Julie's shoulder to prevent her from raising her head.

5

With my torso now upright and having established a stable base with my legs, I bring my right arm over Julie's head and brace my right hand on her neck. I also maintain the overhook on her right arm with my left arm. These actions prevent Julie from driving into me and forcing me to my back again. From here I can easily rise to my feet and resume the fight in the standing position.

UNDERHOOK

As its name implies, the underhook half guard uses a different arm position than the overhook. Establishing a leg hook and an underhook from the half guard gives you control of half your opponent's body, which provides you with a great deal of leverage. You can then use that leverage to mount attacks and launch several sweeps that will achieve a dominant position. I generally look to establish the underhook half guard when my opponent is playing away from my body or if he allows me to create some separation between our torsos.

ESTABLISHING THE UNDERHOOK HALF GUARD

As I stated in the previous section, I like to take a more active approach and establish a half guard position that allows me to mount attacks and sweeps. However, achieving an underhook is only part of the position. To attain full control from the underhook position it's also necessary to achieve a butterfly hook on your opponent's leg. This affords you complete control of the far side of his body. Unable to pass over the far side of your guard, your opponent will be forced to stay in front of you. This makes his reactions predictable, and will open many offensive opportunities.

I'm on my back with Julie in my half guard. Both of my arms are underhooked under her armpits. I have both of my legs wrapped around her right leg, and I've hooked the crook of my left leg over my right foot.

Since Julie is playing away from me, I will attempt to utilize the space to insert a leg hook under her right thigh. I unhook my legs and base my left foot on the ground for leverage.

I plant on my left foot and move my hips to my left. This creates the space I need to sneak my foot inside her thigh.

I hook my left foot on the inside of Julie's thigh. My right leg stays in between Julie's guard. Having established a left butterfly hook and left underhook, I have greater control than I would when in the traditional half guard.

TRIANGLE FROM UNDERHOOK HALF GUARD

One of the key advantages of the underhook from the half guard position is that it allows you to elevate your opponent's upper body. In this technique, I demonstrate how to capitalize on that ability by driving your opponent off balance, forcing him to post out on his hand, and then using that space you just created to slide your leg through for a triangle. Flexibility is important for this technique. Without adequate hip flexibility, you will be unable to fully retract your leg from underneath your opponent's body, which will cause you to be unsuccessful with the technique.

1

I am on my right hip with Neil in my underhook half guard. I have double underhooks with my arms and my left shin is inserted between Neil's thighs.

2

To upset Neil's balance, I rotate my hips to my right and lift my left arm to throw Neil off his base. This accomplishes two things—it makes him base his left arm out so I can trap it, and it creates the space I need to pull my right leg free from underneath his hips.

3

When Neil's left hand hits the ground, I extend my right arm and grab his left wrist with my hand.

4

With Neil's wrist trapped and his balance off center, I have the room I need to pull my right leg out from underneath his hips. I begin to retract my right leg, pulling it out from underneath Neil's body.

5

I continue bending my right knee until my foot clears Neil's shoulder. Note that I am keeping a firm grip on Neil's left wrist. If I release his wrist at this point, he will likely bring his left elbow back in and block my right leg from sliding underneath his armpit.

6

With my right leg clear of Neil's armpit, I wrap it over his left shoulder. At the same time, my left arm remains underhooked under Neil's right arm to ensure he doesn't rip out of the submission. For the submission to be successful, I need to maintain control of Neil's right arm throughout the maneuver.

7

Now that I have my right leg over Neil's left shoulder, I release my grip on his left wrist. To retain control of his upper body, I hook my right hand behind his left triceps, and slide my left hand down to his right triceps.

8

Using my right underhook, I pull Neil's left shoulder into my body. At the same time, I bring my left leg up to establish the triangle position.

9

I hook my right foot underneath my left leg, wrap my hands over Neil's left shoulder to control his posture, and pinch my knees together to apply the submission.

BASIC SWEEP

The underhook half guard is not a dominant position. However, it is an excellent platform from which to attack with sweeps and attain a dominant position. While there are many different methods to reverse your opponent, I'm going to explore two sweep options from the underhook half guard. The basic sweep has some risks because when you sneak your hand behind your opponent's leg, he can execute a cross-face and push your head down, which makes the sweep very difficult. You have to explode into your opponent and get him off balance as soon as your arm is underneath his leg. Otherwise, your opponent will flatten out his hips and unleash strikes on your now unprotected head.

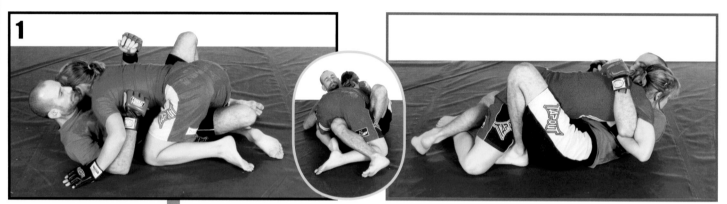

1

I am on my hip with Julie in my underhook half guard. I have double underhooks with my arms and my left shin is inserted between her thighs.

2

Because Julie's left knee is riding high near my arm, I sneak my right arm down and hook it underneath her left thigh. At this point I am vulnerable to a cross-face and elbow strikes, so I have to explode into her hips and sweep her the second I get a grip on her thigh. If I linger, I will almost certainly find myself in a bad position.

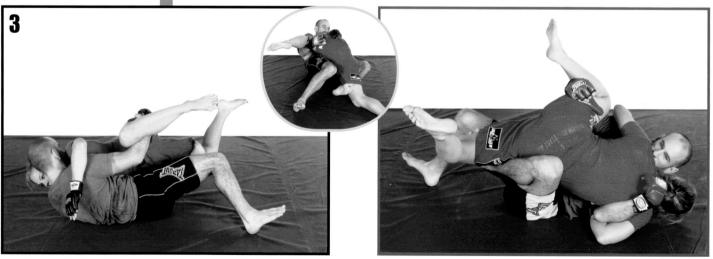

3

I plant my right foot on the ground while lifting my right arm to elevate Julie's hips. As I explode my hips off the mat, Julie begins to rotate to her back. Because of the dynamic movement involved in this sweep, it is extremely difficult for Julie to post out and prevent the sweep.

HALF GUARD / UNDERHOOK

With Julie off balance, I continue to drive with my right foot and roll her over. I maintain the hook with my left shin on her thigh to prevent her from moving her hips and attempting to pull guard.

As Julie hits her back, I quickly rotate my hips toward her head to enable me to secure side mount. With my hips tight to her torso, Julie will be unable to pull guard.

I keep rotating my hips and end in scarf hold with my right arm underhooked under Julie's left armpit to complete the sweep. I use my left hand to control her right arm, which prevents her from throwing strikes.

SHIN SWEEP

When sweeping, you will find that your opponent can counter your attempts to off-balance him, no matter how perfectly you nail the technique. To do this, however, your opponent must lean drastically to counterbalance himself. By practicing sweeps in alternating directions, you can counter this tendency. If your opponent leans drastically to prevent a sweep to your left, simply transition into a sweep to your right. The shin sweep demonstrated below moves in the opposite direction of the basic sweep demonstrated in the previous sequence. With this technique you will still sneak one arm underneath your opponent's leg as before, but rather than lifting his thigh up, you simply pick his ankle, which prevents him from basing out as he rolls toward his free leg. This is a great technique to employ either in conjunction with the basic sweep or when your opponent forces his outside knee near your head. With his foot in such close proximity to your hand, it is a simple matter to scoop up his ankle and sweep him over.

I am in the underhook half guard with Neil on top of me. My left arm is hooked under his right armpit, while my left shin is in between his thighs. Because Neil's left knee is riding very close to my head, I slightly bend my torso, extend my right arm underneath Neil's left leg, and hook underneath his left ankle.

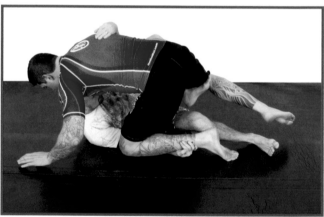

To off-balance Neil, I simply need to extend my left leg while retracting my right hand. This combination of actions simultaneously rolls Neil's center of gravity to his left while taking away his base to his left.

I continue extending my leg to roll Neil over. Because I've maintained my grip on his ankle, he is incapable of stopping the roll. My head stays tight against his chest, and I use my head to assist in driving him to his back.

4

When Neil's back hits the ground, I let go of his ankle and plant my right hand on the mat to establish my base. My left shin drops down across Neil's left thigh, pinning his bottom leg to the ground.

5

I base my right leg out wide to prevent Neil from rolling back into me. At this point, my weight is mostly on my left leg, which traps his right leg so he can't roll in either direction. Notice that I have maintained my underhook with my left arm. If I were to lose this control, Neil could easily turn into me and put me right back in the bottom position.

6

To complete the sweep, I rotate my hips toward Neil's head until both of my knees are flat on the mat. I pull my knees in tight to his rib cage in order to attain the side mount position.

TEETER TOTTER ESCAPE

As I've mentioned before, sometimes your opponent can counter your technique no matter how well it is executed. However, rather than simply admitting defeat, it's most often possible to utilize their counter to attack another weak spot. This technique is initiated when you attempt the basic sweep and your opponent counters by posting out his hand and raising his base. By employing the teeter-totter, you can take advantage of the space your opponent creates by sneaking your upper body out the back door. The risk with this move is getting caught in a triangle as you turn and go out through your opponent's legs. For that reason, be sure to pull your arm out as you turn and escape.

I am underneath Neil in an underhook half guard. My left leg is inserted between Neil's thighs. My left arm is underhooked under his right armpit, and I have already slipped my right arm under his left leg.

I rotate my hips to my left and lift with my right arm in an attempt to execute the basic sweep shown earlier in this section.

Neil blocks the sweep by basing out his right hand and left leg and dropping his weight into my body. However, by doing this, Neil has created a big opening for me to escape. I have to switch to the backup plan and take advantage of the opportunity my opponent presents me with. Instead of using my right arm to lift Neil, I now use it to keep his left leg elevated.

I release my underhook and post my left hand on Neil's chest. As I extend my left arm, it off-balances Neil, giving me just enough time to escape out the back door.

As I roll in a counterclockwise direction to my left knee, I retract my left arm so it doesn't get trapped between Neil's legs. At this point, I don't want him to spin around, so I retain my hook over his left leg with my right arm. I post on my left hand and knee, preparing to take his back.

I quickly let go of Neil's left leg and transition to his back. Notice that my right leg is still underneath Neil. I don't want to base it out too far because it's in perfect position to secure a leg hook as I move to his back.

I wrap my arms around Neil's back to complete the transition. From here I will attempt to secure my left leg hook over Neil's left thigh or, if that fails, simply seek to secure top position.

GET-UP

Like the sweeps and the escape we just looked at, with the get-up you use your leg to lift your opponent off the ground and then escape out to the side through the space you've created. Like all get-ups shown in this book, the keys to success are using your arms to create and maintain space while circling your hips away from your opponent as you extract your bottom leg and base out into the standing position.

1

I am underneath Neil in an underhook half guard. My left leg is inserted between his thighs and my left arm is underhooked under his left arm. I have already slipped my right arm underneath his left leg.

2

In one explosive movement, I extend my left leg and left arm in order to elevate Neil's hips, pushing him away from my hips.

3

I retract my right arm and pull it underneath my body as I continue to extend my left leg, forcing Neil away from me.

4

I post my right elbow on the mat to act as a post for my torso. Due to the space created between our bodies, I'm now able to slide my right leg out from underneath of Neil's hips and post my right knee on the mat. Notice that I still have my left shin against his right thigh so he can't drive back into me and block my escape.

5

Once I am on both knees I have essentially escaped. From here I can push him over and get on top of him, get to my feet and strike, or disengage completely.

INSIDE HALF GUARD (SUBMISSIONS)

Now we'll turn the tables and look at the options you have when you find yourself inside your opponent's half guard. This is a common position to be in during a fight, especially after a clinch, takedown, or scramble. While the top of half guard is a great position to launch a ground-and-pound attack, my primary goal in this chapter will be to demonstrate the submissions available to you.

ARM TRIANGLE CHOKE

The arm triangle choke is a very effective, low-risk submission and is therefore often one of the first submissions you should try. Even if you fail to obtain the choke, attacking your opponent's neck can preoccupy him and allow you to pass his half guard unhindered. If you obtain the choke but fail to finish, you will still have transitioned into a dominant top position. During this move, keep your weight down and your chest tight to your opponent's chest to elevate his arm. This will prevent him from wrapping his arm over your head to defend the choke.

I am in Tom's half guard. To prevent him from attacking me and forcing his agenda, I slide my right elbow toward his hip and grab his left wrist with my right hand.

With Tom's left wrist trapped, I force his arm down and pin it to the mat. Next, I dive my head underneath his armpit and drive his arm upward. Note that my left arm is wrapped over Tom's head. It will remain in this position throughout the duration of the technique.

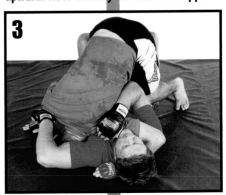

Now is a good time to free my leg from Tom's half guard. To initiate the pass I simply release Tom's wrist and place my right hand out wide on the mat, while raising my hips into the air. Because my head is isolating Tom's left arm, he's unable to steal my base and roll me over as I attempt this move.

I bring my left knee up and cut my shin across Tom's stomach to establish another point of leverage. With my left shin driving against his stomach and his shoulders pinned flat, the twisting motion of my hips makes it extremely difficult for him to retain his grip with his legs.

5

With the tremendous pressure prying my right leg out of Tom's guard, his grip breaks and my right leg pops free. As my right leg hops over Tom's guard, my left shin slides the rest of the way over his stomach and lands on the ground by his left hip.

6

Now I pull my right leg out wide and begin to walk my legs toward Tom's head. With my head trapping Tom's left arm between our heads and my torso at a ninety-degree angle to his torso, I now simply need to lock up my grip and finish the submission.

7

To secure my grip, I grip my right biceps with my left hand, and then place my right hand behind my head. With my arms triangled together, I sink my hips and squeeze my elbows together, cutting off blood flow to Tom's brain.

KNEE BAR FROM HALF GUARD

When you are in the top half guard position, your opponent's legs are frequently vulnerable. Oftentimes, he will ride his knee up close to your hips as a defensive measure, so with a quick pivot, you can trap his leg and submit him. The knee bar is a great submission that is designed to hyperextend your opponent's knee joint. However, the knee bar is a difficult submission to secure in MMA because it leaves your opponent's upper body open and gives him the opportunity to sit up, strike, or execute an escape. So it's important to pin your opponent's shoulders for as long as possible as you posture up and spin over his leg.

1

I am in Tom's half guard. He has his legs wrapped around my right leg and his left knee is riding up high against my right hip.

2

Before I try to pivot and grab Tom's knee, I have to pin his shoulders to the ground to prevent him from sitting up and blocking my spin. I push off his shoulders, posture up, and back away. If necessary, this is a great position to soften Tom up with some punches and elbows to distract him before spinning for the kneebar.

3

I bring my left knee off the mat and post on my left foot. I will use this leg to move my hips as I pivot around Tom's leg. Now that I have committed to the knee bar, I slide my left hand down Tom's arm to secure his right wrist. With this wrist pinned to his chest, he will be unable to grab my leg as I spin over his body.

4

I quickly pivot on my right knee and step my left leg over top of Tom's body. This movement must be quick, or Tom will have the opportunity to counter.

5

I continue to pivot until I'm facing Tom's feet and reach down with my right hand and grab his left calf. All of my weight is resting on Tom's stomach and my left hand is based out in case he tries to roll away from me.

6

As I drop to my left side, I pull Tom's left leg tight into my chest and bring his foot up to my left ear. Notice how his knee is lined up over my stomach and I lock my legs together—this isolates his leg. To finish the submission, I pull my hands tight to my chest, curl my legs, and drive my hips forward. This hyperextends Tom's knee joint, causing him intense pain and forcing him to tap.

BRABO CHOKE

This brabo choke is a very effective counter when your opponent establishes a deep underhook from the bottom half guard position. If you look at the photos below, you'll notice that as my opponent establishes an underhook, he comes up onto his hip and attempts to drive his underhook high to set up an escape. However, by doing this, he exposes his neck and gives me an opportunity to trap his head and submit him. The brabo choke works like an upside down arm triangle. You're effectively using your biceps and your opponent's own biceps to cut off the blood flow to his brain, causing him to pass out. Using your chest to maintain weight on your opponent's arm is a critical element of this submission. The pressure of your body weight driving through your chest is what forces your opponent's arm into his own throat. Without that forward pressure from your chest, the choke will only restrict half of the blood flow, allowing your opponent to fight through the submission.

I am in Tom's half guard. He has his legs wrapped around my right leg and he has secured double underhooks with his arms.

Tom rolls onto his right hip and drives his left arm deep underneath my armpit. This is a common movement from the bottom of half guard to secure space to execute various sweeps and submissions.

I wrap my right arm over Tom's right arm and feed my right hand underneath his neck. At the same time, I move my left arm over Tom's head.

I now clasp my hands together, trapping Tom's left arm and neck.

Once I get my right arm underneath Tom's chin, I grab my left biceps with my right hand, and then place my left hand up by his left shoulder.

To apply pressure to the choke I must drive my chest into Tom's left arm. I spread my base and flatten my chest while squeezing my elbows together. This cuts off the blood supply to Tom's brain, forcing him to tap out.

STRIKES

There are some great advantages in striking from the top of the half guard vs. striking from the full guard. In the half guard you are closer to your opponent's head and it's easier to pin his hips with your own legs. This frees your hands to deliver punches to your opponent's head, which in turn will often help you set up a guard pass. We'll cover passes in the next section; for now we'll look at the striking options you have when in your opponent's half guard.

SHOULDER BOMB

The shoulder bomb doesn't generate as much force as a traditional hand or elbow strike. Because of the small space between your opponent's head and your shoulder, it tends to be a low-velocity strike. However, it's hard to defend, which allows you to land it quickly and repeatedly. The shoulder bomb won't knock your opponent out, but it's a great tool to harass and distract him when you're trying to pass his guard to side or full mount. It is important to note that you must keep your hands clasped together behind your opponent's head to prevent him from simply shifting his head away or using the space you create to bring his hand in and block the strike.

I am in Tom's half guard. He has his legs locked over my right leg and my hands are clasped behind his head. I have secured an underhook with my right arm to prevent Tom from moving his hips.

I elevate my chest to create the space I need to deliver the strike.

I contract my left arm to bring Tom's head toward my shoulder, adding momentum to the strike. At the same time, I drop my weight down and strike his face with my left shoulder.

ELBOW TO HEAD

The elbow to the head is probably the most effective strike in the half guard. The key to landing this strike is to maintain control of your opponent's upper body until the final momentum before the elbow is delivered. By maintaining a tight underhook on his far arm, and by pinning his head down with your striking arm, you can keep your opponent pinned on his back as you unleash an elbow to his head. If executed with proper control, this elbow strike can have a devastating effect.

1) I am in Tom's half guard. He has his legs locked over my right leg and my hands are clasped behind his head. I have secured an underhook with my right arm to prevent him from moving his hips. 2) I unclasp my hands and wrap my right hand around Tom's shoulder. This provides me with an anchor to secure my underhook. 3) I put my left hand on Tom's neck and extend my arm while raising my chest off of his torso. This enables me to create space to throw the strike while keeping him pinned flat on his back. 4) I flex my arm while dropping my weight toward the mat. As my hand slides off Tom's face, my elbow lands on his chin with the full weight of my upper body.

ROUND KNUCKLE

If your opponent hips out in an effort to return to full guard or execute an escape, the round knuckle is the perfect strike to deliver because he will often expose his head while escaping. If you look at the photos below, you'll notice that my opponent turns onto his right hip and pushes on my left knee using his right hand. His goal is create the space he needs to escape to full guard, but his actions make his face extremely vulnerable to my left hand. To capitalize on this opening, I deliver a powerful round knuckle to his face. However, it is important to note that in order to be effective with this technique, you must pin your opponent's head in place to prevent him from slipping away as you strike and escaping back to full guard. To accomplish this, you want to drive your head into your opponent's head, pinning it to the mat.

I am in Tom's half guard with my right arm underhooked under his left arm. He has his legs locked over my right leg and he is pushing down on my left leg to keep me from passing to side mount.

To pin Tom's head in place, I push his head to the mat using my left hand, and then drive the top of my head into his chin to fix it in place.

With his head isolated, I bring my left hand up to deliver the strike.

I retract my arm, turning my knuckle over as I strike Tom's face with my left fist. To maintain this control, I must keep my underhook tight while stapling Tom's head to the mat with my head. If your opponent defends the strike by raising his right hand, it will make it dramatically easier to execute a pass into side mount.

COMBO TO BODY

Although many fighters emphasize strikes to the head, landing strikes to the body can be just as effective. In the half guard you are in a good position to trap your opponent's hands and deliver a great deal of punishment to his body. One of the great things about this combination is that it can force your opponent into making a mistake. By trapping his arms and striking the same spot repeatedly, you will cause him a great deal of pain, which will sometimes cause him to unhook his legs and try to escape. This often opens an easy guard pass, allowing you to attain a more dominant position.

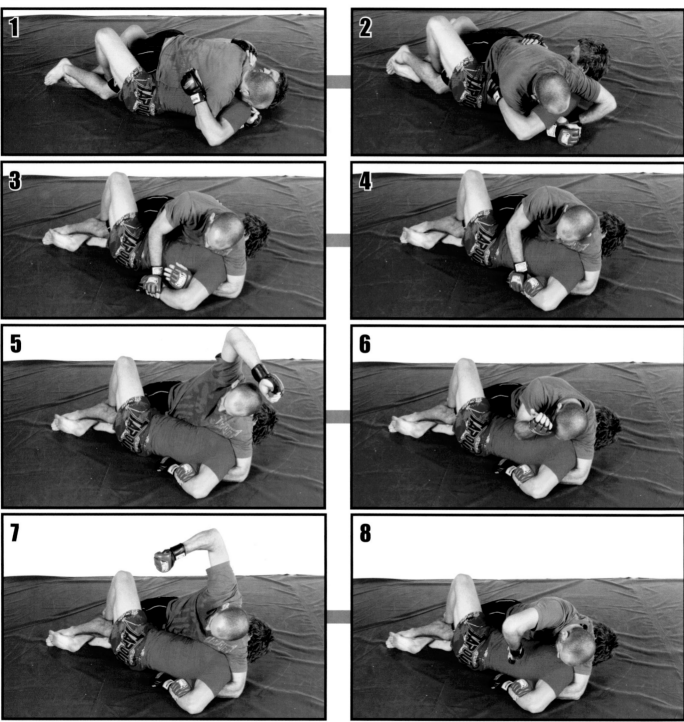

1) I am in Tom's half guard. He has his legs locked over my right leg I have secured an underhook with my right arm. 2) I reach over Tom's head with my left arm and wrap it underneath his left arm. This effectively isolates his left arm away from his torso. 3) I grab Tom's left wrist with my right hand and then pin it to the mat to immobilize it. I then wrap my left hand underneath his armpit as if I were attempting to secure a Kimura. 4) I quickly grab Tom's wrist with my left hand and pull his arm underneath his back. If this move is not done quickly, Tom will likely extend his arm to free it from my grasp. 5) With Tom's left arm now trapped, I have a clear path to strike with my right arm. I elevate my right arm in order to generate velocity for an elbow strike. 6) I bring the point of my elbow down into Tom's ribs. 7) I recoil my right arm quickly to throw another strike. 8) I land a punch to the same spot on Tom's ribs. By throwing uninterrupted strikes at the same spot, I can force him into a panic, which can cause him to do something stupid. If he fails to free his arm or attempt an escape, I will continue to punish his midsection for as long as possible.

PASSES

All of the half guard passes shown in this section work off the same basic premise—isolate and immobilize one of your opponent's legs, which allows you to free your trapped leg and pass his guard. There is some variety to these passes, however. Depending on which way you decide to move, and which options your opponent allows, you can pass to either side mount or the full mount, both of which have options to submit or strike your opponent. Like all positions, I advocate combining attacks. If your opponent is successfully stopping your guard pass, he may leave an opening for you to throw strikes. When he moves to defend your strikes, he may become vulnerable to guard passes. Don't forget about including the strikes from the previous section should they become available.

HALF GUARD PASS

The goal of this technique is to free your trapped leg by prying your opponent's legs apart and then twisting your hips until you secure a scarf hold position. To accomplish this pass you need to have an underhook on your opponent's outside arm. If you fail to secure the underhook, your opponent will come to his knees as you free your leg and initiate a scramble.

1 I am in Tom's half guard. My chest is flat on his chest and I have an underhook with my left arm. He has his legs wrapped around my left leg so I must free this leg to successfully pass his guard.

2 I switch my head to my right and place my forehead on the mat. I want to minimize space between our heads, so I place my left ear against Tom's left ear. This shifts my center of gravity to my right, preventing Tom from rolling me to my left as my hips rise for the pass. By switching sides and pushing against his head, I can get better leverage and limit his options for counters.

3 I place the top of my right foot across Tom's left thigh to pin his knee down. This pries apart his legs, reducing the amount of pressure he can apply to my trapped left leg. Additionally, my right hand is wrapped around Tom's left arm. This prevents him from reaching down to block my leg as it passes through his guard.

4 I elevate my hips and force them forward, which allows my left leg to slip through Tom's now weakened half guard. This movement also pins his upper body and keeps him from rolling away. Because my hips are now elevated, Tom's best counter would be to roll me to his right. To prevent this I must keep my head flat on the mat to keep my center of gravity low.

5

I slide my left leg out from between Tom's legs and pull it up to my stomach.

6

By kicking my left leg out, rotating my hips, and dropping my weight onto Tom's body, I put myself in a side mount and open up a number of submission options.

HALF GUARD HOOK PASS

Sometimes your opponent chooses to control your trapped leg with his foot (usually called a butterfly hook), which effectively prevents you from moving your hips forward. To initiate a pass, you must first gain control your opponent's leg and eliminate his hook. When executing this pass, it is important to watch your base. If you are sloppy, there is a chance you will get swept in the transition. The risk in attempting this maneuver is you have to drop your hand to pry off your opponent's hook. As you do this, you expose your head to strikes. However, since your opponent must release his underhook to throw strikes, he'll be forfeiting control. To mitigate this risk you should keep your head tucked against your opponent's chest as you carry out this pass.

1

I am in Tom's half guard. He has secured an underhook with his left arm and a butterfly hook with his left leg. While in this position, I am very vulnerable to being swept to my back.

2

My first course of action is to lower my hips to lessen the risk of being swept. I accomplish this by flattening out of my left leg and lying on my left hip. I then quickly underhook Tom's left leg and grip underneath his left thigh. By immobilizing this butterfly hook, I've set myself up to free my leg.

In one quick movement I pull Tom's leg toward his chest and donkey kick my leg backward. This frees my right leg from Tom's half guard. Notice that I keep my left knee in tight against his hip so he can't pull guard.

While maintaining my grip on Tom's left leg, I quickly switch my legs and roll onto my stomach in side mount. Notice how I keep my head tight against his torso to protect it in case he decides to throw strikes as I'm passing.

I slide my knees in tight to Tom's body and control his head. Notice I still have control of his left leg as I'm attaining side mount.

I release Tom's left leg and secure side mount.

KIMURA FAKE PASS

This technique is a great example of utilizing deception to achieve your ultimate goal. The kimura fake pass deceives your opponent into thinking you're trying to secure a submission when in fact a pass to full mount is the real goal. By attacking his arm, you can force him to shift his priorities and defend the most immediate threat. While he's distracted, you slip your leg through his guard and end up in the full mount. Don't disregard the kimura. Although you don't have as much leverage on your opponent's arm in the half guard as you do from side mount, it's still possible to create enough torque on the shoulder to force your opponent to quit. It is important to note that you want to hold onto the kimura grip throughout the pass. Not only is it a good control, but it's also a solid backup plan if the pass fails. Also, once you've achieved a full mount, your opponent may try to escape by rolling in the opposite direction. This will only tighten the kimura and make it easier for you to submit him.

I am in Tom's half guard. My chest is flat on his chest and I have secured an underhook with my right arm. Tom's legs are hooked over my right leg, which prevents me from passing his half guard.

I bring my left arm over Tom's head so I have both arms on the left side of his body. This will make it possible to attack his left arm. My chest stays tight to his chest to keep his shoulders pinned to the mat.

I isolate Tom's left arm by grabbing his wrist with my right hand and wrapping my left arm underneath his triceps. Because I'm directly attacking his left arm with no setup, he will likely recognize that I'm attempting the kimura and defend my submission attempt.

As I continue to work for the kimura, I roll up onto my left hip. This will provide me with the leverage I need to slip my right leg out from between Tom's legs.

With Tom's attention on defending his arm, I rip my right leg upward in an attempt to free it from his half guard. Notice how I press my left shin on his thighs for counterpressure to extract my right leg. It is important to note that this move should be done quickly. The instant you begin trying to free your leg, your opponent's attention will most likely shift from defending the kimura to defending your guard pass.

I slide my right knee up to my chest, pulling it free from Tom's guard, and place my right instep against his left thigh. This will allow me to keep pressure on his legs, helping me to pin his hips as I pass to mount. Notice that I haven't let go of the kimura. If my transition to mount should fail, the kimura submission will be a good backup plan.

Once my leg is free, I rotate my hips and drive my right knee over Tom's torso, sliding to mount. I still have a hold of the kimura in case he attempts to scramble free as I'm transitioning.

I complete the pass by sliding my right foot over Tom's body and placing it on the mat. Now that I've achieved a full mount, I have the option of applying the kimura submission or releasing my hold to strike.

PUNCH PASS TO MOUNT

Much like the previous pass, the punch pass to mount initiates a half guard pass by faking the kimura submission. However, this technique also incorporates strikes to the body to force your opponent to open his legs. As his leg pressure decreases, you can slip your leg through his guard and move straight to mount. I always advocate an active defense and offense. When you're not punching your opponent, you should be looking for a pass and vice versa. This move is a good combination of both punching and passing, and it is especially useful against wrestlers who have been taught to bridge to get out of bad situations.

I am in Tom's half guard with my chest flat on his chest. He has his legs wrapped around my right leg and has secured a left underhook.

2

I bring my left arm over Tom's head so I have both of my arms on the same side or his body, making it possible to attack his left arm. It is important to mention that I am keeping his back pinned to the mat using the weight of my upper body.

3

I roll onto my left hip, putting my full weight on Tom's chest. At the same time, I isolate his left arm by grabbing his left wrist using my right hand and wrapping my left arm underneath his triceps. I want to make it obvious that I plan to secure a kimura so Tom focuses on his arm instead of his guard.

4

Here's where this move diverges from the fake kimura pass. Instead of locking up the kimura, I grab Tom's left forearm using my left hand to keep it pinned to the mat. This control will allow me to release my right grip on his wrist and begin landing strikes.

5

With Tom's upper body pinned and his left arm isolated, I elevate my right arm for a strike. Notice that I keep my elbow aligned with my fist to deliver more power with the strike.

6

I retract my arm, rotate my shoulders, and drop my weight through my right hand into Tom's midsection. With his left arm firmly secured, I will continue landing strikes until he opens his guard and attempts to escape this compromising position.

Realizing that he's unable to stop my strikes with his left arm, Tom breaks his guard and puts his left foot on the mat. His goal is to use this foot as a base to bridge off the mat and attempt to reverse me. However, as soon as he opens his guard, I make my move to pass to the mount.

Because Tom has broken his own guard, I can now easily pull my right leg out of his half guard and swing it over his body. While transitioning into the mount, I retain my grip on his left arm with my left arm. Note that my right foot is planted behind me to give me a wider base in case my timing is off and Tom is able to bridge into me. This will prevent him from rolling me over.

I continue the rotation, throw my right leg completely over Tom's body, and finish the transition in the full mount.

PUNCH PASS TO SIDE MOUNT

We'll look at another pass that uses strikes to free your leg from your opponent's half guard and land you in a dominant position. However, this time I demonstrate how to pass to the side rather than straight to the full mount. Like other punch passes, this technique utilizes strikes to elicit a response from your opponent. As your opponent unlocks his legs and attempts to push you away to defend against your strikes, he'll momentarily lose control over your hips, allowing you to slide past his legs. This move is useful against jiu-jitsu practitioners who raise their legs up to protect themselves when faced with a postured-up striker. When your opponent does this, you can grab a hold of his leg and slide past his guard. The great strength of this pass is that there's very little downside to attempting it. If your opponent remains mobile and manages to block your pass, you can posture up and continue to rain down strikes.

I am in Tom's half guard. My chest is flat on his chest and I have secured and underhook with my right arm. He has his legs wrapped around my right leg, but my left leg is free.

2

The first thing I need to do is rain down some strikes to get Tom to unlock his guard. To accomplish this, I bring my left hand up and place it on his chest to create separation between our bodies.

3

I extend my left arm, elevating my torso while at the same time pinning Tom's shoulders to the mat. I raise my right hand to strike, making sure to keep my elbow aligned with my hand to get more force behind the punch.

4

I extend my right arm, delivering a right cross to Tom's face. This puts him in a predicament—he must stop my punches as quickly as possible or risk having the fight stopped by the referee.

5

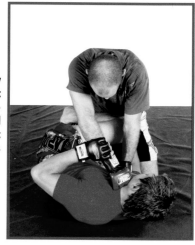

As I had hoped, Tom instinctively unlocks his legs and places his left shin against my stomach to prevent me from moving forward and throwing more strikes. This slight mistake will allow me to pass his guard.

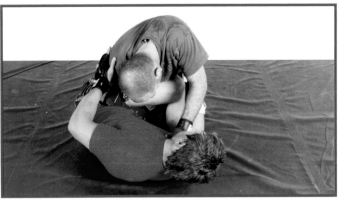

I quickly wrap my right arm over Tom's left leg to control it, and then immediately drop my shoulders down on top of his leg. My overhook on his left leg, combined with my weight driving down onto his hip, prevents him from regaining guard.

With Tom's leg out of commission, I now drive the top of my head into the side of his head. This will keep his back flat on the mat as I slide past his guard.

I now slide my right leg past Tom's half guard and sit through. As my leg passes his legs, I unhook his left leg and prepare to bring my right arm up to secure an underhook.

I sit all the way through with my hips turned toward Tom's head and bring my right arm up high into his armpit to secure an underhook. I have now fully passed Tom's half guard and am ready to deliver strikes to his head or attempt a submission.

CHAPTER THREE: SIDE MOUNT

When you pass your opponent's guard and establish side mount, you effectively neutralize his legs and cut his defensive options in half. With your body lying perpendicular to his body, you have a great amount of leverage and can use all four of your limbs to attack his arms. It also puts you in a great position to attack his head and neck with strikes and submissions. Despite all the advantages side mount offers, retaining the position can often be difficult, which is why body control must be a priority. Realizing your advantage, your opponent will try to escape, sweep, or even submit you, and if you lose control of his body, his chance at success increases significantly. So to reiterate, always secure the position before going on the attack with submissions, strikes, and transitions to more dominant positions.

BASIC SIDE MOUNT

In the photos below, I demonstrate the basic side mount. My body is at a ninety-degree angle to my opponent, I have one arm wrapped under his head, and the other arm underhooking his far arm. To limit his movement, I clasp my hands together underneath his far shoulder. To limit his escapes and keep him pinned to the mat, I drop my weight fully on his chest and press my knees tightly against his rib cage and near hip. Lastly, I drive my shoulder down into his chin to make it difficult for him to turn into me and attack. Once I secure this position, I am ready to begin my attack.

SUBMISSIONS

As I mentioned, establishing side mount neutralizes your opponent's legs, making it a good time to attack his arms or head. It is certainly possible to attack your opponent's legs from side mount (the reverse heel hook shown in this section is actually one of my favorite submissions from the position), but with his head, neck, and arms closer and trapped underneath your weight, they are not only easier to target with an attack, but they also usually require you to give up less control.

AMERICANA

Although the Americana is similar to the kimura, it's important to note that the Americana is not just a hyperextension of the elbow. Once you establish a figure-four lock on your opponent's arm, you want to use your grip to pull his elbow toward his hip as you apply the submission. This places pressure not only on his elbow, but also his shoulder. The Americana is very useful in the side mount because in this position you can use your body weight to trap your opponent's upper torso, which frees up your arms to attack his vulnerable arm. The side mount also gives you the leverage you need to put a lot of torque on his arm and force the submission. If your opponent tries to push your head while in the side mount, it actually helps you isolate and trap his arm for the submission.

1

I am in side mount on top of Tom. My right arm is under his head and my left is under his right arm.

Tom tries to push my head away from his body to create separation to execute an escape. This puts his right arm in a vulnerable position. While he manages to create a slight amount of separation, he's actually isolated his own arm.

I break my grip and swing my right arm over Tom's head.

I bring my right arm to the inside of Tom's right arm to control it and prevent him from retracting his limb. At this point Tom will likely realize he's in danger and attempt to pull his right hand back to his body.

I bend my right elbow, bringing my right hand onto my forehead. With my right elbow on the mat, and my right hand firmly attached to my head, my arm now creates a block to prevent Tom from retracting his arm.

With Tom's arm trapped between my hands, I push forward with my legs pin his arm to the mat using my body weight rather than using arm strength. This also keeps my full body weight on his chest so he can't roll away or pull guard.

7

Now I flip my hand over and grasp Tom's right wrist with my right hand. At the same time, I adjust my weight, allowing my head to rise upwards and my hips to sink. This will prevent Tom from rolling me over with a powerful bridge.

8

Because I retained my left under-hook throughout the entire movement, my left arm is in position to secure the figure four grip. With my left arm laced underneath of Tom's right arm, I grab my right wrist with my left hand.

9

To complete the submission I pull Tom's elbow to his hip while lightly twisting my shoulders. This puts a tremendous amount of torque on both Tom's elbow and his shoulder joint, forcing him to tap out.

DOUBLE-KNIT CHOKE

The double-knit choke is as simple as it gets. Rather than attempting to change position and secure a rear naked choke, or secure a head an arm to attempt a strangle, this choke is easily finished from the top of side mount. It's a straightforward submission that applies pressure to your opponent's throat if he makes the mistake of keeping his chin high in side mount. It's unorthodox, but it's quick and effective and can end a fight when your opponent has a lapse in focus. There's not much risk to this move since you don't change your body position or give up any control. If you fail to finish the choke, your hold may very well make your opponent so uncomfortable he becomes reckless in his attempt to escape, which will often present you with a high percentage submission opportunity.

1

I am in side mount on top of Tom. My right arm is under his head and my left is under his right arm. My hands are clasped together above his right shoulder.

2

I can tell that Tom is keeping his chin up high and his neck is unprotected, so I extend my left leg to drop my left hip. This will give me the space I need to extract my arm and attempt the choke.

3

I release my left underhook and bring my left arm to the inside of Tom's Right arm.

4

I place my left forearm under Tom's chin and across his neck to cut off his airway.

5

I connect my arms together by grasping my right shoulder with my left hand and my left elbow with my right hand. This creates a complete circle with my arms, making it extremely difficult for Tom to loosen my grip.

6

I complete the choke by dropping my left elbow to the floor and driving my right shoulder into Tom's neck. This levers my left forearm into his neck, creating pain and choking off his air supply. From this position Tom must either tap out or attempt a drastic escape in order to prevent passing out.

THE GROUND GAME

ARMBAR

When in side mount, your opponent's far side arm is his most vulnerable limb to attack because you can use both of your arms and upper body to isolate it. The most common defense against this is for your opponent to roll into you instead of away from you. However, this creates an opportunity for you to secure a submission. As your opponent turns into you, it's a simple matter to trap his arm, pivot, and spin for the armbar. It's important to ensure you have a firm grip on your opponent's arm before attempting this move. If you don't, you might find yourself on your back scrambling for position. This move requires a very delicate balance of speed and control. You have to give up some of the control you have over your opponent to secure the submission, so you have to make up for it by moving fast. Too much emphasis on control or too little on speed can cause this move to fail.

1

I am in side mount on top of Tom. My right arm is under his head and I've secured a left underhook on his right arm. My hands are clasped together above his right shoulder.

2

I move my right arm over his head to attack his far arm (throwing an elbow into his face as I bring my arm over is a good way to distract him while I go for the submission).

3

Realizing that I am attempting to secure his arm, Tom turns into me to avoid the submission. But with my left arm underhooked under his right arm, I still have the advantage. I push off of the floor with my hand to elevate my hips over his head while simultaneously pulling Tom upward by his right arm. With Tom's arm securely fastened, I stand on my feet.

4

I rotate my body counterclockwise, keeping a firm grip on Tom's left arm by holding it close to my chest. At the same time, I move my right leg further around to his right side.

5

I rotate my hips one hundred eighty degrees and fall backward with my left leg draped over Tom's head. At the same time, I raise my right leg to place it over Tom's body. Again, it's critical to keep your opponent's arm close to your chest or he'll likely spin free and escape the submission.

6

I lean back, squeeze his arm between my thighs, thrust my hips upward into his elbow, and pull down on his wrist. This puts tremendous pressure on his elbow joint.

REVERSE HEEL HOOK

This is one of my all time favorite moves. When you're in side mount, a common defense is for your opponent to bring a knee up to prevent you from moving to full mount. It's a smart move, but it also leaves that knee vulnerable to being controlled and twisted into submission. Like the armbar previously shown, you can use speed and control to isolate your opponent's leg and submit him with a reverse heel hook before he is able to recognize the situation and counter. Like the armbar, this move is risky because you give up some control momentarily. To mitigate this risk, be sure you have a firm grip on your opponent's upper knee before falling backward to finish the technique.

1

I am in side mount on top of Tom. My right arm is under his head and I've secured a left underhook on his right arm. My hands are clasped together above his right shoulder.

2

To prevent me from transitioning to full mount, Tom brings his left knee up high against my hip. To isolate that leg, I raise my left knee and place it underneath his left leg. This prevents him from lowering his leg.

3

I break my grip and sit up. My left hand traps Tom's knee against my left knee while my right hand posts on his chest to prevent him from scrambling to escape the position.

4

Now I must move fast. With Tom's left leg trapped between my left knee and left arm, I come up onto both feet, fall backward, and pull his leg to my chest. Notice that my left knee is underneath his left leg.

5

As I fall backward, Tom's left leg becomes trapped in between my legs. When my back hits the floor, I bring my right foot up and place it on Tom's left hip. This will prevent him from moving forward and freeing his leg.

6

I lock my right foot underneath my left knee to isolate Tom's leg. This gives me a more secure grip on his limb, allowing me to more easily control his left leg. Now I'm ready to submit him.

7

I slide my left arm up Tom's left leg until his toes are trapped in my armpit. To finish the submission I simply extend my back, twisting Tom's ankle. This applies pressure to his knee and ankle joint, causing him to tap out.

GUILLOTINE

Another common defense when you achieve side mount is for your opponent to transition to guard by slipping his inside knee underneath your body. While this is great defensive measure, it can cause your opponent to have a lapse in concentration. It's possible that as he moves back to guard, he forgets to defend the most vulnerable part of his body—his neck. This move is great to use against jiu-jitsu players who always revert back to the guard when trapped on the mat. The great thing about this technique is there is a built in backup plan—if you can't secure the guillotine, you will still end up in a full mount position.

1

I am in side mount on top of Tom. My right arm is under his head and I've secured a left underhook on his right arm. My hands are clasped together above his left shoulder.

2

Tom rolls into me and tries to pull guard by slipping his right knee between our bodies.

3

I change position by bringing my left arm over Tom's head and wrapping it around the back of his neck. This compresses Tom's body, momentarily stopping him from moving back to the guard position.

4

I walk my lower body towards Tom's hips while swinging my right leg over his midsection. At the same time, I clasp my hands together under his neck and post on my head on the mat. This prevents me from rolling over to my back as I leap into the mount.

5

I complete the submission by dropping my weight back down on Tom's midsection and pulling up with my arms. If he attempts to roll me over to my back to avoid the submission, I will simply finish the guillotine choke from guard. If he doesn't roll and I fail to finish the choke from the top, I will still have secured the full mount position.

STRIKES

Strikes from side mount can be very effective as long as you maintain a strong position. You do not want to allow your opponent to achieve half or full guard while you strike, so stopping him from countering your dominant position has to be a priority before initiating a striking attack. The trick to mounting a successful striking attack from side mount is finding the balance between maintaining ample control while creating enough space to deliver damaging strikes.

SHOULDER BOMB

Despite the fact that the shoulder bomb is not a conventional strike, it should not be underestimated. The shoulder bomb can have a debilitating effect when executed properly. I covered the shoulder bomb from the top of half guard previously. While in this technique the execution is essentially the same, the results are drastically different. From the side mount you can generate more force because you can push off with your legs and drop your full body weight down onto your opponent's head as you throw the strike. You can also use your hand that's under his head and pull his head up into the strike to add to the impact. This makes the shoulder bomb an excellent strike from the side mount position.

I am in side mount on top of Tom. My left arm is underhooked under his right arm and my right arm is under his head. My hands are clasped together above his right shoulder. My knees are tight against his side and my weight is dropped onto his chest.

Without unclasping my hands I raise my right shoulder and head to prepare for the strike. My chest comes off of Tom's chest just enough to create a small amount of space.

When I drop my shoulder into Tom's face, I also drop my weight down on top of him and pull his head up into the strike.

ELBOW TO HEAD

This is a very effective strike that can cause your opponent a great deal of pain, but you have to be careful. In competition MMA you cannot elbow the back of your opponent's head, so if he suddenly turns his head away from the strike, you cannot follow through with the elbow. To make this strike more effective and to prevent your opponent from escaping while you throw it, extend your leg closest to your opponent's legs for added leverage and stability.

1) I am in side mount on top of Tom. My left arm is underhooked under his right arm and my right arm is under his head. My hands are clasped together above his right shoulder. My knees are tight against his side and my weight is dropped on his chest. 2) I extend my left leg to give me added stability and leverage for the strike. This also drops my full weight onto his chest and makes it very difficult for him to pull guard. 3) I release my grip and bring my right arm up high. The rest of my body stays tight against Tom to prevent him from moving. I also keep a firm grip on his right shoulder with my left hand so he can't raise it to defend his head. 4) I bring my elbow down into the side of Tom's head. If you have successfully neutralized your opponent's right arm and have a clear path to his head, be prepared to deliver this strike several times in succession.

ELBOW TO FACE

This is another very effective strike because it pins your opponent's head to the ground until the moment you decide to throw the elbow. As you drop the elbow down, you can deliver your full body weight into the shot. To make this strike more effective, you need to keep a hold of your opponent's far shoulder and drive your weight forward. This eliminates his far arm from the equation, allowing you land an unanswered elbow directly to his face.

I am in side mount on top of Tom. My left arm is underhooked under his right arm and my right arm is under his head. My hands are clasped together above his right shoulder. My knees are tight against his side and my weight is dropped on his chest.

I unclasp my hands and put my right hand on Tom's face to immobilize his head.

By pushing down on his head I not only create the space I need to drop the elbow, but I also keep his head immobilized.

As I allow my hand to slide off of Tom's face, I drop my elbow into his chin and my upper body weight onto his chest. It's not just an arm strike, but a full body movement.

ATTACKS FROM HEAD FLANK

The head flank is a modified side mount where you turn onto your side so your chest is facing your opponent's head. Once established, it gives you a number of options to attack. However, due to your orientation, the majority of your attacks will focus on your opponent's arms and neck. From this position, it is easy to use your entire body weight to isolate your opponent's arm and finish him with a submission.

BASIC POSITION

Getting into the basic head flank position is a matter of rotating your hips so your upper body is facing your opponent's head while maintaining control of his upper torso. It is a quick transition that doesn't require much movement, and it's particularly effective when up against an opponent who is attempting to pull you into his guard.

I am in the basic side mount position with my hands clasped together above his right shoulder.

I unclasp my hands and place my right hand on Tom's left shoulder. I then straighten my right leg while keeping my weight on his chest.

I slide my left leg under my right leg and rotate my hips towards Tom's head until my left hip is on the mat. Like the basic side mount, I have established a left underhook on his right arm and grabbed his right shoulder from underneath. My right hand is controlling his left triceps. If he's able to free this arm, he will likely be able to escape the position. My legs are posted out wide to strengthen my base.

KIMURA

In this sequence I demonstrate how to trap your opponent's near arm from the head flank position using your legs, and then attack his far arm with a kimura. With your opponent's near arm trapped, he becomes unable to cross-face you or clasp his hands together, which dramatically increases your chances of finishing him with the kimura. If you look at the photos below, you'll notice that before applying the kimura, I step my leg over my opponent's head and position my foot underneath his neck. This is key for your success. With your body positioned so high up on your opponent's body due to your near-arm-trap, he gains the ability to bridge and roll you off of him. However, by positioning your foot underneath his neck, you eliminate his ability to accomplish this.

1

I am in a head flank side mount on top of Tom. My left knee is underneath his left arm and my weight is dropped on his chest. My left arm is underhooked under his right arm. Tom has raised his left arm out to push my legs away, so I immediately grab his wrist to control it.

2

I bring my right knee up and put it in the crook of Tom's left arm.

3

I step through with my right knee and trap Tom's arm between my legs. My full body weight is now laying flat on his chest. I still have control of his right shoulder with my left hand.

4

With Tom's arm still trapped, I roll back towards his stomach.

5

I crossface Tom using my right hand to create space as well as to immobilize his head. With his arms extended and his head immobilized, he will now be helpless to defend the Kimura.

I step my right leg over Tom's head to completely isolate his right arm.

I now change my hand position. I wrap my right arm underneath Tom's right arm, and I pin his right wrist to the ground using my left hand. Notice that my right foot and left leg are flat on the floor. This prevents him from bridging out or rolling away from the hold.

I grasp my left wrist with my right hand. To finish the submission, I simply rotate my shoulders, bending his arm toward his head. However, it is important to notice that I keep Tom's arm bent as roll my shoulders, and I maintain my leg hook over his head to prevent him from escaping.

ELBOW HUG INTO ROLL-OFF ARMBAR

The head flank is a great position to attack your opponent's far arm. This technique actually attempts two elbow submission consecutively. The elbow hug is a safe way of attempting an armbar without forfeiting your position. You simply attempt to hyperextend the elbow joint using your arm strength. If the elbow hug fails, the roll-off armbar is always an option. The roll-off armbar provides more leverage, but at the risk of losing top control. Timing is the key here. It's similar to the kimura previously shown in that you will step over your opponent in an attempt to control his upper body.

I am in a head flank side mount on top of Tom. My left knee is underneath his left arm and my weight is dropped on his chest. My left arm is underhooked under his right arm. Tom has hooked his left arm over my back to prevent me from isolating it away from his body.

Rather than attempting to pry his arms apart using arm strength, I instead place my forearm in between my head and Tom's head. My goal is to create enough separation to allow me to trap his right arm.

I post up on my right foot to afford me more leverage as I move over top of Tom's body.

I push off the mat using my legs and drive my torso forward to break Tom's grip. Notice that his right arm is trapped over my shoulder.

Tom's right arm is now extended and isolated. With both of my hands wrapped around his elbow joint, all I have to do is squeeze and his elbow will begin to hyperextend. I stay tight against his body and pull his elbow joint into my chest. With adequate pressure, this move alone will force Tom to tap out.

Since Tom has not tapped out from the elbow hug, I decide to execute the roll-off armbar. I let go of my grip and place my right hand on the ground for leverage.

7

I base out with my right arm and right leg to create the space I need to step over Tom's body and initiate the roll-off armbar.

8

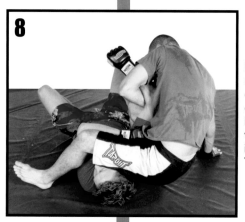

In one quick movement, I rotate my hips, moving to the far side of Tom's body, while maintaining control of his right arm with my left arm. My right foot has the farthest distance to travel so I pivot it around quickly and swing it over Tom's body.

9

I bring my right arm up to control Tom's extended right arm while pinching my knees together tight to prevent him from spinning and escaping the submission.

10

With Tom's arm trapped, I bridge my hips upward, pull his right arm toward my chest using both hands, and pinch my knees together. The combination of my actions places a tremendous amount of pressure on his elbow joint.

WRISTLOCK

When in the top side mount position, your opponent will often attempt to establish a far side underhook by slipping his arm underneath of your body. If your timing is right, this allows you to trap his hand and hyperextend his wrist by applying downward pressure with your chest. It's a very simple technique, but it's an effective move that runs virtually no risk. If you fail to secure the grip needed, or you opponent simply refuses to tap, you are still in a great position to continue attacking.

1 I am in a head flank side mount on top of Tom. My left knee is underneath his left arm and my weight is dropped on his chest. My left arm is underhooked under his right arm and my right arm is underneath his head.

2 Tom moves his right hand in front of my face in an attempt to pummel inside and steal my far side underhook away from me.

3 I lean forward just enough to place my chest over top of Tom's right hand and trap it between our bodies. Notice that I'm now cupping the back of his right triceps with my left hand.

4 I bring my right hand over his head and grab the back of his elbow with both hands. This grip prevents Tom from pulling his arm away.

5 To finish the wrist lock submission, I simply pull upwards with my arms and drive my chest forward. Because Tom's wrist is caught between our bodies, his wrist joint has no choice by to hyperextend, causing him to tap out.

HEAD AND ARM CHOKE

Any time your opponent extends his arms away from his body he creates an opportunity for you to lock in a submission. In this case my opponent attempts to cross face me, and I use the opportunity to trap his head and arm and execute a choke. There's little risk in this move as you're not sacrificing position to attempt it. The head and arm choke can be secured from the side mount, but to make the choke stronger, I like to swing into the full mount to get more leverage behind the final squeeze. If I lose my grip on the way to mount, I will still attain an excellent position.

1

I am in a head flank side mount on top of Tom. My left knee is underneath his left arm and my weight is dropped on his chest. My left arm is underhooked under his right arm and my right arm is underneath his left shoulder.

2

Tom brings his right hand up to crossface me and push my head away. By doing this, he's given me an opportunity to trap his arm and attempt a strangle hold.

3

I quickly drive Tom's right arm upward with my left hand while at the same time dropping my head to the mat.

4

I push my right ear against Tom's arm in order to press his shoulder against his own neck. With Tom's right arm trapped between our heads, I clasp my hands together to secure my grip.

5

I need to drive my head into Tom's arm to apply pressure to the choke. To do that, I cut my left knee across Tom's stomach to move to the opposite side.

6

To complete the submission, I slide my left arm up and then grab my left biceps with my right hand. Keeping one knee on the floor to check Tom's hips, I squeeze my elbows together until he taps. Should this fail to put Tom to sleep, I can continue rotating to his right side to apply even more pressure to the choke, but at the risk of losing the mount.

BENT ARMBAR FROM SCARF HOLD

Sometimes from the head flank position you will be unable to maintain your underhook on your opponent's far side arm. While this presents a risk in losing position, there are still many submissions available from here. The bent armbar from the scarf hold allows you to finish your opponent even after losing your underhook. The key to maintaining control of your opponent from this position is to secure a grip on his inside arm. This allows you to attack him with submissions while keeping him pinned in place. The bent armbar is useful when your opponent attempts to steal your underhook as you come into side mount. As your opponent swims his arm inside, you simply secure his head and initiate your attack on the opposite arm.

1

I am in a head flank side mount on top of Tom. However, Tom attempts to escape the position by forcing his right hand into my armpit in an attempt to steal my underhook.

2

Tom creates space and drives his right arm underneath my left armpit. If I linger in this position, Tom will turn into me and escape the bottom position.

3

By wrapping my left arm underneath Tom's head and dropping my weight fully onto his chest, I've taken his right arm out of the fight. It's important to keep a firm grip on his triceps so he can't escape before I move onto the next step. This is the scarf hold position.

4

I bring my right knee up to trap Tom's left arm and grab his left wrist with my right hand to prepare for the submission.

5

As I bend his left arm down, I drop my head close to Tom's head to prevent him from crossfacing me with his right arm.

6

I bring my left leg over top of Tom's left arm, trapping it in position. It's important to keep a tight grip with my left arm to prevent him from escaping out the back door.

7

Before Tom can force his arm straight, I lock my right leg over my left leg. Now his arm is bent backwards, so all it takes is a little pressure to submit him. I also clasp my hands together to make sure he doesn't pull his head out.

8

I simultaneously pull his head up toward me and thrust my hips forward to rotate his arm, torquing his shoulder and elbow joint.

CRUCIFIX

This is a devastating hold that creates an opportunity to end the fight with a multiple of unanswered strikes. Similar to the bent armbar we just looked at, this move uses your body weight and legs to trap your opponent's arms and leave his head exposed. Body weight control is key for this move. You have to keep your weight centered on your opponent's chest to prevent him from bridging out and escaping the position.

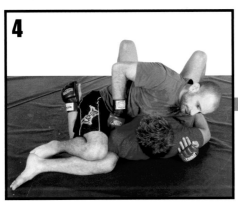

1) I am in a head flank side mount on top of Tom. My left knee is underneath his left arm and my weight is dropped on his chest. I am controlling his right arm with my left hand under his shoulder. I'm also controlling his left arm with my right hand on his shoulder. 2) I want to trap Tom's left arm, so I grab his left wrist and prepare to force it between my legs. 3) I push his left arm down while moving my right leg back to create space. 4) I quickly swing my right leg over and squeeze Tom's left arm between my thighs. This is his best opportunity to escape, so he may try to buck or bridge at this point. I keep my weight fully on his chest and my left hand on his right shoulder to prevent this. 5) Now that his arms are trapped, it's time to strike his head quickly and repetitively. I push his head away to set up an elbow strike. 6) When I drop the elbow, I also drop my body weight so it's not just an arm strike, but a whole body strike. This generates more force and makes the strike more efficient. 7) I follow up the elbow with a hammer fist by bringing my hand up high. 8) When I strike with the hammer fist, I don't drop my weight like I did with the elbow, but instead I pull up on his shoulder with my left hand to force his head into the strike. 9) I follow up the hammer fist with a straight punch by bringing my hand up high and turning my fist over. 10) With this punch I combine elements of the previous two strikes—I drop my weight like I did with the elbow and I pull his shoulder up like I did with the hammer fist.

ATTACKS FROM LEG FLANK

The goal for most of the attacks from the side mount leg flank is the full mount. When you're in side mount and your opponent pummels in and gets an underhook, you're in danger of being swept. You're also unable to execute head flank moves so you have to change tactics and focus on the leg flank attacks. The leg flank position forces you to face your opponent's legs, which can make it difficult to attack with strikes or upper body submissions. All leg flank attacks end up in the full mount, so you have to temporarily disregard strikes and submissions and concentrate your efforts on body control and leverage so you can get yourself into a dominant position without being swept.

BASIC POSITION

When you are in the side mount and your opponent pummels in and achieves an underhook, your primary goal is to block his ability to lift your weight up. By turning your hips down and hooking your opponent's leg, you can prevent him from turning into you and manipulating your body weight. Even if he secures the underhook, if you quickly transfer to the leg flank position, you can prevent your opponent from executing an escape.

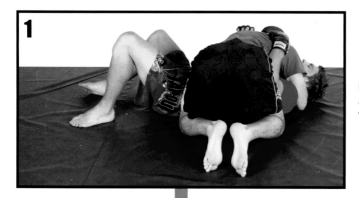

I am holding Tom in side mount. In an attempt to escape, he secures an underhook with his right arm and intends to use it to drive my body weight upward and turn into me.

I reach down and grab Tom's far leg to prevent him from hiking me up.

I pull Tom's leg towards my chest and switch my hips underneath me so they are facing his legs. I keep pressure on his head with my shoulder. This is the basic leg flank position.

FOOT HOOK FROM LEG FLANK

In this technique you trap your opponent's near foot with your foot, which blocks his primary lines of defense and clears a pathway for you to swing into the mount. When executing this move it's easy to get so focused on your opponent's feet that you let your weight come up off of his chest, which gives him an opportunity to escape. So it's important to keep your shoulder in his chin to maintain pressure. Once you trap his ankle, his natural reaction will be to bring his opposite knee up to block the mount. This actually works against him because it gives you a limb to push down on and you can use the momentum to roll into the mount.

1

I am in a side mount leg flank position on top of Tom. He has his left arm underhooked under my right arm. I have my left arm underneath his head and shoulders. I also have my right hand under his left leg, and I use that control to pull his leg up so he can't escape or sweep me.

2

The first thing I do is reach down and grab Tom's right ankle using my right hand. Once accomplished, I hook my left ankle overtop of his right ankle while keeping my weight pressed down on his chest.

3

Sensing that I am about to mount him, Tom brings his left knee up to block me. Immediately I place my right hand on his knee and prepare to push it down.

4

I push Tom's left leg toward the mat using my right hand.

5

As I push Tom's leg down, I use the momentum to swing my right leg over his body.

6

Tom tries to use his left hand to stop my leg. However, because he is on the bottom with no leverage, he will not have the strength to stop me from achieving mount.

7

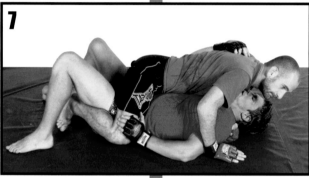

I hook my right foot over his left knee and use it to pull myself over.

8

Once I'm over and have the full mount, I have an array of options to end the fight.

UNCOMFORTABLE MOUNT

When you are in side mount, your opponent will often elevate his near knee to prevent you from stepping over his body and establishing the full mount. In the sequence below, I demonstrate how to use this defense against your opponent. Instead of trying to push his leg back to the mat, you grab his foot and bend his leg painfully toward his head. When you acquire the proper angle with that bend, it gives you enough space to slide your knee over his body and secure the mount position. As I mentioned before, the underlying theme of Jackson's MMA is to use everything your opponent gives you to your advantage.

1 I am in a side mount leg flank position on top of Tom. He has his left arm underhooked under my right arm. I have my left arm underneath his head and shoulders, and I'm using my right hand to pull up on his left leg. Tom raises his right leg to block me from mounting him so I shift my focus to that leg.

2 As I grab Tom's right foot using my right hand, I plant my right foot on the mat to use as a point of base.

3 I pull Tom's right foot towards his chest and he puts his left hand up to block it. This can be an extremely painful movement, as his knee bends in an unnatural manner.

4 When Tom tries to push my hand off and straighten his knee, it allows me to drive my right knee over his torso. This is classic misdirection. My real intention is to force Tom's leg down, so by pulling it up I lead him into the exact reaction I desired.

5 In one quick movement I drive forward and slide my leg over into the full mount.

DOUBLE KNEE SLIDE

Similar to the uncomfortable mount, this technique comes into play when your opponent elevates his near knee to prevent you from stepping over his body and securing the mount. Although this blockade can make it difficult to step your upper leg over his body, it oftentimes allows you to slide your lower leg onto his abdomen. This creates a barrier that drives your opponent's near knee back toward the mat, giving you the space you need to step your upper leg over his body and secure the mount position. However, it is important to mention that this technique momentarily jeopardizes your base, and if your opponent initiates a scramble before you can secure the mount, there is a possibility of him escaping. To reduce the risk, keep your weight down on his midsection, and instead of lifting your hips as you step over his body, slide them across his midsection. This will keep your center of gravity low and make it harder for your opponent to move.

I am in a side mount leg flank position on top of Tom. He has his left arm underhooked under my right arm. I have my left arm underneath his head and shoulders and have my right hand under his left leg. Tom raises his right leg to block me from mounting him.

I pull his left leg toward the outside of his body to open him up and make it hard for him to block me. At the same time, I slip my left knee across his midsection.

My left knee gets fully across his stomach and braces against his legs. I let go of his left leg since I don't need to control it anymore.

With my left knee braced against Tom's legs, I swing my right leg over his body.

Once I get my right leg over, I flatten him out to complete the mount. I get my knees up into his armpits to make the mount more secure.

FAKE KIMURA TO MOUNT

Just like the other fake kimura moves that we saw in the previous chapters, this one forces your opponent to focus on protecting his arm, which in this case creates the opportunity to throw your leg over into the mount. Although this is a fake kimura move, it doesn't mean you should ignore the opportunity to finish the submission. If you manage to get his arm trapped, finish the fight. The kimura attack has to be convincing. You shouldn't just grab his arm and then drop it or your opponent will see through your deception. You have to grab his arm and convince him that you intend to attack it before transitioning to the mount.

I am in a side mount leg flank position on top of Tom. He has his left arm underhooked under my right arm. I have my left arm underneath his head and shoulders and have my right hand under his left leg. Tom raises his right leg to block me from mounting him.

I pull my left arm out from underneath Tom's head and then move it over the top of his head.

I let go of Tom's leg and grab his wrist with my right hand and push it down. At the same time, I wrap my left hand round his left arm.

I place both hands on Tom's wrist to control his left arm. This will get him worried about his arm and take his focus off his legs.

5

Maintaining control of Tom's left arm using my left hand, I quickly change tactics and use my right arm to push his right knee down. This creates the space I need to slide into mount.

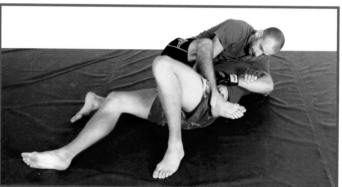

6

By pushing his knee down I can swing my right leg over his torso. Notice I am still controlling his left wrist so he can't use his hand to block my leg.

7

I swing my right leg all the way over and rotate into the full mount.

8

I secure the full mount and I am ready to attack.

ESCAPES AND DEFENSES

As with the other ground positions, we'll now turn the tables and look at the options when your opponent has captured you in side mount. Although side mount is certainly a dominant position for your opponent, you still have ways of escaping or sweeping from the bottom position. However, before attempting an escape or sweep, you want to block your opponent from swinging his leg over into the full mount by elevating your leg closest to his body. As we saw in the previous section, this can be used against you if he decides to transition to a leg flank and attack your elevated knee, so be wary when he suddenly switches positions. Once you have established your defenses, you don't want to stay in side mount for any longer than you have to. Your primary goal is to get out of this position by escaping or sweeping. We'll look at both, but first we'll explore some easy ways to use hand control to block your opponent's attacks.

HAND POSITION DEFENSE

The easiest way to block your opponent's attacks and conserve energy in side mount is with good hand positioning. There are three basic hand control defenses—the cross-face, wrap-around, and underhook. If you look below, you'll notice that in all three positions I keep my right forearm against my opponent's hip so she can't step over my head or knee me in the face.

BASIC POSITION

CROSS FACE

WRAP AROUND

UNDERHOOK

1) BASIC POSITION—I am in Julie's side mount. Her left arm is under my head and her right arm is underhooked under my left arm. Her hands are clasped together. I have my right knee up and have put my right foot across my left knee to prevent her from swinging her legs over to mount me. My right forearm is against her hip so she can't step over my head or knee me in the face.

2) CROSS-FACE—With the cross-face I simply slide my left hand up and press it up underneath her jaw. This creates space, which makes it harder for her to strike my head and starts off some of the escapes we will look at next. I have to be wary of her left arm in this position because, as we saw previously, she can grab my left wrist and try an Americana submission.

3) WRAP-AROUND—By wrapping my left arm around Julie's head and pulling it closer to me, I do the opposite from the cross-face and eliminate the space between her head and my shoulder. This makes it hard for her to posture up and will almost always cause her to cross-face me to break my grip.

4) UNDERHOOK—By underhooking her right arm, I pull her weight higher on my torso, which protects my arms from submission attacks and opens me up for a number of escapes. However, it can also make me vulnerable to leg flank attacks.

ESCAPE TO FULL GUARD (SHRIMPING)

Getting back to full guard from side mount is a core move that has to be trained regularly. The most common way is shrimping, which is very useful at getting you out of a bad situation. Of all the ways to escape to full guard, shrimping is the first move you should try because even if you're not successful at pulling yourself into full guard, you will be able to keep our opponent off balance and gain an underhook. Shrimping starts with the cross-face that we just looked at. It creates the space you need to get underhooks and pull your close leg underneath your opponent and get to the full guard.

I am in Julie's side mount. Her left arm is under my head and her right arm is underhooked under my left arm. Her hands are clasped together. I have my right knee up and have put my right foot across my left knee to prevent her from swinging her legs over to mount me. My right forearm is against her hip so she can't step over my head or knee me in the face.

I bring my left hand up and shove my forearm underneath Julie's chin to cross-face her and push her head away. This creates the space I need to force my hand under her right armpit.

I quickly slip my left hand underneath her right armpit.

With double underhooks, I have control of Julie's upper body.

Julie counters by bringing her left leg in and pressing it up against my right arm. This actually makes it easier for me to get her off balance.

I push off with my planted left foot and force my right knee into her midsection to knock her off balance.

I continue pulling her off balance using my underhooks. This creates the space I need to sneak my right leg underneath her body.

I quickly rotate my lower body underneath Julie, scoot my butt toward her hips, and force my right knee across her midsection.

I grab her left triceps with my right hand to prevent her from blocking my leg from coming through her guard. I brace my right knee against her thigh so I can get my left foot on her right thigh.

I continue rotating around and pull Julie forward.

I move my right leg over her thigh to complete my escape to full guard.

ESCAPE TO FULL GUARD (THE PEEKABOO)

This is an in-depth attack that illustrates many of the core principles of Jackson's MMA—every move has a backup, you should plan more than one move ahead, and some moves can be used to get your opponent to react in a predictable way. This move starts the same as the previous move—by shrimping and pulling one leg inside your opponent's guard. But this is just a feint to get leverage for the armbar. If your opponent pulls his arm out to block the armbar, then you have the space you need to rotate into full guard. It's a move within a move within a move. This isn't to say you shouldn't take the armbar submission if it's there, but if it's not because your opponent properly defends against the submission, you will find yourself with the space you need to transition to guard.

1

I am in Julie's side mount. Her left arm is under my head and her right arm is underhooked under my left arm. Her hands are clasped together. I have my right knee up and have put my right foot across my left knee to prevent her from swinging her right leg over to mount me. My right forearm is against her left hip so she can't step over my head or knee me in the face.

2

As with the previous move, I bring my left hand up and shove my forearm underneath Julie's chin to cross-face her and push her head away.

3

I rotate my hips and bring my right knee up inside her torso and brace it against her midsection for leverage.

4

Julie thinks I'm trying to achieve guard and drops her weight onto my right leg to prevent it from coming underneath her. This is what I wanted her to do because it gives me leverage to attempt the armbar. I quickly change tack and push against her midsection with my right knee, which gives me the leverage I need to swing my left leg up toward her head.

I swing my left leg over to the left side of Julie's head.

As I drive Julie's head downward using my left leg, I grab her right arm using my left hand and trap it to my chest. In order to avoid the armbar, she needs to posture up and pull her arm free. In such a scenario, she would give me the space I need to transition to full guard.

Julie is a smart fighter and recognizes the impending submission. She postures up and pulls her arm out.

When she rips her arm out, it creates a lot of space between us and it gives me momentum to rotate on my back in a clockwise direction. I bring my left leg back over her head.

I swing my right leg through and put it on her hip. I could pull her into full guard, but since she's farther away than normal I put my feet on her hips and assume a spider guard.

SEATBELT ESCAPE TO REAR MOUNT

Getting out of your opponent's side mount is one thing, but staying closely engaged and transitioning to a dominant position is another. This technique uses one explosive movement to get you in a position where you can rotate your body around and get your opponent's back. The key to this technique is getting your knee closest to your opponent inside his guard. This provides you with the positioning needed to slip your arms underneath your opponent's body, which in turn provides you with the leverage needed to control his body weight and move around him. Personally, I find this technique very useful against opponents who keep their arms over your head instead of under it, which is common with fighters who like applying far-side Americanas or kimuras when in side mount.

1

I am in Julie's side mount. Her left arm is over my head and her right arm is underhooked under my left arm. Her hands are clasped together. I have my right knee up and have put my right foot across my left knee to prevent her from swinging her legs over to mount me. My right forearm is against her hip so she can't step over my head or knee me in the face.

2

I rotate my hips and bring my right knee inside Julie's guard and brace it against her midsection. This will give me the leverage I need to reposition my arms.

3

With my knee pushing against her midsection, I place both hands on her left rib cage.

4

This step happens all at once. I quickly push off with my right knee, plant my left foot, sit up, base out with my right hand, and wrap my left arm over Julie's back.

I scoot my hips out to my right, which creates a little space between us to maneuver my legs. I don't want to move too far away because then Julie can turn into me and use her body weight to drive me flat to the mat.

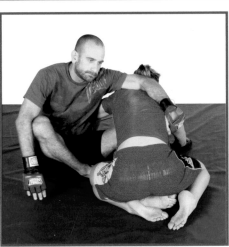

I bring my right leg back and prepare to wrap it over her back.

My left arm sneaks under her neck and my right hand wraps around her back. As I turn my hips and torso to face her, I push off of my right foot and get up on my left knee to use it as a pivot point to rotate my body around behind her.

I complete the escape by wrapping my right leg over her right hip and get my hooks in. From this position I can attack her neck and attempt a number of submissions.

SINGLE-LEG ESCAPE TO SIDE MOUNT

This technique takes you from side mount to the top position, but it is a little different from the other escapes. In this escape, you already have double underhooks on your opponent. This gives you more leverage to throw him off to one side and control his upper torso, which allows you rotate your hips and get off your back. There's a little risk in this move because when you rotate your body around it's possible to expose your neck to your opponent. To prevent this, you have to be sure to get control of your opponent's leg as you turn over.

1 I am in Julie's side mount. Her left arm is under my head and her right arm is over my left arm. I have achieved double underhooks under her armpits. I have my right knee up and have put my right foot across my left knee to prevent her from swinging her right leg over to mount me. My right forearm is against her hip so she can't step over my head or knee me in the face.

Using the double underhooks I have already established, I throw her upper body up over my head and disrupt her balance.

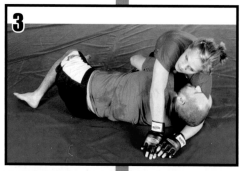

I quickly rotate my hips to face her and get my right knee underneath me.

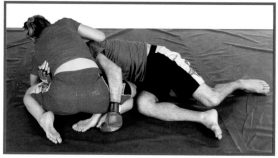

My left hand slides down to her right leg. This is important because controlling her leg keeps her from rotating around to my back.

Maintaining control of her right leg using my left arm, I keep rotating until my knees are underneath me.

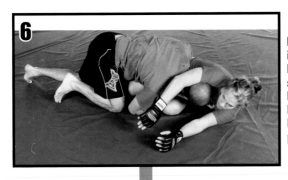

6 I grab Julie's left foot using my left hand to prevent her from basing out. At the same time, I drive my upper body into her body and force her off balance. Notice how I keep tight to her chest to protect my head.

7 I pop my head out from underneath Julie's right arm and continue to roll her over until I'm in the side mount.

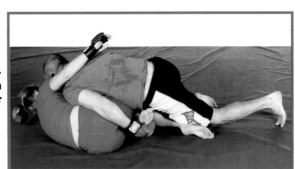

OCTOPUS FOOT LOCK

This technique starts off in a fashion similar to the back door escape, in which you use one knee as a brace against your opponent's midsection while you slide your arms underneath of his body. Instead of using your arms to escape to a rear mount, however, you use your arms to grab your opponent's foot and attack it with a foot lock. It's a simple move that's effective against an opponent who leaves too much space between your bodies, as in the previous moves, and doesn't sprawl his legs out behind him.

1 I am in Julie's side mount. Instead of wrapping her left arm under my head, she has it over my head. So I already have one hand inside her guard.

2 As before, I rotate my hips, put my right knee into her midsection, and brace it against her stomach.

3

I slide my left hand underneath Julie's body and brace my arms against her left side.

4

I continue to rotate and reach for her left foot.

5

I grab the top, outside portion of Julie's left foot with my right hand, wrap my left arm over her instep and then grab my right wrist with my left hand. This gives me a figure-four lock. To apply the submission, I pull her instep toward me using my left forearm and drive her toes toward the mat using my right hand.

CHAPTER FOUR: HEAD CONTROL

Head control is a dominant position, but it's also a trade-off. Although it affords you complete control of your opponent's upper body, it offers almost no control of his legs. However, head control is a good launching point for many attacks. The biggest risk with head control is giving your opponent enough space to escape by rolling to one side or the other. To prevent this, keep your arms tight against his sides and your weight dropped down on his chest.

TRANSITION FROM SIDE MOUNT TO HEAD CONTROL

If you have an opponent who's good at driving his knee inside your guard when in the top side mount position, it will often allow him to recover the full guard. To prevent such an outcome, the instant he begins making a move toward full guard, you should consider transitioning to a new position that still affords you control. One such position is head control. It's still a dominant position, and it is easy to rotate around to if you think you can't keep your opponent in side mount.

1

I have Tom in side mount with one hand under his head and the other underhooked under his right arm. My knees are tight against his ribs.

2

Tom rotates his hips and brings his left knee inside my guard.

3

I counter by dropping my left arm in front of his right leg, which blocks his knee from sliding across my midsection. At the same time, I begin circling in a counterclockwise direction around his body.

4

I rotate my body around to his head and drop my chest onto his chest.

SUBMISSIONS

Submissions from head control target the neck and arms because they're within close proximity to your own arms, so it doesn't take as many movements to attack them. Leg locks from head control are possible, but they take more motion to achieve. We'll look at four submissions from head control. The first two start from the chest-to-chest head control position, and the second pair start when you have head control but your opponent is on all fours.

KIMURA

I like this as a first option from head control because if it doesn't work, I still retain top control. If anything is going to go wrong with this move, it will be keeping control of your opponent's lower body, because he will be free to maneuver his legs and roll to either side. To counter that, you have to maintain very tight control of the arm you are bending and control his opposite arm with your shin. If he tries to escape by rolling away from his isolated arm, the submission will actually become tighter because you can rotate his arm behind his back. Obviously, to execute a kimura you must isolate one of his arms, so that's the first step. Once you do that, it becomes an issue of posturing up quickly and locking it in before he can pull his arm out.

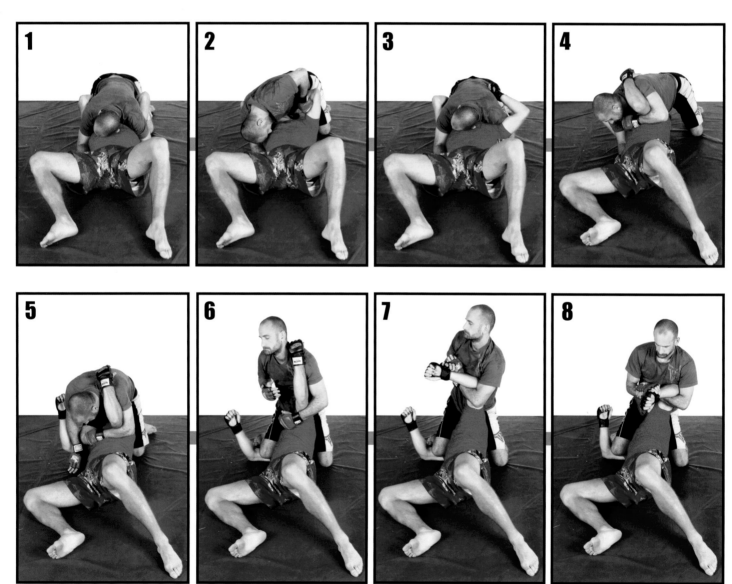

1) I am in a head control position with Tom underneath me. My arms are tight against his sides and my head is against his midsection for protection. My weight is dropped on him fully to prevent him from rolling to either side. 2) I isolate the arm I want to attack by forcing my left arm in between his left arm and my body. Notice that I don't posture up when I do this. I keep my weight on top of him and my head in his midsection. 3) By underhooking my left arm under his left arm, I've isolated it and have control of it. 4) I pull Tom's left arm up onto my shoulder using my left arm. 5) Keeping Tom's left arm trapped using my left arm, I place my right knee over his right arm to pin it to the mat. This severely limits his mobility. 6) As I rise up, I keep a firm grip on his left arm so he can't free it. Notice how his left arm straightens as I increase my elevation. 7) I slide the crook of my left arm up to the crook of Tom's left arm. Next, I grab his left wrist with my right hand. Finally, I grab my right wrist with my left hand, giving me the figure-four lock I need to apply the Kimura. 8) Keeping Tom's left elbow pinned to my chest, I drive his left forearm toward the outside of his body using my right hand, putting a tremendous amount of pressure on his left shoulder.

ARMBAR

This submission is preferable when your opponent keeps his arms in tight to his sides and prevents you from attempting the kimura. It's also a good backup for the kimura when you are unable to trap his opposite arm with your shin in the way we just looked at. There are two risks with this move. First, your opponent will instinctively roll away when he feels the armbar coming, so keeping a firm grip on his arm is important. The other risk is that he'll rip his arm away as you lean back. Again, keep a firm grip to prevent that. Speed is also key. You want to rotate around your opponent's body and bring your legs underneath before he can see the move coming. If he senses your intentions, there is a good chance that he will block the submission.

1

I am in a head control position with Tom underneath me. My arms are tight against his sides and my head is against his midsection for protection. My weight is dropped on him fully to prevent him from rolling to either side.

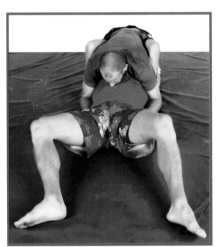

2

I pummel my left arm in between his left arm and my side.

3

I wrap my left arm around Tom's left arm to isolate it. Notice how I establish a firm grip on his arm by wrapping the crook of my arm around his triceps.

4

Now that I have his arm, I have to take advantage of it by putting myself in a position to bend it. I start by lifting Tom up and rolling him away from the arm I've isolated (his left one).

5

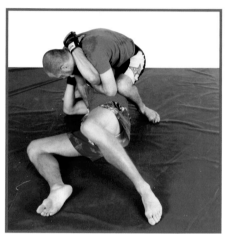

I plant my right arm on the ground and get my legs underneath me for the eventual positional change. At this point Tom could attempt to escape by rolling right, so I keep firm control on his left arm to prevent such an escape.

6

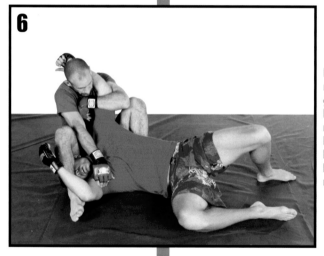

In one quick movement I change direction and lean back. My right leg goes over his head to cross-face him so he can't roll into me. For now, my left leg stays up against his back to control his movement. Notice how I use my left arm to keep his left arm trapped tight to my chest.

7

To complete the submission, I swing my left leg over his chest and lean back to hyperextend his elbow. Squeezing his arm between my thighs increases the pressure on his arm and makes the submission more efficient.

ANACONDA CHOKE

This submission and the next one begin with a different start position. Instead of being chest to chest with your opponent, you will start with your chest against his back, but still in head control. I like the anaconda choke submission because it can be applied quickly and with minimal movements. You don't have to give up any control to attempt it, and once it's secure, it only takes a rollover to tighten it. This submission is useful against an opponent who tries to reach for your legs instead of protecting his neck, which is common among wrestlers.

 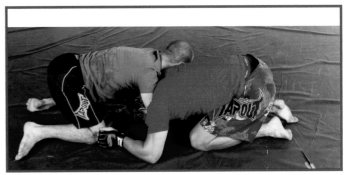

I have Tom in head control with his head on my chest. Note that my right arm is already against his neck. If you find yourself with both arms under his armpits, the first thing you need to do is get one under his neck. My left hand is on his right elbow for control. My knees are far enough back that he can't grab them.

 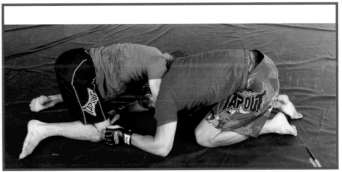

I drop my weight so my chest is on his head and so I have more room to wrap my arm around his neck. My right arm slides all the way under his neck so my biceps is fully against his Adam's apple. At the same time, I move my left arm forward so I can grab my left biceps with my right hand.

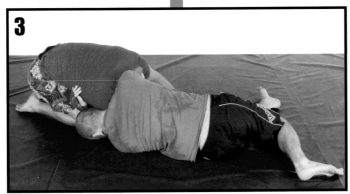 

After I secure a firm grip, I roll over my left elbow and drag Tom with me.

I continue to roll and force Tom over with me. As we roll, my grip on his neck gets tighter.

Tom lands flat on his back, and I want him to stay there, so I stop dragging him and rotate my lower body around him in a clockwise direction.

With his head and neck trapped, I push off with my legs and walk them in a counterclockwise direction. Notice how this drives his right arm into the side of his neck.

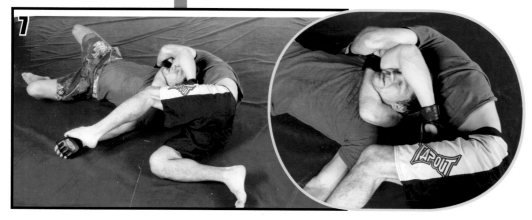

I put my left foot on his hand to prevent him from using it to break the grip. With my right arm digging into the left side of his neck and my grip forcing his right arm into the right side of his neck, blood flow is severed to his brain, forcing him to tap in submission or pass out.

GUILLOTINE (ARM IN)

If your opponent prevents you from dropping your weight for the anaconda choke or you simply can't establish the correct arm positioning, the guillotine choke is a good alternative. The risk with the guillotine is that you must give up your dominant position to attempt it. So it's important to have a very secure grip before you attempt it or your opponent can pop his head out and obtain the top position. While the normal guillotine choke places your opponent in your guard, with my version, you do not wrap your legs around his hips when applying the submission, which means he could pass your guard and secure side mount. Although this weakness might make my version of the guillotine seem less appealing, I find placing my knee across my opponent's midsection allows me to gain more counterpressure for the choke. For this reason, it is very important to secure your grips tight before abandoning your dominant position. If you look at the photos below, you'll notice that the other modification that I like to make is to pull my head up at a forty-five-degree angle to cut off my opponent's airway. I find this dramatically increases your success rate with the submission.

I have Tom in head control with his head on my chest. As with the previous move, my right arm is already against his neck. This move doesn't work unless you have one arm against your opponent's throat. My left hand is on his right elbow for control. My knees are far enough back that he can't grab them.

I drop my weight so my chest is against his head and slide my right arm farther under his neck. I lock my hands under his right armpit so he can't break the choke when I roll back.

With my hands secure and one arm against his neck, I get up on my left leg and start to roll my weight back.

I roll backward and drag Tom with me. His instinct is to lean back to prevent the choke. My left leg stays inside his guard instead of wrapping around him in a full guard posture.

I lean completely back and place my left leg on Tom's back to trap his right arm and prevent him from escaping my guard to side mount. I pull his neck up at a forty-five-degree angle and use my right leg to press against his midsection. This adds counterpressure and makes the submission more effective.

TRANSITION TO REAR MOUNT

This is an important transition because it takes you from head control to the rear mount, which increases your options for finishing your opponent. Obtaining the rear mount also takes away your opponent's ability to put you on your back and allows you access to the rear naked choke, a very high-percentage finishing hold.

1

I have Tom in head control. My right arm is against his neck and my left hand is on his right triceps for control. My knees are far enough back that he can't grab them.

2

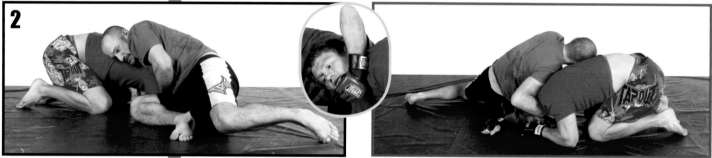

It's hard to see, but my right hand is cupped under his chin to control his head. I don't want him to pop his head out while I move so my hand will stay here throughout the technique. My left hand is on his right triceps for control as well. Many things happen at once here. I slide my right shoulder in between his right shoulder and his neck. At the same time, I pull his chin toward my right side using my right hand and push his right arm toward my right side using my left hand. This clears a path for me to circle around his body in a clockwise direction. Notice how I have dropped my right hip all the way to the mat to block him from moving his right arm out to his side and catching my body.

3

Using my right knee as a base, I throw my left arm over Tom's back and rotate my torso around his body to his back.

4

I slide my right arm between his chin and shoulder, slide my left arm under his left arm, and clasp my hands together in the center of his chest. From here, I will swing my left leg over his back and sink my hooks in to complete the transition.

ESCAPES

Now we'll turn the tables and look at ways to escape head control. In all three of the following moves the goal is not to disengage, but rather to escape your opponent's head control and achieve a dominant position of your own, or even a submission.

ESCAPE TO TRIANGLE

This technique works well against an opponent who keeps his weight back on his butt instead of keeping pressure on your chest. It also works well against an opponent who keeps his head too high and leaves space between your bodies. In either scenario, you have an opportunity to get your legs back in the fight. By pushing against your opponent's shoulders, you can swing your legs up and wrap them around his head for the triangle. Once your legs are in a position to spin your torso, you will utilize the ninety-degree cut that we saw in chapter 1 to put you in position for the submission. Arm control is crucial for this submission to work. Throughout the move you have to control one of your opponent's arms so you can trap it for the triangle choke.

Julie has me in head control with her head on my chest. However, I can sense that her weight is back over her buttocks instead of on my chest.

I slide my arms down to her shoulders so I can push against them and get enough leverage to lift my legs up.

I bring my shins up to each side of Julie's ears to prepare for the next step.

4

Now it's time to change position. I bring my left arm across her midsection and get it on her right side. This will give me the leverage I need for the ninety-degree cut. At the same time, I control her right arm by grabbing it with my right hand.

5

I spin my upper torso in a counterclockwise direction by pushing against her body until I am perpendicular to her. I bring my left leg inside her guard and place it against her right armpit. I am still controlling her right arm with my right hand and will continue to do so throughout the move.

6

I continue to rotate until I am squared up and facing Julie. I still have control of her right arm and have brought my right leg up next to her head. It is important to notice that I use my right hand to force her right arm toward the right side of my body. This will allow me to move straight into the triangle.

7

Two things happen at once here: I pop my left leg out from underneath Julie's torso and I wrap my right leg across the back of her neck. Now I have her in a position to finish the submission. Notice how I still have her right arm positioned on the right side of my body.

8

I hook the crook of my left leg over my right foot, hook my right arm underneath her left arm, wrap my left arm over her right arm, and complete the ninety-degree cut by rotating in a counterclockwise direction. Once accomplished, I squeeze my legs tight to lock in the triangle choke.

ESCAPE HEAD CONTROL TO HEAD AND ARM LOCK

Just like the previous submission, this technique is effective against an opponent who keeps his weight too far down your body or digs an arm over your shoulder to attempt a submission. It has elements similar to the anaconda choke in that you obtain control of your opponent's head and arm and roll him 180 degrees against his will. However, it's more of a sweep because it ends with you in a dominant position instead of a submission. The key to success with this technique is catching your opponent by surprise with explosive movement.

Julie has me in head control. Her head is on my stomach, but she's not keeping enough pressure on me to prevent me from moving.

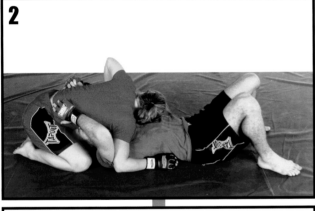

Julie brings her left arm up, forces it over my left shoulder, and wraps it around my arm. This is a common tactic to set up a submission from head control.

Julie has her left arm completely over my left shoulder. I have to act quickly before she can use her hold to her advantage.

My left arm has an unobstructed path to her neck, so I wrap it around behind her head and clasp my hands together. This traps her right arm, preventing her from basing out on that side.

5

I swing my legs to the left, but this is just a feint. It gets Julie to shift her weight to her right to block my movement, which sets me up for the big roll over.

6

Speed is key for the rest of this move. I rotate my hips and plant my feet to get leverage for the roll.

7

In one explosive movement I bridge my back, push off with my feet, and roll with all my might to the right. My grip on Julie is tight and I use that to pull her upper body as I roll.

8

I keep rolling until she's on her back, and I maintain the tight grip I have on her head and arm.

9

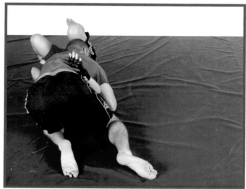

Once I have Julie on her back, I get my knees underneath me and establish control. Now I'm in head control and can transition to one of many submissions.

ESCAPE HEAD CONTROL TO REAR MOUNT

This technique allows you to escape head control and obtain the rear mount, and it works best against an opponent who is simply holding you down rather than attacking. The key to success with this technique is forcing your opponent as high up as possible on your body before attempting to throw your legs over his head. If you attempt this technique while your opponent's head is down by your hips, you will not be successful.

Julie has me in head control. Her head is on my stomach, but she's not keeping enough pressure on me to prevent me from moving.

I first roll left to lower my weight. As I do this, I place my hands on Julie's hips and push off, forcing her as high up on my body as possible.

I roll to my right, further lowering my weight. At the same time, I extend my arms into Julie's hips to prevent her from driving forward and eliminating the space I created.

I flatten both of my feet on the mat and prepare to throw my lower body over Julie's head.

5

I crunch my abdominal muscles and use the grip I have on her torso to bring my legs up high.

6

I keep rolling and use my back as the pivot point.

7

I roll over my left shoulder to prevent injuring my neck and plant my left knee on the mat by Julie's left shoulder.

8

I release the grip I have and quickly rotate my right leg over her thigh to get a hook in.

9

I shift my weight toward Julie's feet, establish a left underhook to prevent her from bucking me forward, and slide my left foot to the inside of her left thigh, establishing my second hook. I now have control of her back.

CHAPTER FIVE: REAR MOUNT

The rear mount is one of the best positions in unarmed combat because it gives you the ability to control and attack your opponent with very low risk of counterattack. It's also advantageous because your opponent cannot see you or your strikes coming and therefore has difficulty defending them. The rear mount can be achieved in either a sitting-up position or supine position, with your opponent's front toward the ground. In both of these positions, strong leg control is key.

The biggest risk with the rear mount is that your opponent can turn his hips over and end up on top of you if he's quick and strong, but if you stay sharp and active, you can keep this from happening. Unlike the other chapters, we will not look at one basic rear mount position, but instead we'll explore moves from a few of them.

SUBMISSIONS

The rear naked choke is the most common submission from the rear mount because it is so effective. There are two variants of the RNC for the different body types you might encounter—the standard rear naked choke is useful against normal body types, whereas the fat boy RNC is (as it sounds) meant for opponents with thicker necks. Obviously arm position is the most critical aspect of the RNC. The choke doesn't work unless your arm gets fully underneath your opponent's chin. A smart opponent will recognize the RNC and tuck his chin against his chest to block you from slipping your arm underneath it. There are several ways to get him to raise his chin for the choke, such as punches or a neck crank.

REAR NAKED CHOKE SETUP

The first version of the RNC uses incremental advances to move your hands up to a position where you can finish the choke. Before you try this, however, you first have to establish control of your opponent's lower body. Bringing both your legs around his pelvis helps you stabilize his body so you can better advance your choke, while minimizing his chances of escape.

I've established a right overhook on Tom's right arm and a left underhook on his left arm. Instead of being directly on top of him, I've moved off to his right side and placed my right knee on the mat. It is important to notice that I've clasped my hands together on his chest.

I rotate around to Tom's side by sliding my right knee underneath him. This gives me the leverage I need to pull him off balance.

I drop back to my butt and pull Tom with me using my arms. As his back comes down on my chest, I slide my right arm underneath his chin. Notice that I am still grabbing my left wrist with my right hand.

When my back hits the ground, I swing my right leg over Tom's right leg.

I hook my right leg over Tom's right hip to attain control of his lower body. At this point, Tom sees the choke coming and tucks his chin to block it.

I want to get my other hook in without Tom blocking it, so I lift his left arm up using my left arm. This allows me to bring my left leg up to hook it over his left hip.

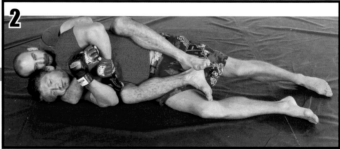

Now I've got both hooks in so I have control over Tom's torso. I keep my legs tight around him to prevent him from rolling over and facing me. From here, I will work to finish the rear naked choke.

REAR NAKED CHOKE (ITSY BITSY SPIDER FINISH)

I grab Tom's left wrist using my left hand, and then pull his arm tight to my chest.

In an attempt to defend against the choke, Tom grabs my right wrist with his right hand and attempts to pull my arm away from his neck.

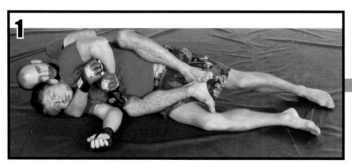

The next few steps take a little time. The goal is to get my right hand up to Tom's left shoulder, so every time he relaxes I crawl my right fingers up his left arm like a little spider.

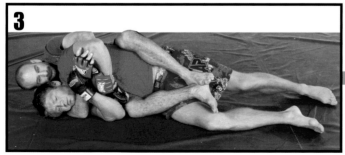

Tom relaxes momentarily, and I walk my fingers up his left arm.

Again, Tom relaxes momentarily, and I walk my fingers up his left arm.

Tom relaxes one last time, and I manage to get my hand near the top of his shoulder.

I wrap my right hand over Tom's left shoulder, giving me an anchor point to sink the choke in.

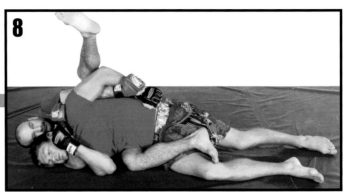

With my right forearm against Tom's throat and my right hand anchored on his shoulder, I force his left arm toward his hips using my left arm and then begin throwing my left leg over his left arm to trap it.

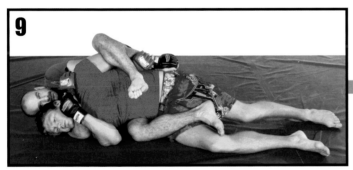

My left leg comes over his left arm to immobilize it.

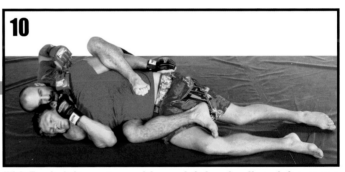

With Tom's left arm trapped by my left leg, I pull my left arm out from under my leg.

I slide my left arm over the top of my right hand.

I slide the back of my left hand behind Tom's head, and then grab my left biceps with my right hand. To finish the choke, I squeeze my arms tight, severing blood flow to his brain.

REAR NAKED CHOKE (FAT BOY WITH BODY LOCK)

This is a variation of the previous move that is designed for opponents with thick necks that are hard to get your arms around. Instead of placing a hand behind your opponent's head, grabbing your biceps, and squeezing, as you did in the previous move, you clasp your hands together and pull your forearm into your opponent's throat. If you look at the photos below, you'll notice that instead of keeping my regular hooks on my opponent's legs, I establish a body lock by triangling my legs around my opponent's midsection. This lock not only makes it very difficult for your opponent to spin around and into your guard, but it also restricts his breathing.

1

I start from the rear mount position with Tom on his side, both of my hooks in, and my right arm around his neck.

2

The first goal is to wrap my legs around his torso and squeeze him. The body lock cannot be on the ground, meaning the upper leg cannot be the one that is placed across his stomach. Therefore, I bring my right leg up and place it across his stomach.

3

Just like a triangle choke, I hook my left leg over my right foot.

4

It's hard to get enough leverage on his stomach by just crossing my legs, so I need to tighten the hold by bringing my left foot up higher. In order to accomplish this, I begin pulling my left arm out from underneath his left arm.

5

I reach down and grab my right foot using my left hand.

6

I pull my right foot up until it's in position in the crook of my left leg. This allows me to cinch my legs tighter, which not only restricts Tom's breathing, but also makes it very hard for him to spin and face me.

With my legs secure around his midsection I can concentrate on the choke. My left hand comes back up toward Tom's head.

Since this is a fat boy RNC against an opponent with a thicker neck, I'm not going to bother trying to sneak my arm in like the last version. Instead I simultaneously clasp my hands together and place my head against his head to act as counterpressure.

With my hands clasped together and my head against his, I pull up to squeeze his neck.

By squeezing on Tom neck, I sever blood flow to his brain, and by keeping my body lock tight around his midsection, I restrict his breathing. He has no choice but to tap out.

ARMBAR

This armbar is effective from the rear mount when you can't secure the rear naked choke. It works best when you are in a rear mount underneath your opponent with your back on the ground. From this position you can rotate your body similar to the ninety-degree cut that we saw in chapter 1, swing a leg over your opponent's head, and isolate an arm. It is important to mention that when executing this technique, it is possible for your opponent to roll over and end up on top, but as long as you keep a firm grip on your opponent's captured arm, the risk is usually worth the reward.

I have a rear mount on Tom from underneath. Both of my hooks are in, and my arms are underhooked under his.

I want to spin my body underneath him, so to set that up, I free my right arm and bring it over his left shoulder so I can push against it.

I roll Tom to his left side so I have the space to swing my right leg over.

As I rotate my body in a clockwise direction underneath Tom, I throw my right leg over his head and pull his left arm toward my chest using my left arm.

I slide my left leg up to Tom's chest, grab his arm with both hands, and lean back.

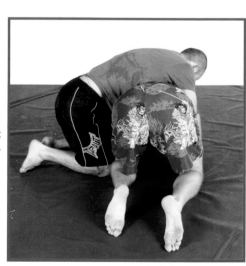

To finish the armbar, I pin Tom's arm to my chest, squeeze my knees together, and arch my hips upward, hyperextending his elbow. It is important to notice that I have his left thumb positioned upward.

CALF CRUSHER

When you achieve a rear mount, your opponent will naturally expect a rear naked choke since it has a high success rate. A submission like the calf crusher is unorthodox and unexpected, so there's a good chance your opponent won't recognize you setting it up until it's too late. This move is effective against opponents who "turtle up" and go into a defensive posture to protect themselves.

I have Tom in a rear mount, but I am off to his side without my hooks in. My left arm is under his neck and my right arm is over his back.

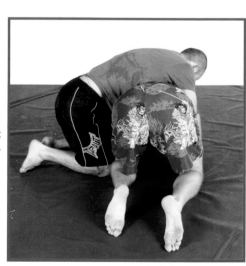

2

Keeping my right knee as a base, I sneak my left leg in between Tom's legs and wrap it around the inside of his left leg, establishing a hook.

3

I slide my upper torso down his body and get my left arm over his back. This will prevent him from rolling out while I lock the submission in. At the same time, I reach down with my right hand and grab my left leg to pull it through his legs.

4

I rotate around so I am facing Tom's legs and sit on my butt to get my weight back. My left leg is across Tom's left leg, with my calf directly behind his knee.

5

With my left leg across the back of Tom's leg, I grab his left foot and pull it up against my leg with both hands. At the same time, I place my right foot on my left heel and drive my right leg into his calf. The combination of these actions puts him in a tremendous amount of pain and causes him to tap.

SLIP-IN GUILLOTINE (ARM IN)

Like the calf crusher, this submission starts from the same hybrid rear mount with your knees on the ground. Only instead of attacking your opponent's legs, it attacks his neck and gives you another option in your toolbox. Speed is key with this move because once your opponent feels an arm wrap around his neck he will instinctively try to block the choke. Therefore, you have to quickly rotate your body from his side to his front and lean back to secure the choke before he can prevent it. As with some other submissions, I like to use my inside leg as counterpressure by pressing it up against his midsection. This stretches my opponent's body out and puts more pressure on his neck. With a guillotine choke there is always a risk of your opponent popping his head out. If your grip on his neck is not tight, he can free his head and possibly gain side mount on you, so maintain a tight grip with your arms as you rotate around to his front to prevent this. If you can't secure the choke, a sweep and another choke are possible, which we'll look at next.

1 I have Tom in a rear mount, but I am off to his side without my hooks in. My left arm is under his neck and my right arm is over his back.

2 Both of my arms change position simultaneously. My left arm slides over his head and neck while my right arm moves to his near side. I clasp my hands together on his chest.

3 I quickly rotate my body around his until we are almost squared up with each other. My left knee slides inside his midsection until I can press it up against his stomach and push him away.

4 I bring my right leg up onto his back to prevent him from rolling away. To complete the submission, I pull his neck upward with my arms while pushing his lower body away from me using my left leg.

SWEEP TO ANACONDA CHOKE

This is a continuation of the move we just saw and is a great backup plan if you cannot gain enough leverage for the guillotine choke. It's not a stand-alone move, meaning the sweep and the anaconda choke should not be your goal. The guillotine choke is the goal, but if that's not achievable, then the sweep and the anaconda become your focus.

I have Tom in a guillotine choke hold with my hands clasped under his chest and my weight back. My left knee is pushing against his stomach and my right leg is on his back. Even though I have a good grip, he's not tapping out.

I put my right foot on the ground to act as a base for the sweep.

The majority of the work is being done by my legs here. My left leg pushes Tom away, while my right leg pushes off the ground. My upper body pulls Tom to my left to sweep him off balance. Notice my hands. Because I intend to secure an anaconda choke, I've unclasped them. My left arm will remain on his neck while my right arm slides up.

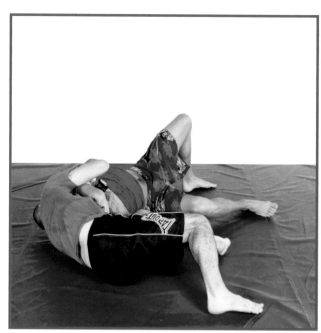

As I force Tom to his back, I grab my left biceps with my right hand. This acts like a lever against his neck. By flexing my right arm, my left arm gets tighter against his neck and cuts off his blood flow.

Keeping my arms tight, I walk my hips toward Tom's hips. This will prevent him from rolling away and puts more pressure on his neck.

STRIKES

Strikes from the rear mount rarely produce a knockout, but they can be used to harass your opponent and get him to make a mistake. Land enough strikes and sometimes it will frustrate him enough that he tries something drastic to get away, which plays into your hands. For example, if he bases an arm out to stand, you can grab that arm and attack it with a submission. However, striking an opponent from the rear mount is tricky. Under unified MMA rules, you cannot strike an opponent in the back of the head, but the more he covers up, the harder that is. You have to be careful to strike the side of his head and not the back. Whenever I strike from the rear, I keep one hand on my opponent for control so he does not have an easy way to roll away or escape. I never strike with both hands at the same time unless my hooks are in.

STRIKING A TURTLED OPPONENT—BASIC PUNCHES

Turtling up is a term that describes getting on all fours in a defensive mode to protect the head and prevent hooks from being established. When an opponent does this, he's usually tired and frustrated already, so you can usually get several shots in without a response. A strong base is important when throwing strikes from this position, so before I start striking, I base a leg out. It's also important to keep your weight dropped down on your opponent's back while striking to prevent him from rolling to guard.

1) I have Tom in a rear mount, but I am off to his side without my hooks in. My left arm is on his left arm and my right arm is over his back. **2)** Before I start striking, I base my left leg out so he can't roll into me and sweep me over. At the same time, I place my right knee tight against his side and drop my weight down on his back. **3)** With my right arm over his back for control, I bring my left hand up high for a strike. **4)** I punch him in the side of the head with the round knuckle punch. **5)** I use the momentum from the strike to bring my hand up high for another strike from the other side. **6)** I strike the side of his head with a hard hammer fist.

STRIKING A TURTLED OPPONENT—KNEE TO BODY

In this sequence I demonstrate how to land a knee to your opponent's body when he assumes the turtle position. Although it is also possible to land knees to your opponent's head, such strikes have been outlawed in MMA competition in the United States.

I put my left hand on Tom's left hand to immobilize it so he can't protect his mid-section. At the same time, I move my right leg away from his body to set up the strike. It is important to notice that my right arm is under his right arm, and I'm grabbing his right forearm.

I move my body over Tom and drive a short knee into his rib cage.

STRIKING A TURTLED OPPONENT—PUNCH UNDER ARM

The under-arm punch is effective when your opponent maintains an open defense that leaves enough room for you to sneak punches in. Here I've transitioned back to a position of control with my right knee against Tom's side.

I bring my left hand up for a strike. Notice that the left side of my body comes up with my arm, but the right side of my body is still dropped down on his back for control.

I strike under Tom's armpit and into his face.

STRIKES FROM THE REAR MOUNT

Striking from the rear mount while on the bottom is different from the top for several reasons. First off, you don't have the advantage of using your weight to hold your opponent down as you did before. Your opponent will also have both feet on the ground, which allows him to push off his feet and move from side the side the moment you release your grips to strike. To prevent your opponent from escaping as you attack with punches, you must keep your hooks very tight and use one hand to control his upper body (preferably underhooked). If you release both of your upper-body grips, your opponent will most likely escape his compromising position.

I have Tom trapped in a rear mount with my back on the ground. My hooks are in over his hips and my left arm is underhooked under his left armpit. My feet are not crossed.

He reaches his right arm toward my feet to remove my hooks, leaving the right side of his head unprotected. To capitalize, I deliver a round knuckle to the side of his head.

Immediately Tom protects his head from further strikes.

To get around Tom's guard, I throw my right arm around his right arm and strike his chin.

ESCAPES

When caught in a rear mount, your first priority is to protect your neck since that's the first thing your opponent will most likely attack. Your second priority is to escape. Frequently, doing one will lead to the other, so we'll look at two ways to get out of the rear mount that start by protecting your neck. Believe it or not, there's also a simple way to submit your opponent from the rear mount, which we'll look at last.

BRONCO ROLL

The Bronco Roll is a move designed to get an opponent off of your back when his weight is too far forward or before he establishes underhooks on your arms. Many times, a fighter will achieve a rear mount but opt to strike instead of going for a choke. This escape can get him off of you and into the top north-south control position. Just as it sounds, it involves a vigorous bronco-bucking motion to get your opponent off balance and then get him into a position where you can exert your own control.

Julie has me in rear mount. She has her hooks in, but doesn't have any upper body control established.

I raise my hips and stand up on my feet. This throws her balance off and forces her forward.

Julie's hands hit the ground and she tries to maintain her base with them.

Before she can recover, I grab the back of her neck with my right hand.

5

I pull her neck toward me to get her shoulders above her head. This will make it difficult for her to recover her balance and she'll have no choice but to keep rolling forward.

6

By dropping my hips one at a time Julie is forced to give up the control she had with her hooks.

7

By driving forward into her upper torso, I force Julie to roll onto her back. My hands are under her arms so when she lands I can control them.

8

Julie lands on her back and I establish the north-south control position.

TIPPING THE SCALE

When your opponent establishes the rear mount, gets his hooks in, and manages to get an arm underneath your head, it is one of the worst positions for you to be in. While your first goal should be to protect your neck, at the same time you also want to work to escape, which is what this technique teaches you how to do. If you are successful, it will usually have a huge psychological effect on your opponent because he had a very advantageous position and you managed to get out of it. Of course, the biggest risk with this escape is getting choked, so keep your chin down in case you lose control of your opponent's wrists.

Julie has me in a rear mount. She has a left underhook, a right overhook, and has clasped her hands in the center of my chest for control. To begin my escape, I roll to my right and straighten out my right leg to make it more difficult for her to maintain her right hook on my leg. At the same time, I plant my left foot on the mat for leverage.

The first thing I want to do is pry Julie's arms away from my neck, so I grab her right wrist with my left hand and pull it toward my hips.

I slip my right hand in between my chest and her hands with my palm facing out. Once I get my right hand in there, I grab her right wrist and push it away from me.

I release my left grip on Julie's wrist, reach over my right shoulder, and grab her right elbow using my left hand. Now I'm in a position to pry her hands off of me.

Using both of my grips, I move Julie's right arm over my head. Notice how I immediately drop my head to the mat to prevent her from reestablishing her control.

I continue to drive Julie's right arm toward my left side using my grips.

I remove my right hand from Julie's right wrist and place it on her left knee. Notice how I maintain control of her right arm using my left hand. This prevents her from climbing on top of me and establishing the mount.

I straighten my right leg out so my right hip comes off the ground and Julie's heel falls off. This is important. By passing her hook, I can now turn into her to complete the escape.

In one quick movement I push her left knee away from me, pull on her right elbow, and spin into her. My right heel acts as a base to push off of.

With her off balance, I keep turning into her.

When I'm upright and in Julie's full guard, I get my knees underneath me to finish the escape.

CROSSING THE FEET

This is not an escape from the rear mount, but it's a quick and easy move that can end in a submission when your opponent isn't paying attention. Inexperienced grapplers and tired fighters will sometimes cross their feet when they achieve a rear mount. If you recognize it, immediately pounce on the opportunity by locking a foot over his and leaning back. This puts a lot of pressure on your opponent's feet, and will often cause him to tap out. There's virtually no risk to this move because you're not giving up anything to try it and if it doesn't work, you're no worse off than you were before.

1) Julie has me in a seated rear mount. She has established a left underhook, a right overhook, and clasped her hands together in the center of my chest. Although she is in an excellent position, she has made the mistake of crossing her feet. 2) I bring my right leg over her feet to trap them in place. 3) I hook my right foot underneath my left knee to give me added leverage. 4) I bend my left leg to increase the pressure on her feet and lean back. Notice how I push off of my planted leg to increase the power in the move. Due the pain, Julie taps out.

CHAPTER SIX: FULL MOUNT

The full mount is the most dominant position in MMA because it affords you significant striking and control advantages. Because you are striking down onto a stable opponent, body weight and gravity become huge allies. Like all positions, the mount has several variations, depending on what your opponent is doing and what you seek to accomplish with the position. The mount can still offer danger to the person on top, so it's important to keep sharp and watch for counters.

There are high mounts and low mounts, and each has benefits and risks. A mount that is high on your opponent's upper torso allows you to trap his arms underneath your knees so he can't strike back. The high mount, though, allows him extra maneuver space to escape out the back door. A low mount can give your opponent the opportunity to sit up and fight back, which isn't always a bad idea. If you're fighting someone who can be baited into leaving an arm exposed, then a low mount can be used to let him sit up and stick an arm out for you to trap and submit.

FULL MOUNT POSITIONS

There are four different full mount positions. The difference between all of them is where you place your feet. Each position allows you to launch different attacks and achieve different goals, so the type of person you're fighting will determine the type of mount you go into. If you seek a TKO, then the basic full mount is best. But if you want to submit your opponent, the grapevine and saddle mount are more flexible for maneuvering.

BASIC MOUNT

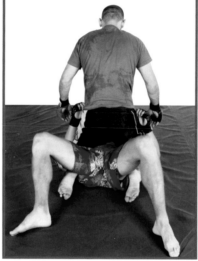

In the basic mount I position my knees high up on Tom's armpits to keep him from using his arms effectively. My weight is down so I'm basically sitting on his chest so he can't roll to either side or try to sweep me. This is the best type of full mount for a ground and pound assault.

GRAPEVINE MOUNT

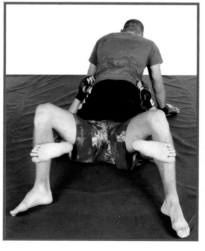

In the grapevine my hips are farther down on Tom's torso and my feet are wrapped around the backs of his legs. This allows me to flatten him out so he can't plant a leg to base out. It also makes it very difficult for him to sweep because I have control of his legs. However, the drawback is that my legs are wrapped up as well, so if he does start to sweep me, it's hard to stop him. The grapevine also gives me good leverage to attack his neck and arms for submissions.

LEG SCISSOR MOUNT

In the leg scissor my feet are hooked over each other. This allows me to squeeze Tom's midsection, which makes it hard for him to breathe and even harder for him to roll me. The leg scissor mount makes it harder for him to turn over and give up his back and is the best method of leg control.

SADDLE MOUNT

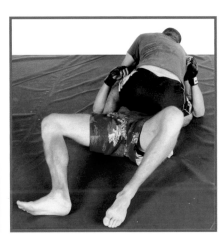

In the saddle mount my weight is higher on Tom's torso and one leg is brought up underneath me. It's your choice which leg is underneath you, so I have pictures of both right and left legs. This is a good position to mount submissions such as the roll-off armbar and the mounted triangle because it affords you more mobility than the other mounts.

SUBMISSIONS

Submissions from the mount rely on stability and the positioning of your body for success. Once you mount your opponent, his primary goal is to escape, so he will try everything to get you off balance to roll, sweep, or shrimp away. Before attempting a submission it's important to establish a solid base and put yourself in a tight mount that allows you to accomplish your objective.

DOUBLE-KNIT CHOKE

The double-knit choke is a quick choke that can surprise an opponent who isn't paying attention to his neck. If you get the choke before he realizes it, you can end the fight. If he blocks it, then he opens himself up to secondary attacks that take advantage of his counters. When applying this choke it's important to keep your hands as open as possible. Like an elbow strike, you don't want to curl your hands up into a fist because that causes your forearm muscles to cover your bone. You want your forearm to drive directly into his throat and cut off the blood flow to his brain.

1) I have Tom fully mounted. My feet are in a grapevine on his legs, but a leg scissor works just as well to prevent him from moving. **2)** I put my left arm across his throat with my forearm directly on his windpipe. **3)** I dig my right arm underneath his neck and snake it through until it's on my left forearm. **4)** By squeezing my hands together and rolling my shoulders back as I press down against his neck, I cut off his air supply and force him to submit. **5)** Close up of the hand position.

ROLL-OFF ARMBAR

This submission is very popular in MMA because many opponents, especially ones who are uncomfortable on the ground, tend to stick their arms up to block strikes from the mount. They don't realize that exposing an arm provides an opportunity for a crafty fighter. This move requires trapping an arm, getting good leg position underneath you, and rolling into the standard armbar position to the side. There's risk involved in this move because you will be giving up the full mount to get the submission. Therefore, you must be certain that you have his arm isolated and immobilized before giving up the mount.

I have Tom in the full mount. My knees are high up on his torso to reduce his ability to sweep, roll, or strike me. He has his arms out to defend himself so I've decided to trap one and submit him.

My hands cross and push down on his chest. Notice that my left arm is over top of his right arm. This submission will not work if he has both hands over top of my arms.

In one quick movement I trap his right arm in the crook of my left elbow (it's not necessary to grab his arm with your hand) and push off of him until I can get my legs underneath me. I then rotate my body ninety degrees to his side.

I lean back until my butt hits the ground and throw my left leg over his head. At this point he'll see the armbar coming and try to grab his trapped hand with his free hand. It's too little, too late.

I trap his left arm with both hands and bring my legs together so I can squeeze his arm between them.

To complete the submission I lean back, squeeze his arm between my thighs, and arch my hips up into his arm. The pressure on his elbow forces him to submit.

LAWNMOWER ARMBAR

If your opponent senses the armbar coming, he will sometimes clasp his hands together to prevent you from isolating his arm and applying the submission. In such a case, the lawnmower armbar is an excellent alternative. By simply switching your leg position, you gain the leverage needed to break his grip, isolate an arm, and apply the armbar.

I have Tom in the full mount. My knees are high up on his torso to reduce his ability to sweep, roll, or strike me. He has crossed his arms on his chest to prevent me from isolating one and submitting him.

I slide my right arm underneath Tom's right arm.

I place my left hand on the mat on the left side of Tom's head and push off. This allows me to come up on my right foot and begin rotating my body in a clockwise direction. It is important to notice that although I am now up on my right foot, I still have my weight riding on his chest.

Continuing to rotate in a clockwise direction, I step my left leg over to the left side of Tom's head. Notice how I still have my right arm hooked underneath of his right arm and my weight is positioned down on his body.

I lean back until my butt hits the ground and pull Tom's arms toward my chest using my right arm. He keeps his hands clasped tightly together, so I must now shatter his grip.

Keeping my right arm hooked around Tom's right arm, I place my left hand on his left biceps and push his arm away from me. This creates an opening between his arms, and I immediately begin sliding my right foot through that opening.

My right leg goes through his grip and ends up on his left shoulder.

I bring my left leg off of Tom's head.

I establish a triangle lock by hooking my left leg over my right foot.

I clasp my hands together and then slide my right forearm up to Tom's right wrist.

I lean to my left to bring his arms above his head until my left elbow hits the ground.

The angle of his upper torso and the squeezing of my legs make it too difficult for Tom to maintain his grip.

Once I break Tom's grip, I lean back, pull his arm toward my chest using both of my hands, and arch my hips upward.

MOUNTED TRIANGLE

The mounted triangle is difficult to achieve, but nearly impossible to escape when you manage to secure it. It involves trapping one of your opponent's arms, passing your leg over top of it, and then wrapping your legs around his head. Throughout the move it's important to maintain control of the arm that will end up inside your legs at the end. If your opponent pulls this arm out at some point, it will be difficult to submit him and he will have the opportunity to escape. It is important to note that during this move, your weight will be very high on your opponent's torso, so there's a risk that he will try to escape out the back door, meaning between your legs, or sweep you. Keeping your weight down on his chest and maintaining control of his arms will prevent this.

1

I am fully mounted on top of Tom. My left hand is behind his head and my right hand has his left arm trapped against the ground.

2

I slide my right hand up to Tom's left wrist to isolate it and step over his left arm with my right knee.

3

Once my right knee is past Tom's left shoulder, I straighten my leg out while lifting on his head with my left hand. I'm practically sitting on his chest at this point, so he can't roll over or sweep me.

4

I place my right hand on the ground and I wrap my right leg behind Tom's head. At this point it's important that I keep my left knee up against Tom's right armpit. If he digs his arm underneath my legs right now, he could sweep me over.

Now I need to get my left leg in a position to lock it over my right. There isn't enough space to simply bring it up and place it over top of my right leg, so I lean forward, place my head on the mat, and pull Tom's right shoulder up using my left hand. In addition to creating space, it also controls his left arm, which has to stay inside my legs to make the submission work.

I bring my left leg forward and hook it over my right foot. Because my head is bearing my weight, my feet are free to move and I can lock in the triangle.

Once my feet are locked, I sit up on my knees and squeeze my legs tight. If Tom doesn't tap from the triangle, I am free to throw downward punches into his face.

REAR NAKED CHOKE

The most common means of defense for an opponent who's mounted is to roll over and give up his back, especially if your striking is having effect. Some opponents would rather take their chances with the rear mount than continue to get punched in the face. This opens up several options for you, the most common of which is the rear naked choke. It's probably the easiest submission to secure when you have your opponent's back because he frequently will have his arms out to his sides instead of protecting his neck as he rolls over. Even if he does protect his neck, there are ways to get him to expose it for the RNC.

I am fully mounted on Tom with my weight low on his torso. I don't have my knees up into his armpits so he has room to maneuver.

He suddenly rolls to his left to escape the mount.

3

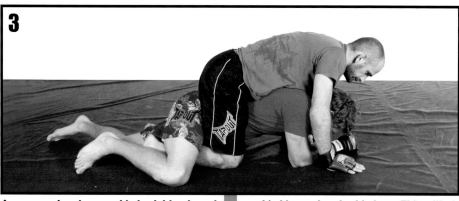

As soon as he gives me his back I hook my legs over his hips and under his legs. This will give me more control during the submission.

4

Tom gets up on his knees. He might try the Bronco Roll escape that we saw in the last chapter, or he may be looking to roll into me. Either way, I don't want to let him up. With my hooks in, I slip my arms underneath his armpits. This will give me the leverage I need to flatten him back out.

5

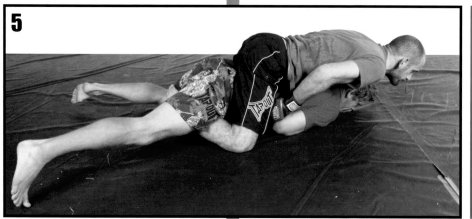

By pushing down with my hips and pulling up with my hands I flatten Tom back out on the mat. This effectively neutralizes his legs and takes away his options for sweeping or escaping.

6

While keeping pressure on his legs so he can't get up, I release my grip under his armpits and reach for his neck.

7

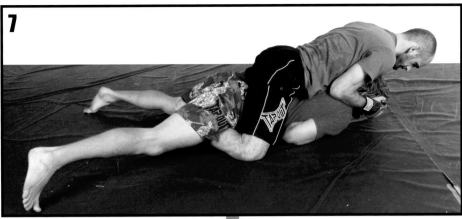

Tom keeps his head down, and I can't simply wrap my arm underneath his neck, so I grab his forehead with both hands to force it up.

8

I lift up on Tom's forehead to expose his neck (kidney punches have also proven useful in this situation, as many fighters will lift their chin when hit with hard body shots).

9

I slip my right arm underneath his neck and press my forearm against his throat.

10

To finish the submission, I grab my left biceps with my right hand, place my left hand on the back of Tom's head, and then squeeze my arms tight. With blood flow severed to his brain, he has no choice but to tap in submission.

STRIKES

Strikes are the bread and butter of the full mount. Even if your opponent manages to block the majority of your shots, they will harass him enough that he can't mount a counterattack. More than any other position in MMA, your opponent will be desperate to escape and just a few solid strikes can cause him to panic and make a mistake.

BASIC PUNCHES

Punches to the face from the full mount only need to adhere to a few basic principles:
-Keep your elbow aligned with your fist to make the punch more effective.
-Punch rapidly so your opponent has no time to come up with a counterstrategy.
-Always stop his escapes, and then continue punching.
-For striking, the regular mount is more effective than the grapevine, leg scissor, or saddle mount.

PUNCHES FROM WRIST CONTROL

Most fighters use their arms to block your strikes once they're mounted. It's a natural instinct. As you can see below, this allows you to grab his wrists, control his arms, and then move them out of the way. Before he can recover his guard, you land a solid punch to his face. This is actually similar to the matador pass that we saw in chapter 1 because you throw your opponent's arms to one side and strike downward.

1) I have Tom mounted with my knees up close to his armpits. He has put his arms up to defend himself and I've grabbed a hold of both wrists.
2) I force both of his arms to my right. Notice that I've used his right arm to block his left arm. **3)** I let go of his left arm and bring my right hand up, elbow high, for a strike. He is unable to bring his left arm back toward his head to block the punch, and his right arm is immobilized.
4) Finish the move with a downward strike to his head.

ELBOWS FROM WRIST CONTROL

Similar to the last move, this is a way to use your opponent's defense against him. When he puts his hands up to protect his head, you can grab his wrists and come over the top of them with downward elbow strikes.

1) I have Tom mounted with my knees up close to his armpits. My hands are on his shoulders to hold him in place. **2)** When he puts his arms up to defend himself, I grab a hold of both wrists. **3)** My right elbow comes up high to prepare for a downward strike. **4)** As I throw my right elbow into his face, I drop my weight.

ELBOWS

Dropping an elbow from the full mount into your opponent's face is a devastating blow. It can cause a lot of damage and is hard to block. Like all elbow strikes, it's important to keep your hand open to cause more damage.

1) I have Tom mounted with my knees up close to his armpits. My hands are on his shoulders to hold him in place. **2)** I bring my right hand up to strike. **3)** I open my hand so my forearm muscle doesn't cover the bone. This will cause more damage to my opponent. **4)** I put my left hand on the ground for leverage as I bring the strike down. **5)** My whole body drops down as I strike into his face with my forearm.

ROUND KNUCKLE

This strike adds another angle for you to attack your opponent. Instead of striking him from top to bottom, the round knuckle lets you strike from outside in, so if he covers up with his hands in front of his face, you can still cause damage by punching from the side. It is important to mention that with the round knuckle, you turn your palm downward instead of upward.

1) I have Tom mounted with my knees up close to his armpits. My hands are on his shoulders to hold him in place. **2)** I raise my right arm to strike, and he covers up, leaving the sides of his head unprotected. **3)** I respond by changing the angle of attack and bringing my hand out wide so I can strike from outside in. **4)** I drop my weight and lean to the left to add momentum to my strike. **5)** I target his jaw and ear and follow through with the strike.

HAMMER FIST

Employing the hammer fist from the full mount comes in very handy when your opponent covers his head but leaves a small gap between his arms. Although you can also punch through that gap, you risk striking one of his elbows and injuring your hand. The hammer fist is a much safer move in such a scenario, and it still packs a lot of power.

1) I have Tom mounted with my knees up close to his armpits. My hands are on his shoulders to hold him in place. **2)** I rise up to strike with a basic punch. This usually causes your opponent to cover his face with his arms. **3)** I change the strike and bring my right fist to a position in front of my face with the bottom of my hand facing Tom. **4)** As I drop the strike I also drop my weight to cause more damage. I aim for his nose.

BOW AND ARROW

In this sequence I demonstrate how to establish the bow and arrow position and then use it to deliver brutal strikes to your opponent's face. It can be difficult to maintain this position for a prolonged period of time, but all you need is a few seconds to land several damaging shots.

1

I have Tom mounted with my knees up close to his armpits.

2

I drop my weight on him while pushing both of his arms to my right. I want to trap his right arm, so I ensure that it is lying across his body.

3

I release my left grip on Tom's right arm, but keep my body weight on his arm to keep it trapped to the left side of his head. Immediately I begin snaking my left hand underneath his head.

4

I reach behind Tom's head and grab his right wrist with my left hand. Notice how this traps his right arm across his neck.

5

I bring my right foot underneath me into the saddle mount that we saw earlier. This will give me a better angle and more leverage for the strikes I'm about to throw.

6

I elevate my right arm to strike. In this position, Tom's unable to roll left because his arm is in the way, and he cannot roll right because my leg is in the way. If he does manage to overpower me, he'll only roll into my rear naked choke.

7

I begin throwing downward strikes to Tom's face.

ESCAPES AND DEFENSES

When you are trying to escape the bottom mount position, it is important to keep the same mentality that you have throughout the fight. Staying in motion helps, but you constantly want to hunt your way out or go for submissions. Keeping those goals in mind and switching from move to move will give you the best chance of escape.

BUMP

The goal of the bump is to not only keep your opponent off balance so he can't throw effective strikes, but to also bring him close enough to establish a grip on his body. This is a defensive strategy and will not solve the overall problem of being mounted, so it's only a temporary solution.

1

2

3

4

1) Julie has me mounted. I am unable to keep her close and she's postured up with the intent to throw a strike down at me. **2)** I bring my right knee up and bump her in the buttocks to throw her off balance. **3)** I keep shoving my knee into her to make her unable to strike and force her close enough for me to grab. **4)** By bumping her weight forward, I have brought her close enough, and I wrap my arms around her and keep her too close to strike me effectively.

DEFENDING STRIKES

Your opponent has mounted you and wants to start a ground and pound attack. Securing a strong grip in the middle of his back and controlling his weight are the best means of neutralizing his strikes. But keep in mind that this is not a permanent solution to being mounted. You can only maintain a defensive strategy like this for a short time because it doesn't get you out from under his mount. You still need to find a way to escape.

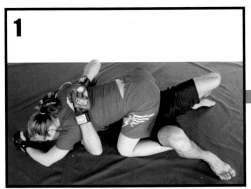  

1) Julie has me mounted. I clasp my hands together in the middle of her back (between her shoulder blades) where I can control her weight and bring her in close to me. **2)** She postures up to throw a punch with her right hand. **3)** I push off with my right leg, roll toward her left right (my left), and pull her toward me. This throws her off balance and stops the strike before it starts.

SHRIMP ESCAPE

The goal of the next two moves is not to escape to a dominant position, but rather to get out of the mount and back to full or half guard. The shrimp escape has two parts. First you will eliminate your opponent's grapevine leg hold. Once that's accomplished, you can free your legs one at a time and get back to full guard.

Julie has me mounted. My hands are clasped together in between her shoulder blades to keep her close so she can't strike while I escape.

My primary goal is to neutralize her grapevine hold and free my legs. I straighten my right leg to shake her left heel off me and free it.

3

I place my right foot on Julie's left heel and apply downward pressure.

4

I push her right foot down and straighten my left leg.

5

I post my right foot on the mat and slide my left hand toward her right knee to establish some control over it.

6

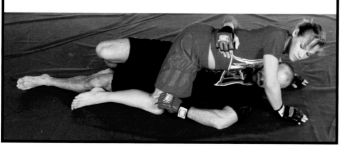

I push off with my right foot and rotate my hips toward my left side.

7

I continue to roll until my hips are facing completely to my left. Next, I hook Julie's right instep using my right foot.

8

I elevate Julie's right leg using my right foot, push on her right knee using my left hand to prevent her from driving it back to the mat, and quickly slide my left leg underneath her right leg.

9

I drop Julie's right leg back to the mat, hook my left leg over the crook of her leg, and then place my right foot on top of her right ankle. This puts Julie in my half guard. Although this is better than being mounted, I want to get her into my full guard.

10

I wrap my left hand over Julie's back to give me some control of her upper body, rotate my hips toward my right, and push down on her left knee using my right hand.

11

Having pushed Julie's left knee down using my right hand, I have created the space I need to pull my right leg underneath her left leg and in front of her left hip.

12

Once my leg is free I wrap it around Julie's waist to establish full guard.

POWER SHRIMP ESCAPE

The power shrimp focuses all of your energy on one of your opponent's knees in order to get out of the mount and pull half guard. It's risky because you drop your hands down to push on your opponent's knee so your head is momentarily un-protected. I don't recommend using this escape while your opponent is striking because you will give him an opportunity to punch you several times in the face without being able to block them.

1

Julie has me mounted. My hands are clasped together in between her shoulder blades.

2

I rotate my hips to my left and drop my left hand down to her right knee.

3

I bring my right hand underneath Julie and place it on her right knee as well. This is where I'm vulnerable to head strikes, so I have to move fast.

In one explosive move, I push down on Julie's knee with both hands, turn onto my left side, and scoot my butt out. Notice how I have created the space I need to pull my left leg out from between her legs.

I quickly get my left leg free and wrap it around Julie's right leg.

I turn toward my right to square my hips up with Julie's hips, wrap my right leg over my left leg to capture her in my half guard, and wrap my arms around her torso. Notice how this gives me two underhooks.

BUCK AND ROLL

In this technique and the three to follow I demonstrate techniques that not only allow you to escape the bottom mount position, but also obtain a dominant top position. In the buck and roll, your opponent establishes a cross-face in order to set up strikes, which is quite common. Although this allows him to break your grip on his body and pin your head to the mat, it allows you to trap the arm he is using to apply the cross-face. If you are able to step your foot over his leg at the same time to trap it, he becomes unable to post his trapped hand or foot on the mat, allowing you to roll him over to his back.

1) Julie has me mounted. My hands are clasped together in between her shoulder blades. **2)** She brings her left arm up and cross-faces me to break my grip and pin my head to the mat. This gives me two advantages: it takes away part of her base and raises her center of gravity, making it easier to sweep her. **3)** I slide my right hand down to her left elbow. At the same time, I move my right foot over her left leg to trap it to my side. **4)** With both Julie's left arm and left leg trapped, I push off my feet and bridge to my right. Notice how this throws her off balance. **5)** I continue to roll her over to my right. With her left hand and leg trapped, she is unable to post on the mat and block the sweep. **6)** When Julie's back hits the ground, I turn my hips over and get my head into her chest to get control. **7)** I end in Julie's full guard, which is much better than being stuck in the bottom mount.

POWER BUCK AND ROLL

The buck and roll demonstrated in the previous sequence is an excellent technique when you catch your opponent by surprise, but if he sees the sweep coming, he will often be able to break the control you have on his arm and post his hands on the mat. In such a scenario, employing the power buck and roll allows you to use his counter to your advantage. As you will see below, the technique requires you to power your opponent over to his back. Although this is quite effective, it is possible for your opponent to catch you in an armbar, so you must keep your head close to his body and your arms tight.

1) Julie has me mounted. My hands are clasped together in between her shoulder blades. 2) Instead of waiting for Julie to cross-face me, I slide my right hand down to her left elbow to trap it and start the buck and roll. 3) I drive off my feet and turn toward my right side. 4) Julie sees the sweep coming, breaks the control I have on her left arm, and posts her hands out to the side to stop her roll. 5) To counter her base, I explode my hips and turn them over quickly. Notice how my right shoulder is still on the mat. It is important to mention that it is at this point in the technique where Julie could potentially step her right leg over to the right side of my head, secure my right arm between her legs, and drop back for an armbar. To avoid this, I keep my head pressed tight to her body and my right arm wrapped tightly around her back. 6) Once I'm on my knees, I drive into Julie's body using my left arm and pull her left hand out from underneath her using my right hand. As her arm collapses, she gets forced toward her back. 7) I continue to roll her over, keeping my head in tight to her chest and my arm wrapped around her body so she can't scramble and secure a submission. I keep rolling until her back is on the ground and I am in her guard.

ANKLE LOCK

No one expects you to try a submission when you're mounted, so this attack on your opponent's foot is both a good way to escape the mount and a potential fight-ender. Whether you secure the ankle lock or not, it will get you out from under your opponent's mount. We'll break it down into steps, but it's an incredibly fast move when you put it all together and should be executed with as much explosiveness as you can muster. It also requires leverage or you'll essentially be bench-pressing your opponent off you. Like the power shrimp, there is risk in this move because your head will be unprotected for a few moments.

Julie has me mounted. My hands are clasped together in between her shoulder blades.

I drop my hands down to Julie's hips to prepare to push her off. Notice that my elbows are underneath my hands instead of out to the sides. This will add strength to the push.

As I bridge my hips, I throw Julie's body forward using my hands.

As I drop my hips back to the mat, I keep Julie elevated above me using my arms. This gives me the space I need to slip my right knee between her legs.

5

As I rotate my body in a clockwise direction, I push Julie in a counter-clockwise direction using my arms.

6

As I rotate my body in a clockwise direction, I push Julie in a counter-clockwise direction using my arms.

Continuing to rotate my hips in a clockwise direction, I throw my left leg over Julie's right leg. Notice how her right foot is now positioned underneath my left arm.

7

I slide my left leg across Julie's midsection to provide the leverage I need for the submission. Notice how this action causes the toes of her right foot to slide up into my armpit.

8

I clamp my left arm down on Julie's toes to trap her foot in my armpit, wrap my forearm underneath her heel, and clasp my hands together over her right leg. To apply the ankle lock, I arch my back.

ABOUT THE AUTHORS

Greg Jackson is the world's most accomplished MMA trainer. He has more than fifteen MMA champions in his stable, including Georges St. Pierre and Rashad Evans, and his athletes have won hundreds of grappling championships.

Kelly Crigger is a Lieutenant Colonel in the US Army and is a columnist for Fight! Magazine. He is the author of *Title Shot: Into the Shark Tank of Mixed Martial Arts*, which details his year-long journey through the world of professional fighting.

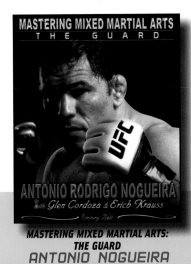

JACKSON'S MIXED MARTIAL ARTS
THE STAND UP GAME

TITLE SHOT
KELLY CRIGGER

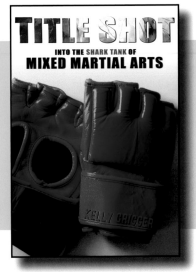

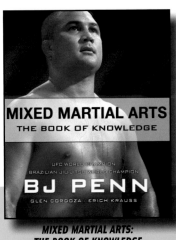

MIXED MARTIAL ARTS:
THE BOOK OF KNOWLEDGE
BJ PENN

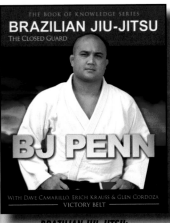

BRAZILIAN JIU-JITSU:
THE CLOSED GUARD
BJ PENN

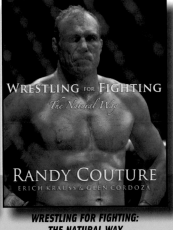

WRESTLING FOR FIGHTING:
THE NATURAL WAY
RANDY COUTURE

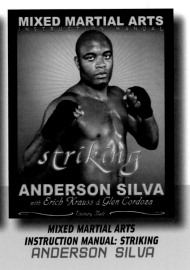

MIXED MARTIAL ARTS
INSTRUCTION MANUAL: STRIKING
ANDERSON SILVA

MASTERING MIXED MARTIAL ARTS:
THE GUARD
ANTONIO NOGUEIRA

GUERRILLA JIU-JITSU:
REVOLUTIONIZING BRAZILIAN JIU-JITSU
DAVE CAMARILLO

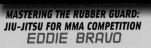

MASTERING THE RUBBER GUARD:
JIU-JITSU FOR MMA COMPETITION
EDDIE BRAVO

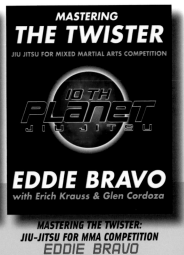

MASTERING THE TWISTER:
JIU-JITSU FOR MMA COMPETITION
EDDIE BRAVO

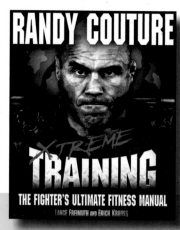

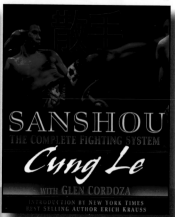
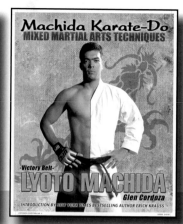

**XTREME TRAINING
THE FIGHTER'S ULTIMATE FITNESS MANUAL
RANDY COUTURE**

**ADVANCED BRAZILIAN JIU-JITSU
MARCELO GARCIA**

**SAN SHOU
THE COMPLETE FIGHTING SYSTEM
CUNG LE**

**MACHIDA KARATE-DO
MIXED MARTIAL ARTS TECHNIQUES
LYOTO MACHIDA**

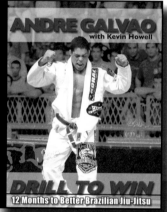
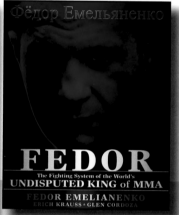
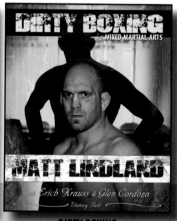

**JIU-JITSU UNIVERSITY
SAULO RIBEIRO**

**DRILL TO WIN
12 MONTHS TO BETTER BRAZILIAN JIU-JITSU
ANDRE GALVAO**

**FEDOR: THE FIGHTING SYSTEM OF THE
UNDISPUTED KING OF MMA
FEDOR EMELIANENKO**

**DIRTY BOXING
FOR MIXED MARTIAL ARTS
MATT LINDLAND**

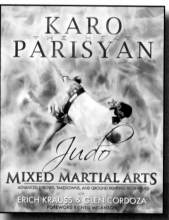
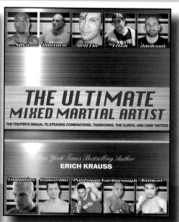

**THE X-GUARD
GI & NO GI JIU-JITSU
MARCELO GARCIA**

**JUDO FOR MMA: ADVANCED THROWS,
TAKEDOWNS, AND GROUND FIGHTING
KARO PARISYAN**

**THE ULTIMATE MIXED MARTIAL ARTIST:
THE FIGHTER'S MANUAL TO STRIKING
COMBINATIONS, TAKEDOWNS,
THE CLINCH, AND CAGE TACTICS
ANDERSON SILVA
RANDY COUTURE
FORREST GRIFFIN
JON FITCH
GREG JACKSON
SHAWN THOMPKINS
DAVE CAMARILLO
KARO PARISYAN**

**MASTERING THE RUBBER GUARD DVD:
JIU-JITSU FOR MMA COMPETITION
EDDIE BRAVO**